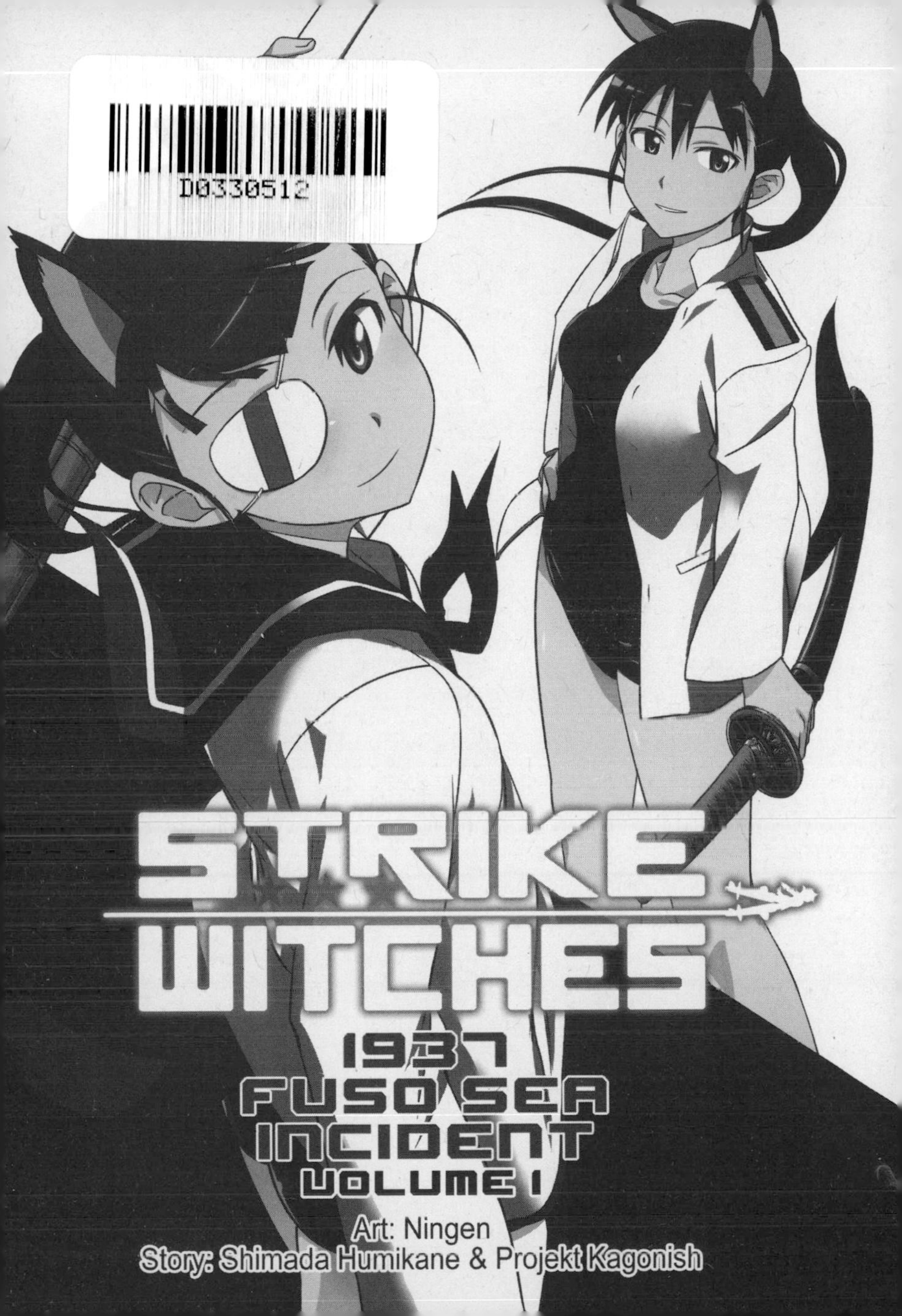

STRIKE WITCHES

1937 FUSO SEA INCIDENT

VOLUME 1

Art: Ningen

Story: Shimada Humikane & Projekt Kagonish

CHAPTER 1:
PROMISE IN THE SKY

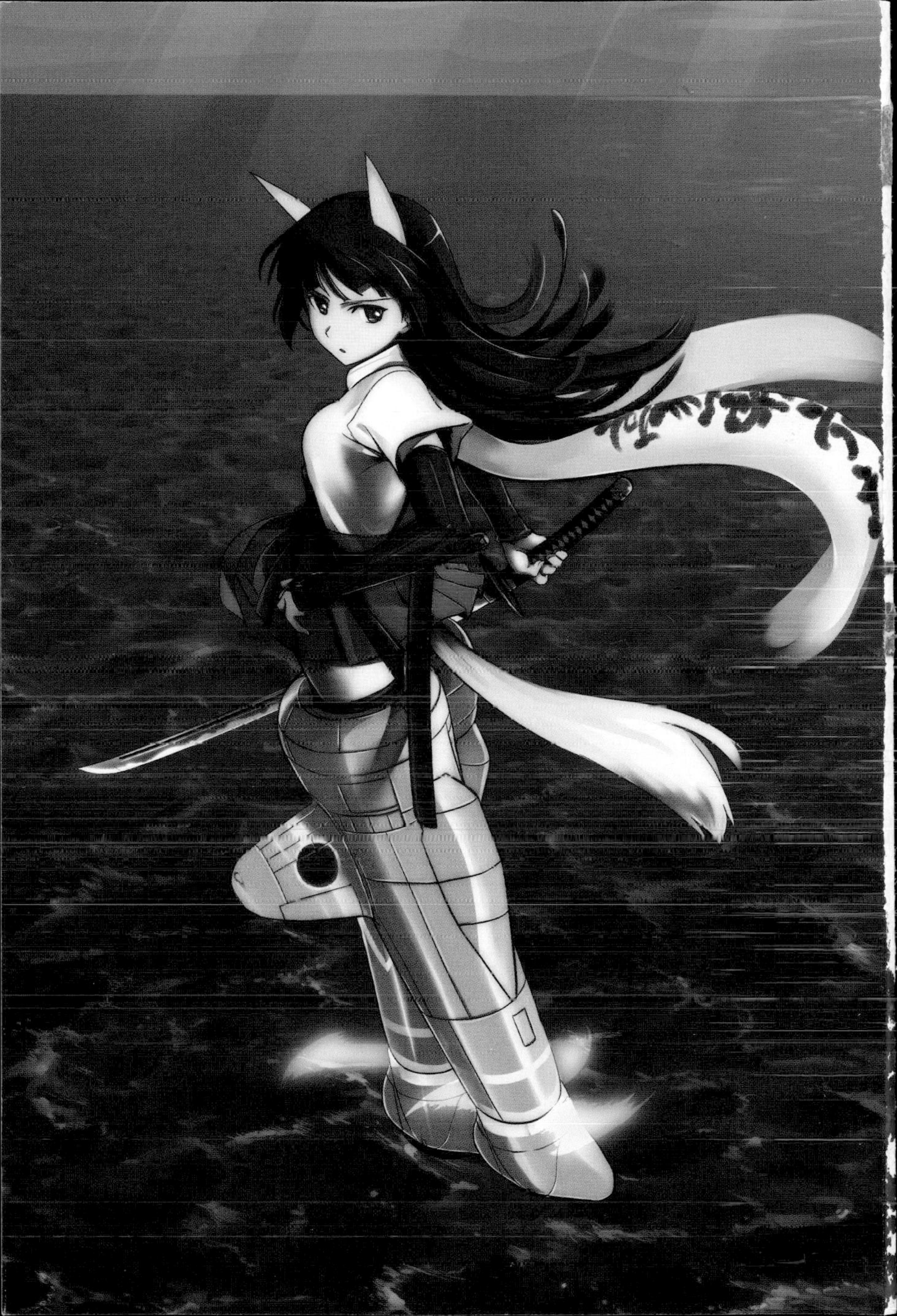

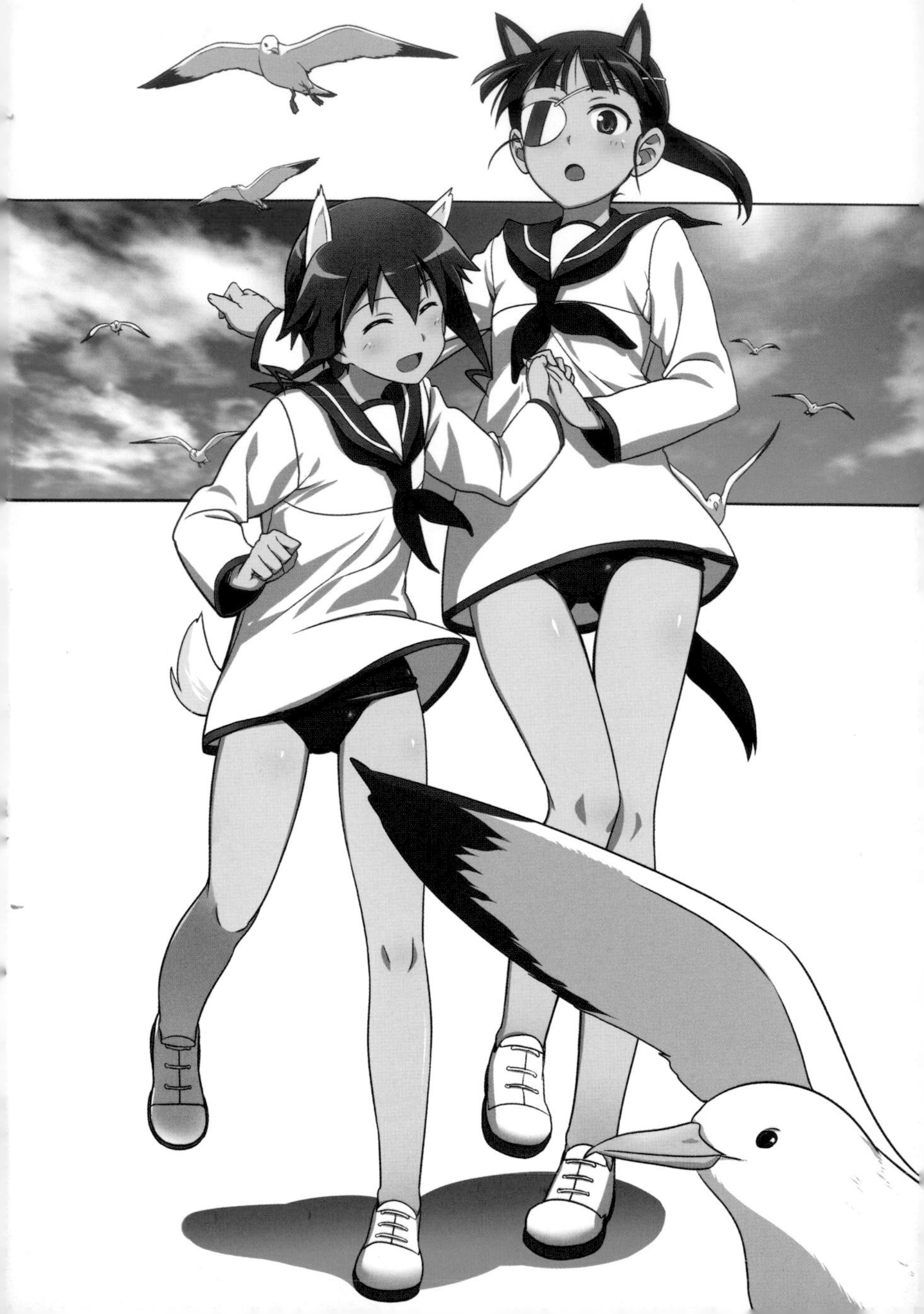

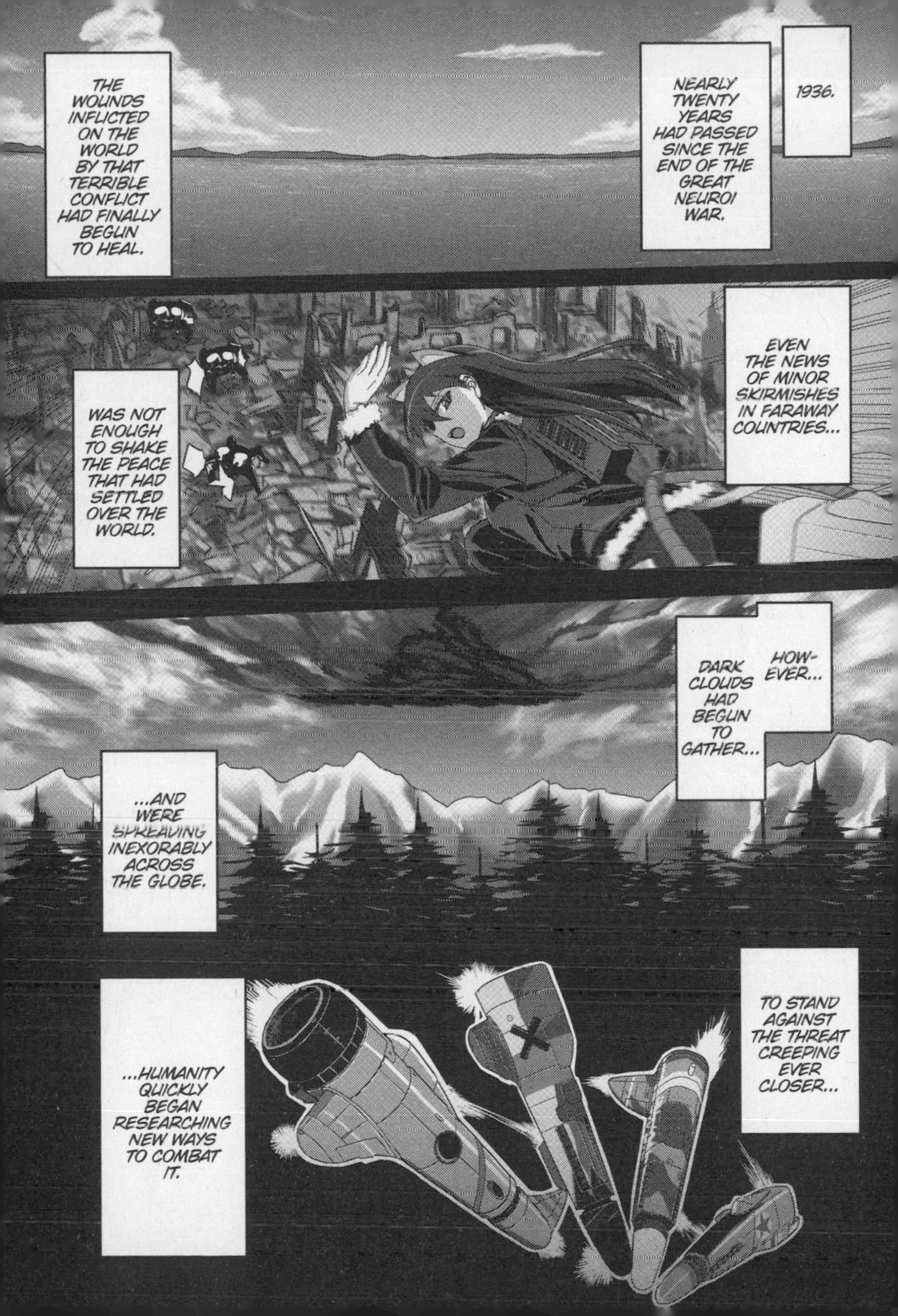
1936.
NEARLY TWENTY YEARS HAD PASSED SINCE THE END OF THE GREAT NEUROI WAR.
THE WOUNDS INFLICTED ON THE WORLD BY THAT TERRIBLE CONFLICT HAD FINALLY BEGUN TO HEAL.
EVEN THE NEWS OF MINOR SKIRMISHES IN FARAWAY COUNTRIES...
WAS NOT ENOUGH TO SHAKE THE PEACE THAT HAD SETTLED OVER THE WORLD.
HOW-EVER...
DARK CLOUDS HAD BEGUN TO GATHER...
...AND WERE SPREADING INEXORABLY ACROSS THE GLOBE.
TO STAND AGAINST THE THREAT CREEPING EVER CLOSER...
...HUMANITY QUICKLY BEGAN RESEARCHING NEW WAYS TO COMBAT IT.

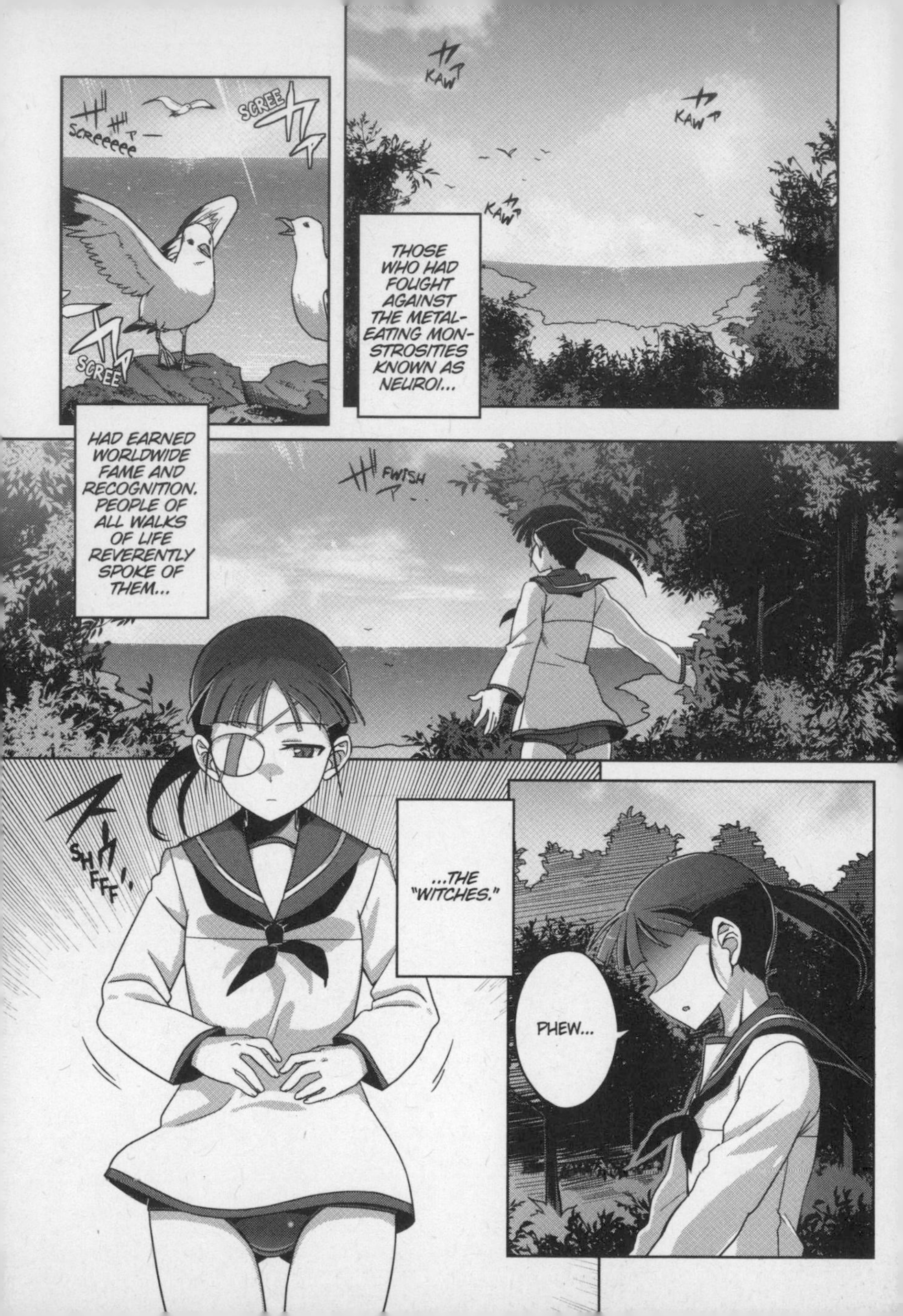
KAW
KAW
KAW
THOSE WHO HAD FOUGHT AGAINST THE METAL-EATING MONSTROSITIES KNOWN AS NEUROI...
SCREE
SCREEEEEE
SCREE
HAD EARNED WORLDWIDE FAME AND RECOGNITION. PEOPLE OF ALL WALKS OF LIFE REVERENTLY SPOKE OF THEM...
FWISH
...THE "WITCHES."
PHEW...
SHFFF

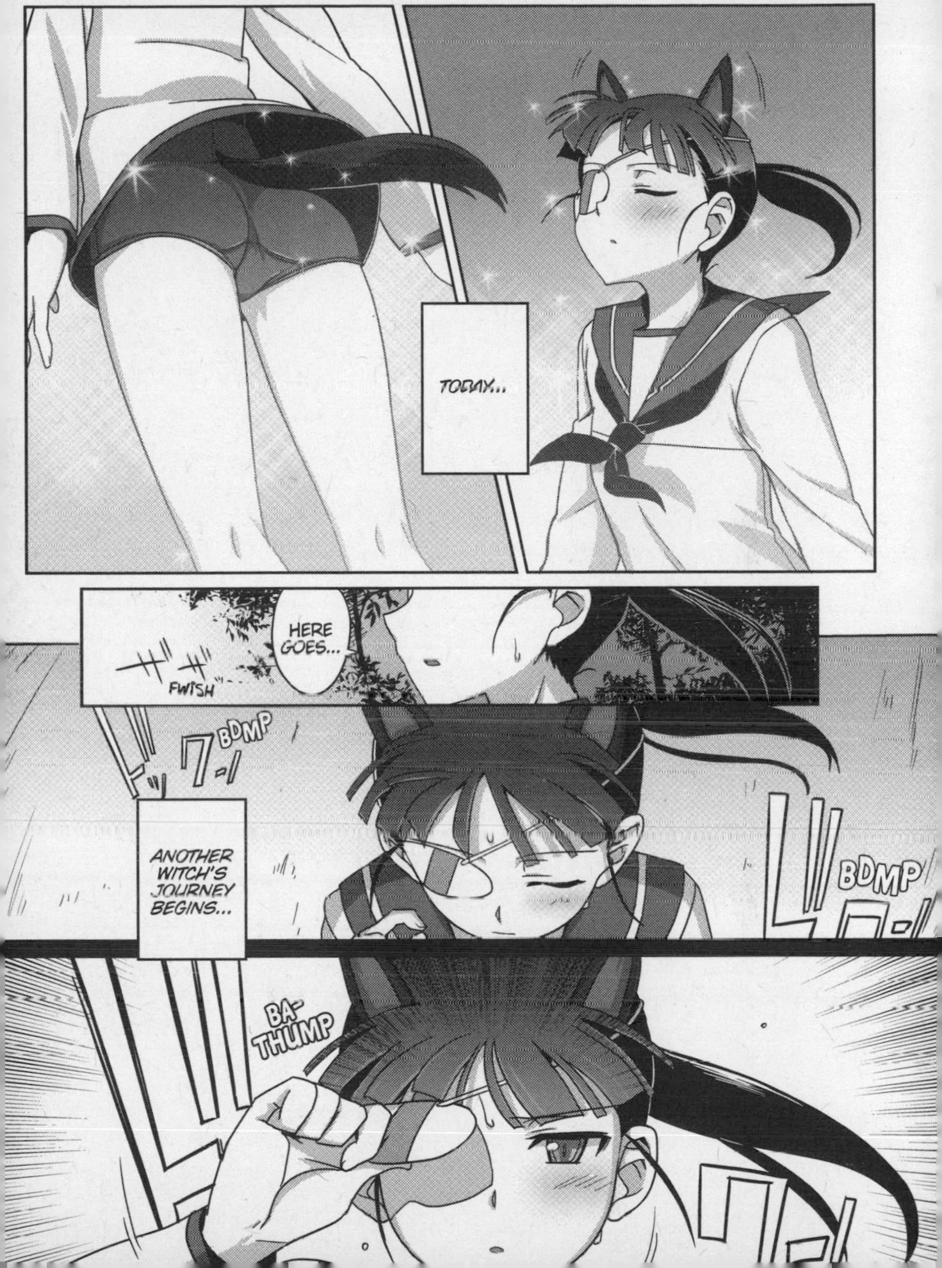
TODAY...
HERE GOES...
FWISH
BDMP
BDMP
ANOTHER WITCH'S JOURNEY BEGINS...
BA-THUMP

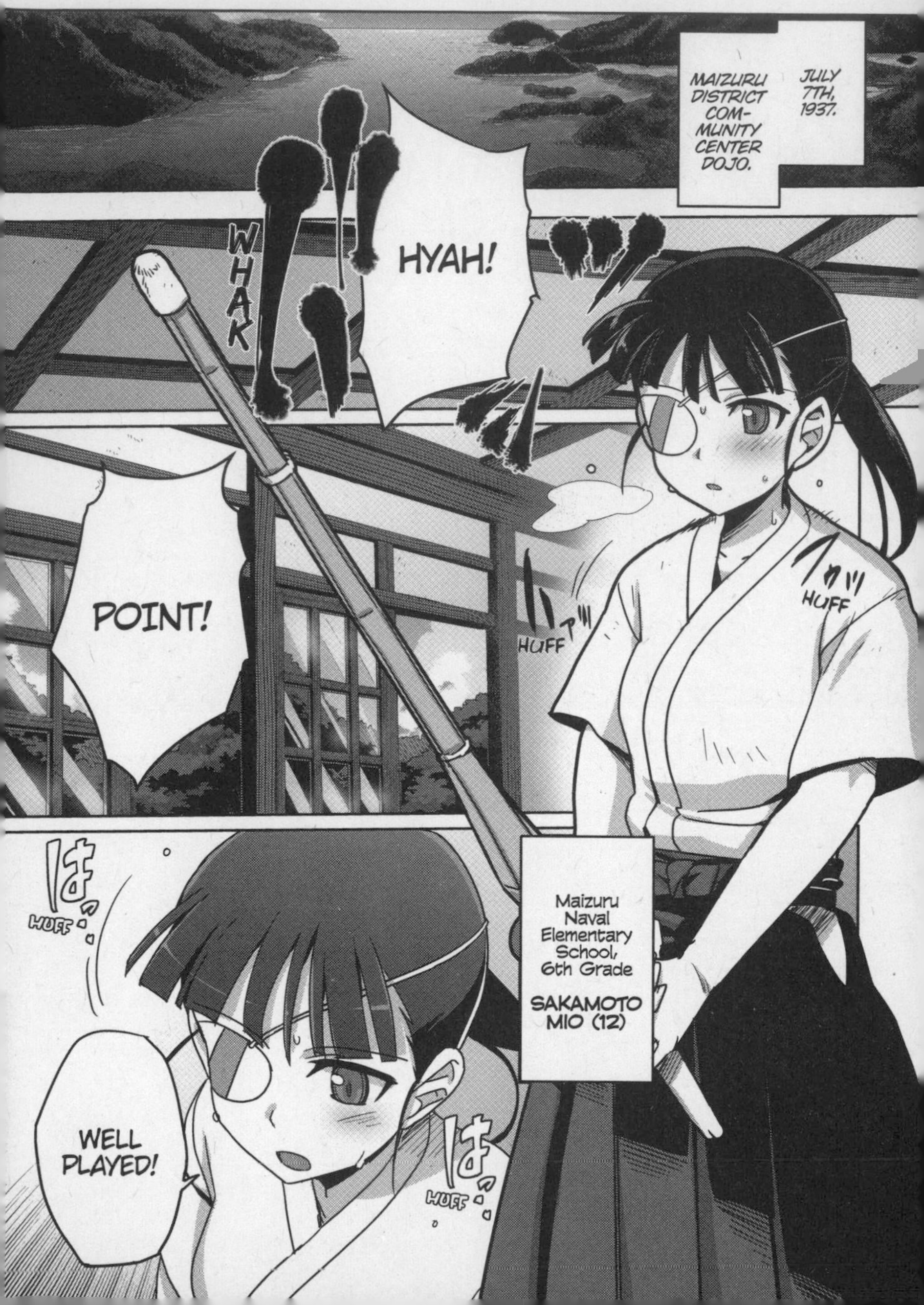

JULY 7TH, 1937.
MAIZURU DISTRICT COMMUNITY CENTER DOJO.
HYAH!
WHAK
POINT!
HUFF
HUFF
Maizuru Naval Elementary School, 6th Grade
SAKAMOTO MIO (12)
WELL PLAYED!
HUFF
HUFF

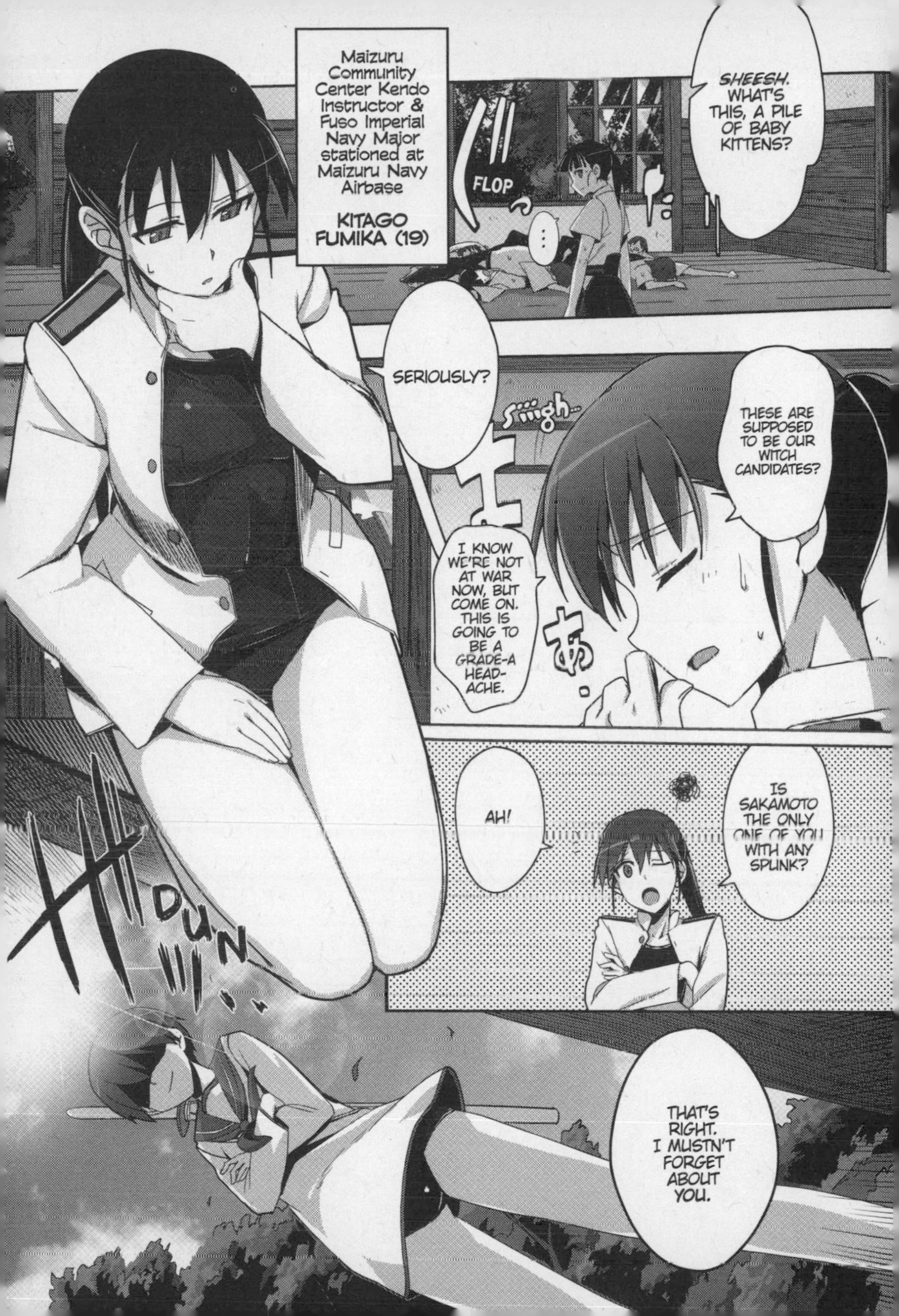
SHEESH. WHAT'S THIS, A PILE OF BABY KITTENS?
FLOP
...
Maizuru Community Center Kendo Instructor & Fuso Imperial Navy Major stationed at Maizuru Navy Airbase
KITAGO FUMIKA (19)
SERIOUSLY?
sigh...
THESE ARE SUPPOSED TO BE OUR WITCH CANDIDATES?
I KNOW WE'RE NOT AT WAR NOW, BUT COME ON. THIS IS GOING TO BE A GRADE-A HEAD-ACHE.
IS SAKAMOTO THE ONLY ONE OF YOU WITH ANY SPUNK?
AH!
DUN
THAT'S RIGHT. I MUSTN'T FORGET ABOUT YOU.

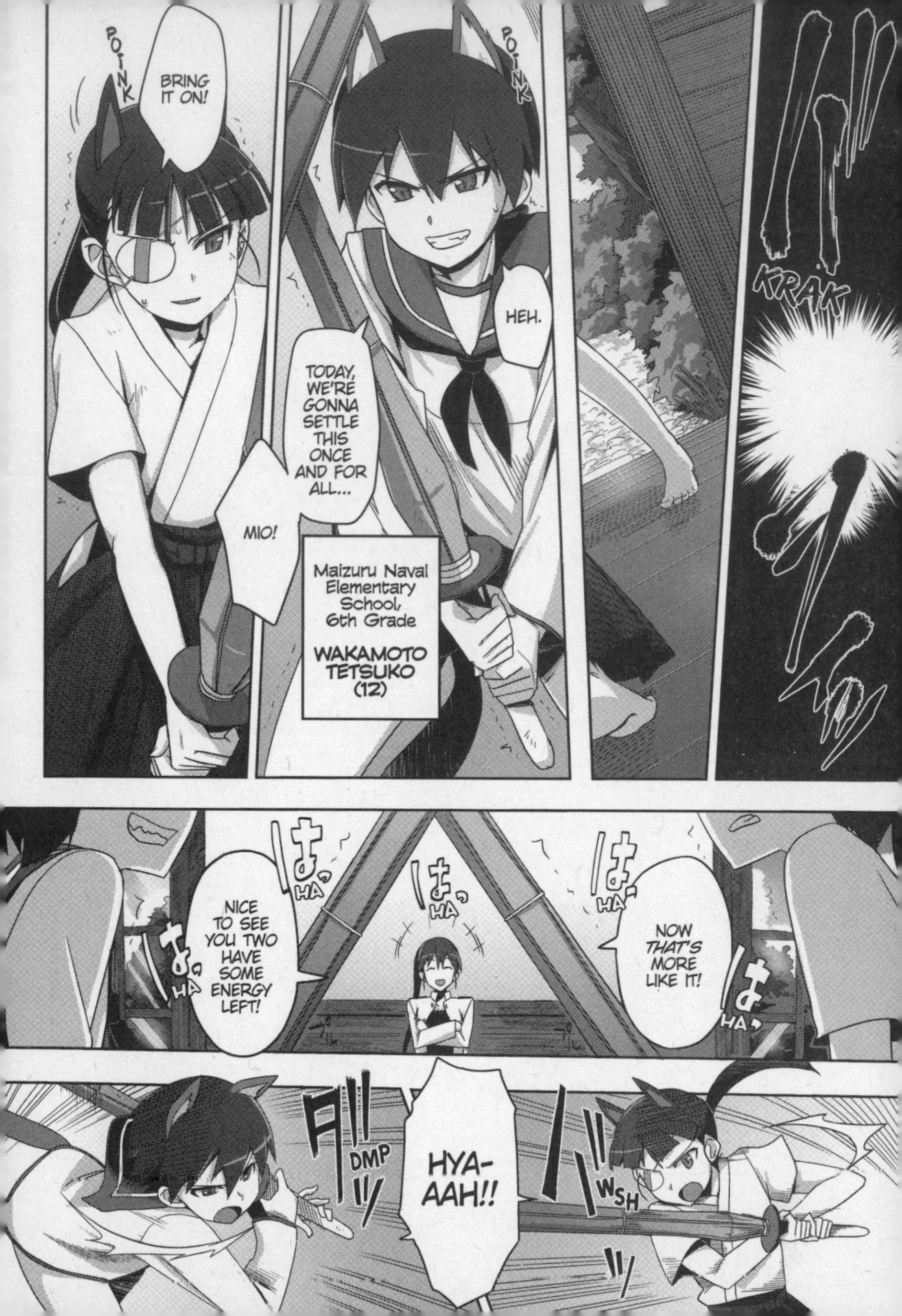
KRAK
POINK
HEH.
TODAY, WE'RE GONNA SETTLE THIS ONCE AND FOR ALL...
MIO!
Maizuru Naval Elementary School, 6th Grade
WAKAMOTO TETSUKO (12)
POINK
BRING IT ON!
HA
NOW THAT'S MORE LIKE IT!
HA
HA
HA
NICE TO SEE YOU TWO HAVE SOME ENERGY LEFT!
HA
WSH
HYA-AAH!!
DMP

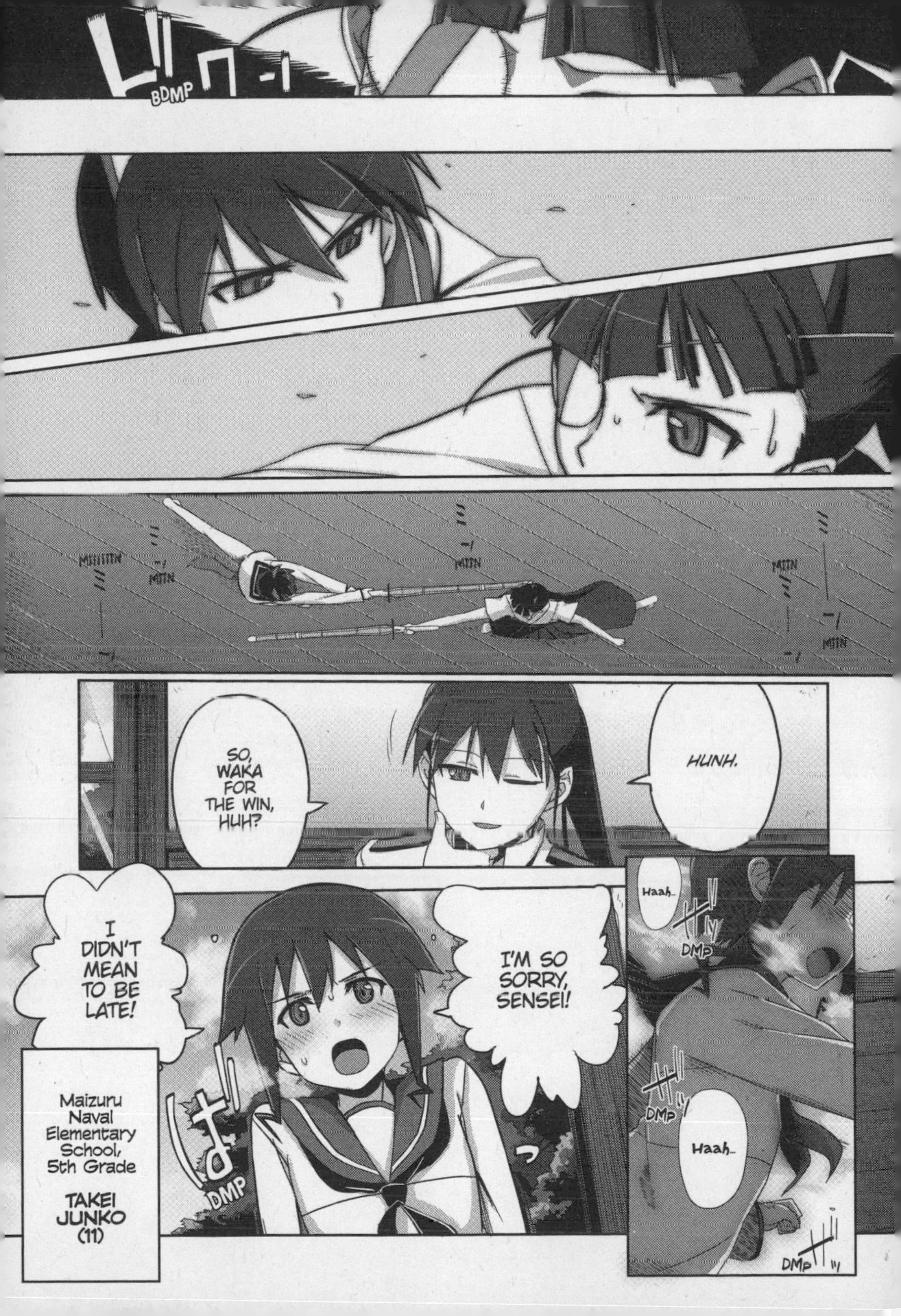
BDMP
MTTN
MTTN
MTTN
MTTN
HUNH.
SO, WAKA FOR THE WIN, HUH?
Haah...
DMP
DMP
Haah...
DMP
I'M SO SORRY, SENSEI!
I DIDN'T MEAN TO BE LATE!
Maizuru Naval Elementary School, 5th Grade
TAKEI JUNKO (11)
DMP

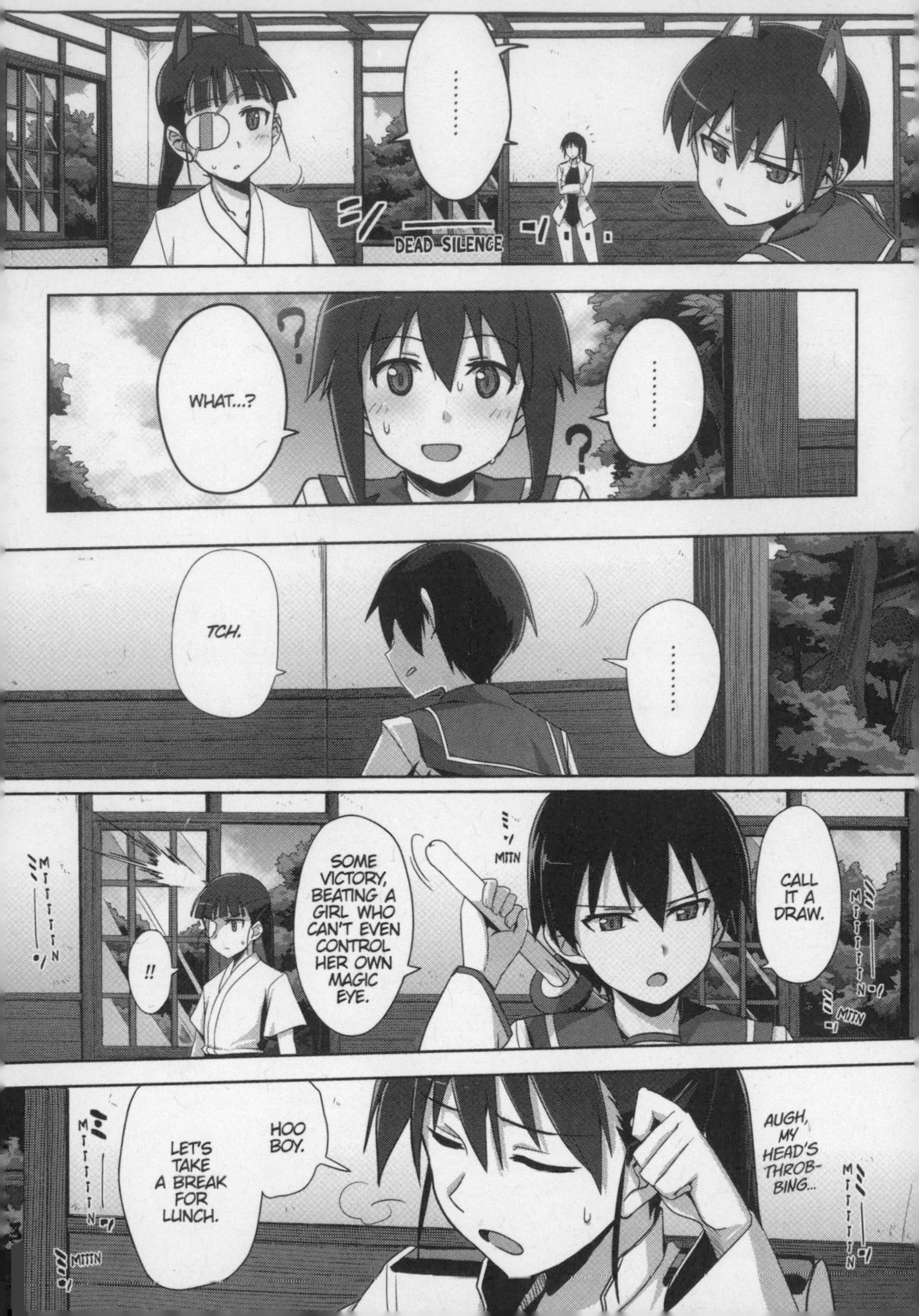
......
DEAD SILENCE
......
WHAT...?
......
TCH.
CALL IT A DRAW.
MIIIIIIN
MIIN
MIIN
SOME VICTORY, BEATING A GIRL WHO CAN'T EVEN CONTROL HER OWN MAGIC EYE.
!!
MIIIIIIN
AUGH, MY HEAD'S THROBBING...
MIIIIIIN
HOO BOY.
LET'S TAKE A BREAK FOR LUNCH.
MIIIIIIN
MIIN

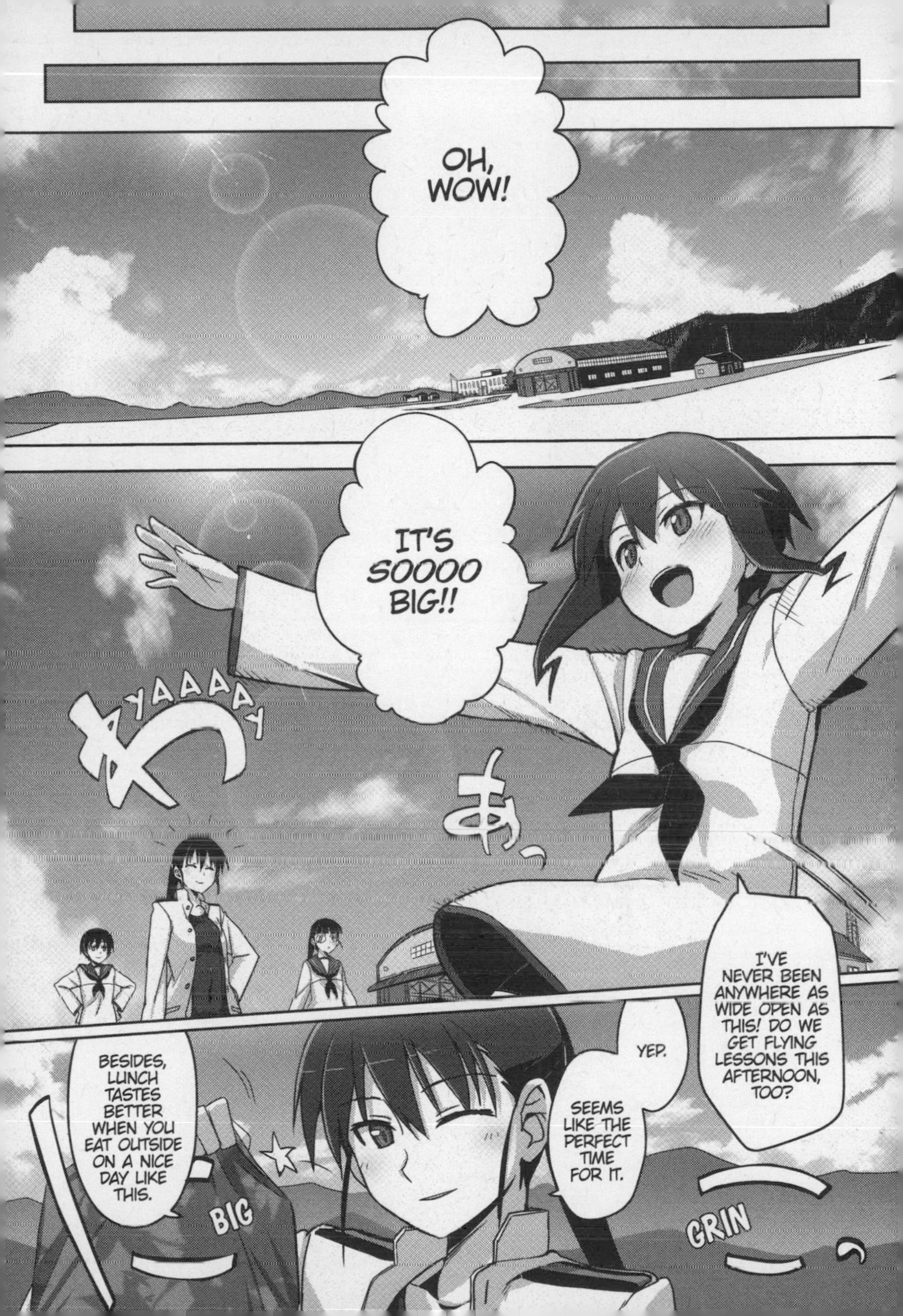
OH, WOW!
IT'S SOOOO BIG!!
YAAAAY
I'VE NEVER BEEN ANYWHERE AS WIDE OPEN AS THIS! DO WE GET FLYING LESSONS THIS AFTERNOON, TOO?
YEP.
SEEMS LIKE THE PERFECT TIME FOR IT.
GRIN
BESIDES, LUNCH TASTES BETTER WHEN YOU EAT OUTSIDE ON A NICE DAY LIKE THIS.
BIG

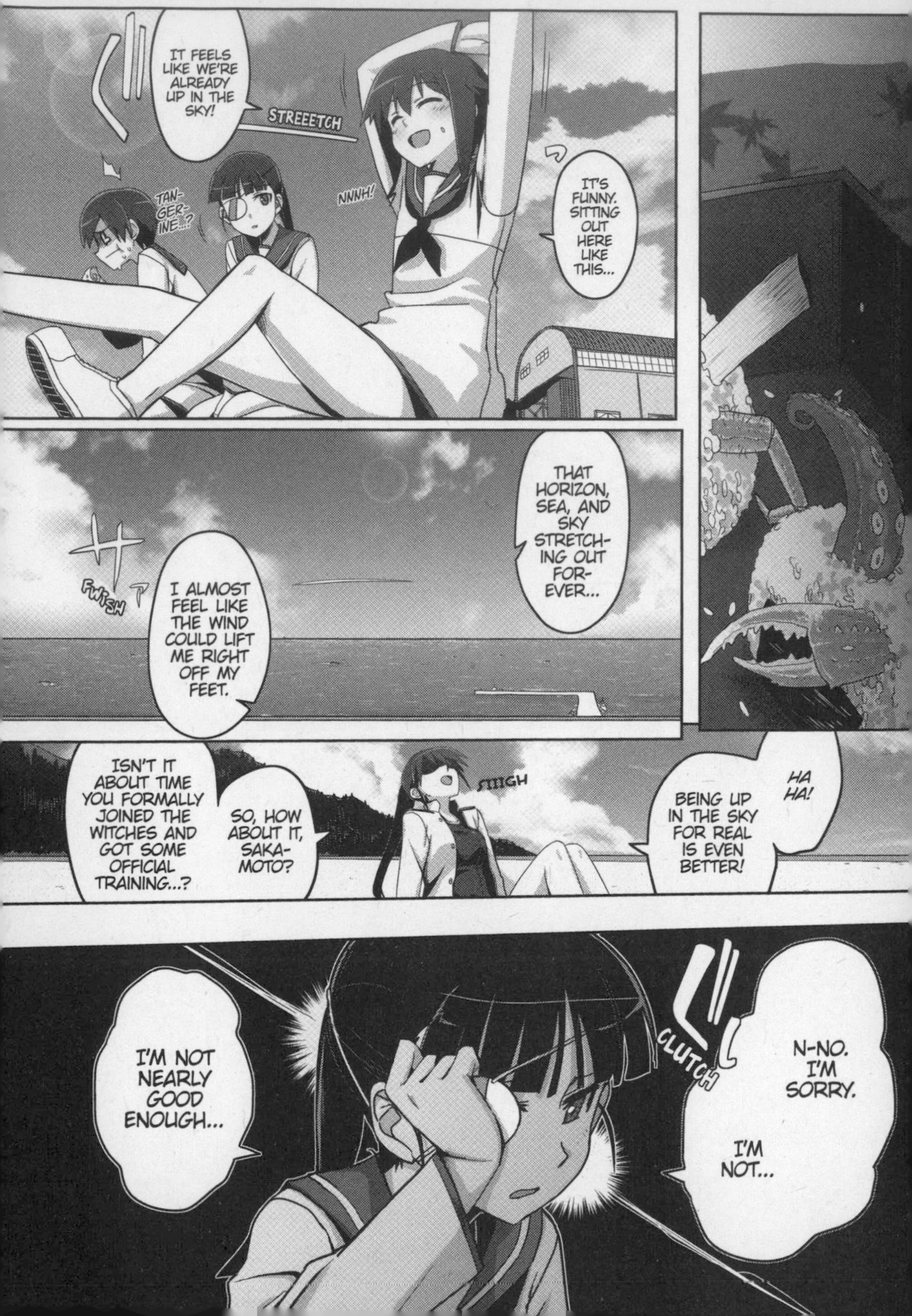
IT'S FUNNY. SITTING OUT HERE LIKE THIS...
IT FEELS LIKE WE'RE ALREADY UP IN THE SKY!
STREEETCH
NNNH!
TAN-GERINE...?
THAT HORIZON, SEA, AND SKY STRETCHING OUT FOREVER...
I ALMOST FEEL LIKE THE WIND COULD LIFT ME RIGHT OFF MY FEET.
FWISH
HA HA!
BEING UP IN THE SKY FOR REAL IS EVEN BETTER!
SIIGH
SO, HOW ABOUT IT, SAKAMOTO?
ISN'T IT ABOUT TIME YOU FORMALLY JOINED THE WITCHES AND GOT SOME OFFICIAL TRAINING...?
N-NO. I'M SORRY.
CLUTCH
I'M NOT...
I'M NOT NEARLY GOOD ENOUGH...

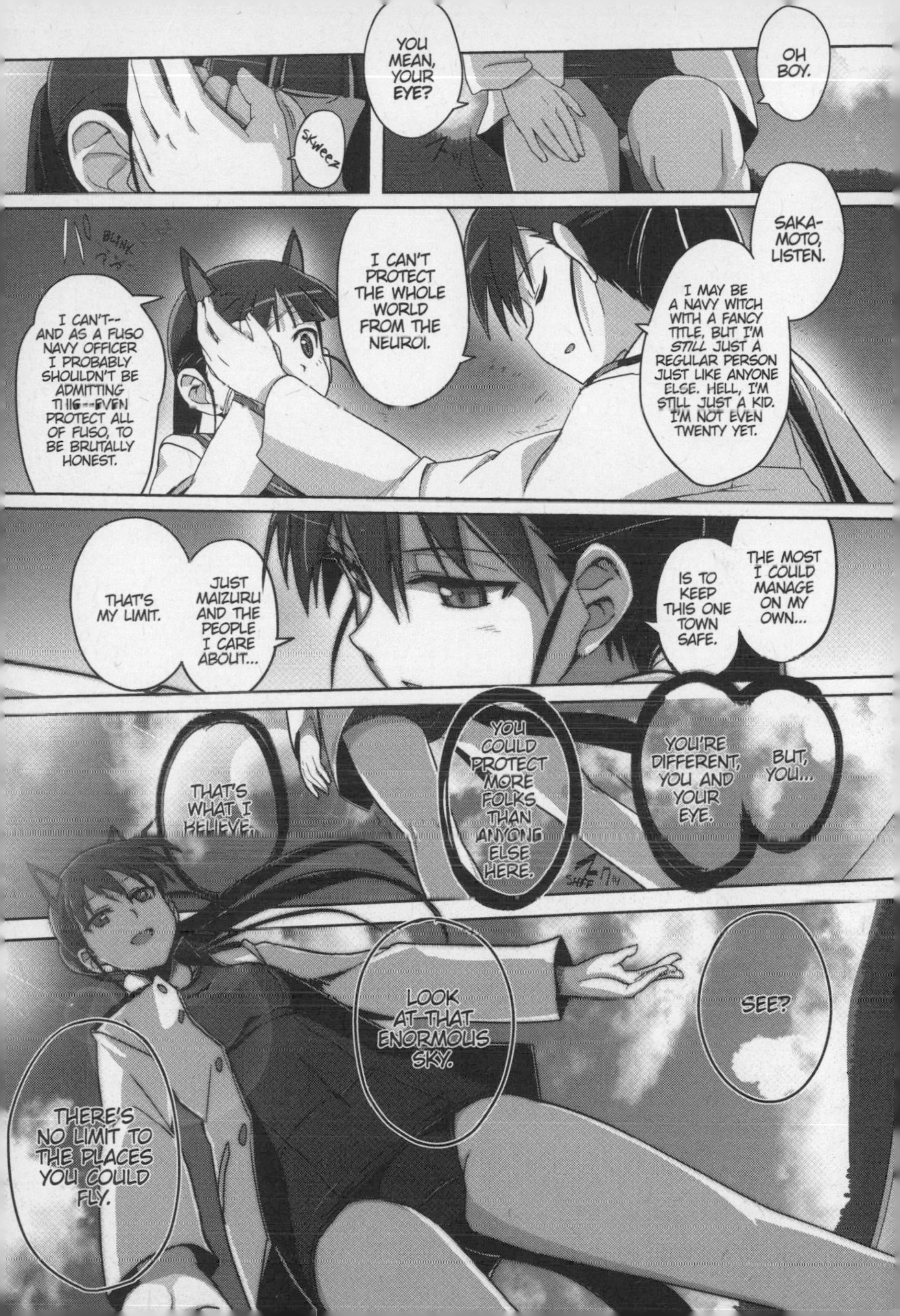
OH BOY.
YOU MEAN, YOUR EYE?
SKWEEZ
SAKA-MOTO, LISTEN.
I MAY BE A NAVY WITCH WITH A FANCY TITLE, BUT I'M *STILL* JUST A REGULAR PERSON JUST LIKE ANYONE ELSE. HELL, I'M STILL JUST A KID. I'M NOT EVEN TWENTY YET.
I CAN'T PROTECT THE WHOLE WORLD FROM THE NEUROI.
I CAN'T-- AND AS A FUSO NAVY OFFICER I PROBABLY SHOULDN'T BE ADMITTING THIS--EVEN PROTECT ALL OF FUSO, TO BE BRUTALLY HONEST.
BLINK
THE MOST I COULD MANAGE ON MY OWN...
IS TO KEEP THIS ONE TOWN SAFE.
JUST MAIZURU AND THE PEOPLE I CARE ABOUT...
THAT'S MY LIMIT.
BUT, YOU...
YOU'RE DIFFERENT, YOU AND YOUR EYE.
SHFF
YOU COULD PROTECT MORE FOLKS THAN ANYONE ELSE HERE.
THAT'S WHAT I BELIEVE.
SEE?
LOOK AT THAT ENORMOUS SKY.
THERE'S NO LIMIT TO THE PLACES YOU COULD FLY.

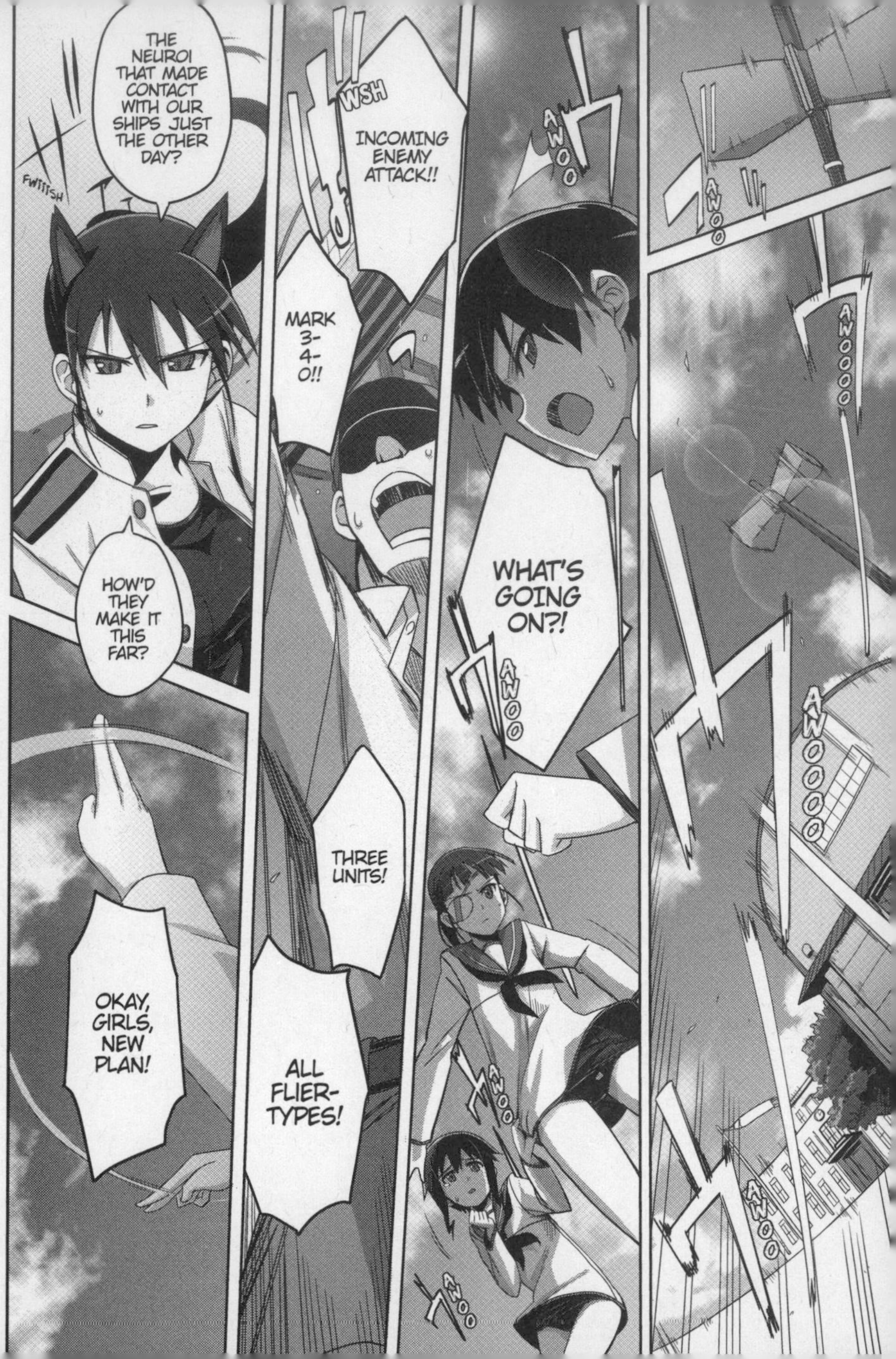
AWOO
AWOO
AWOOOOO
AWOOOOO
AWOO
AWOO
WHAT'S GOING ON?!
AWOO
AWOO
AWOO
WSH
INCOMING ENEMY ATTACK!!
MARK 3-4-0!!
THREE UNITS!
ALL FLIER-TYPES!
THE NEUROI THAT MADE CONTACT WITH OUR SHIPS JUST THE OTHER DAY?
FWIIISH
HOW'D THEY MAKE IT THIS FAR?
OKAY, GIRLS, NEW PLAN!

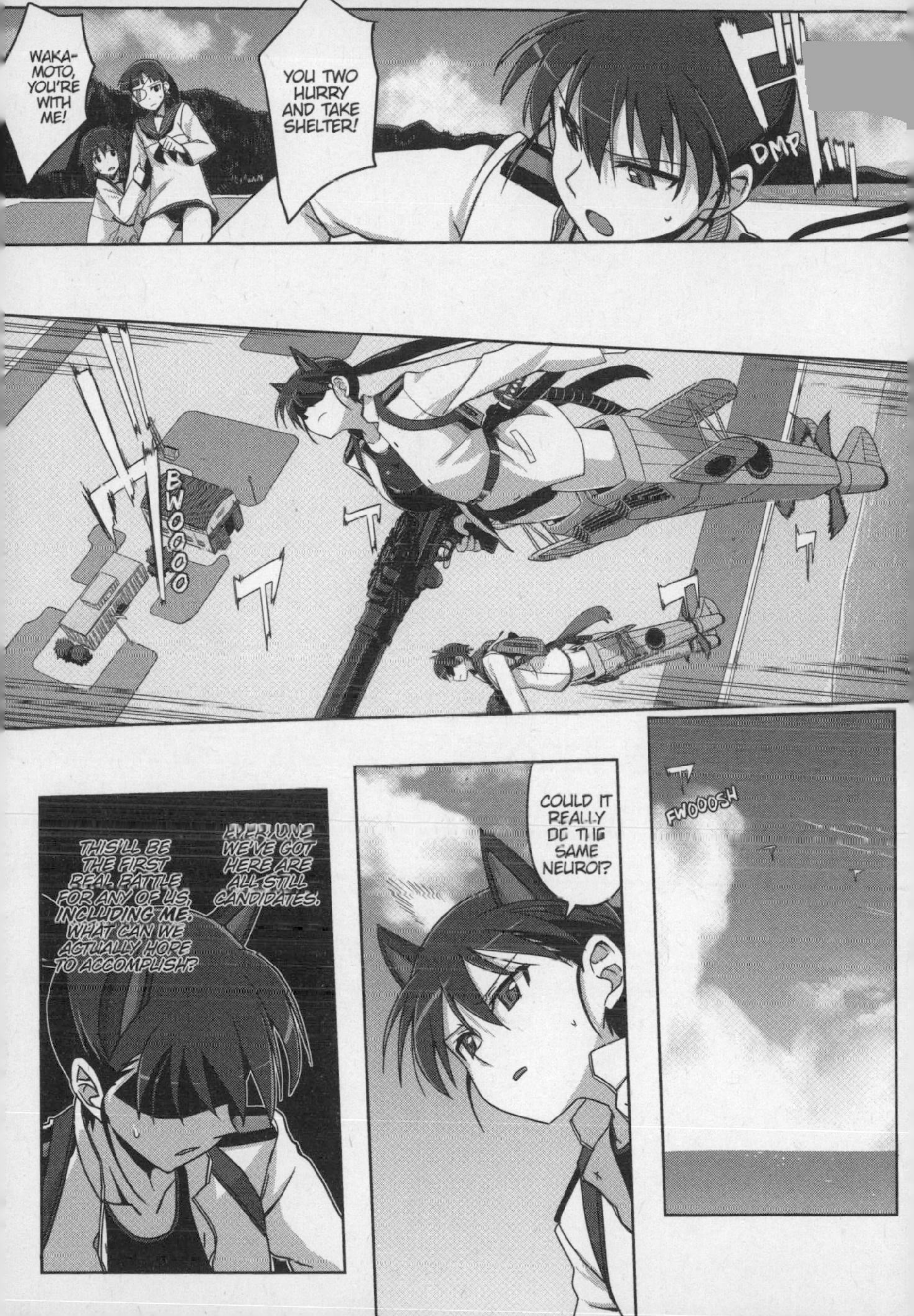
YOU TWO HURRY AND TAKE SHELTER!
WAKA-MOTO, YOU'RE WITH ME!
DMP
BWOOOOO
FWOOOSH
COULD IT REALLY BE THE SAME NEUROI?
EVERYONE WE'VE GOT HERE ARE ALL STILL CANDIDATES.
THIS'LL BE THE FIRST REAL BATTLE FOR ANY OF US, INCLUDING ME. WHAT CAN WE ACTUALLY HOPE TO ACCOMPLISH?

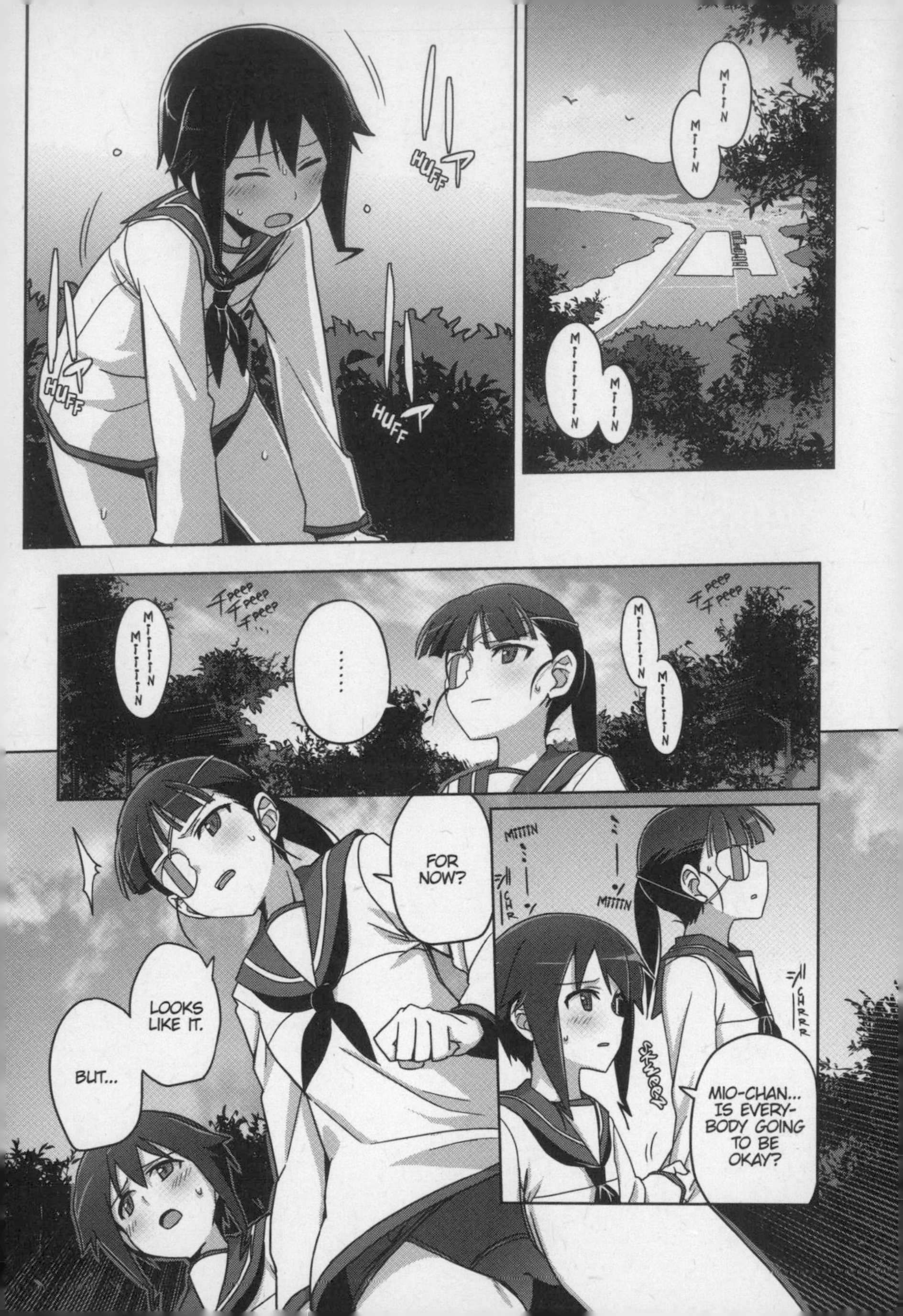
MIIN
MIIN
MIIIIIIN
MIIN
HUFF
HUFF
HUFF
peep peep
MIIIIIN
MIIIIIN
......
peep peep peep...
MIIIIIN
MIIIIIN
MIIIIN
GHRR
MIIIIN
GHRRR
SKWEEZ
MIO-CHAN... IS EVERY-BODY GOING TO BE OKAY?
FOR NOW?
LOOKS LIKE IT.
BUT...

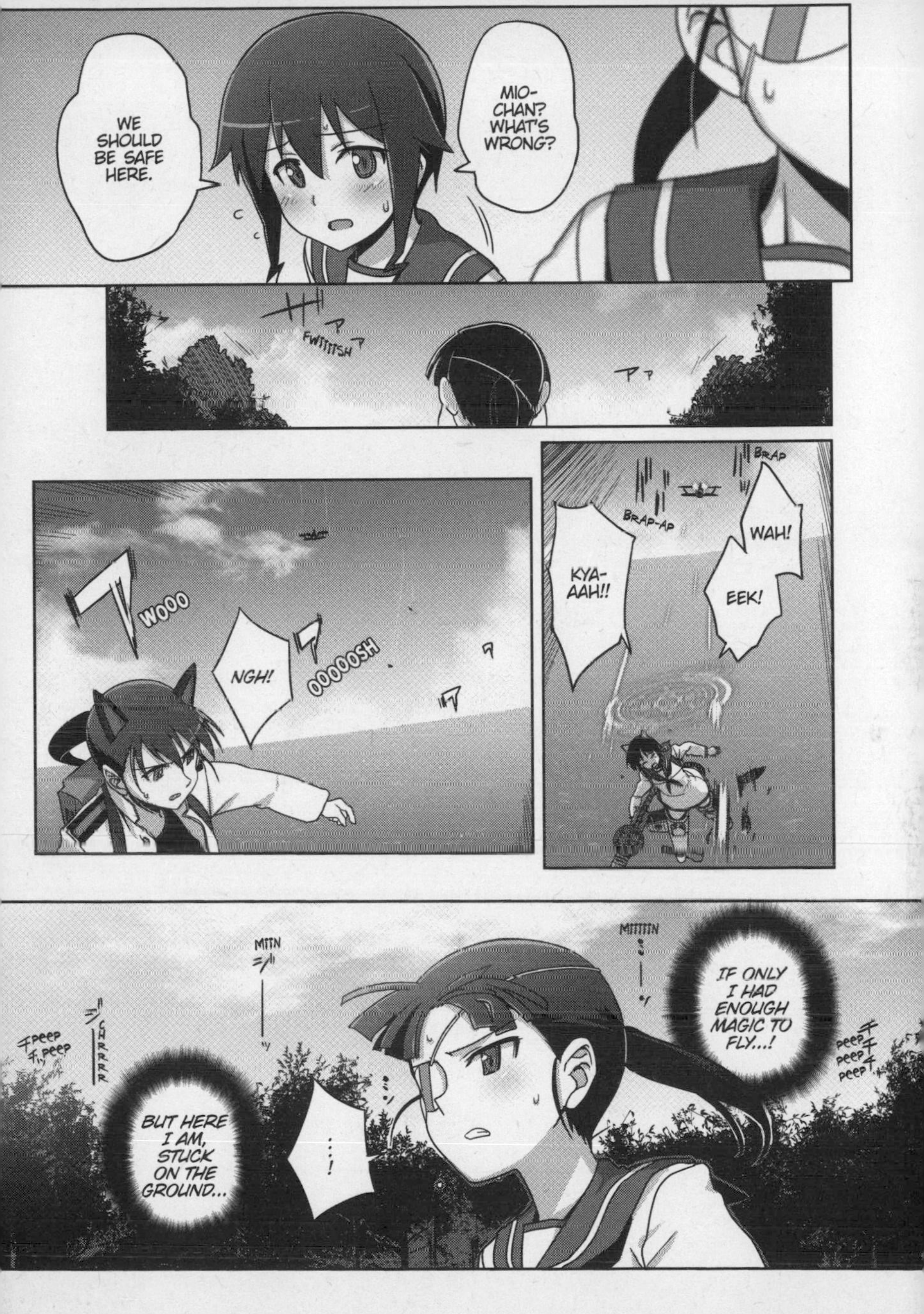
MIO-CHAN? WHAT'S WRONG?
WE SHOULD BE SAFE HERE.
FWIIIISH
BRAP
WAH!
EEK!
BRAP-AP
KYA-AAH!!
NGH!
OOOOOSH
WOOO
MIIIIN
IF ONLY I HAD ENOUGH MAGIC TO FLY...!
PEEP PEEP PEEP
MIIIN
CHRRRR
PEEP PEEP
BUT HERE I AM, STUCK ON THE GROUND...
...!

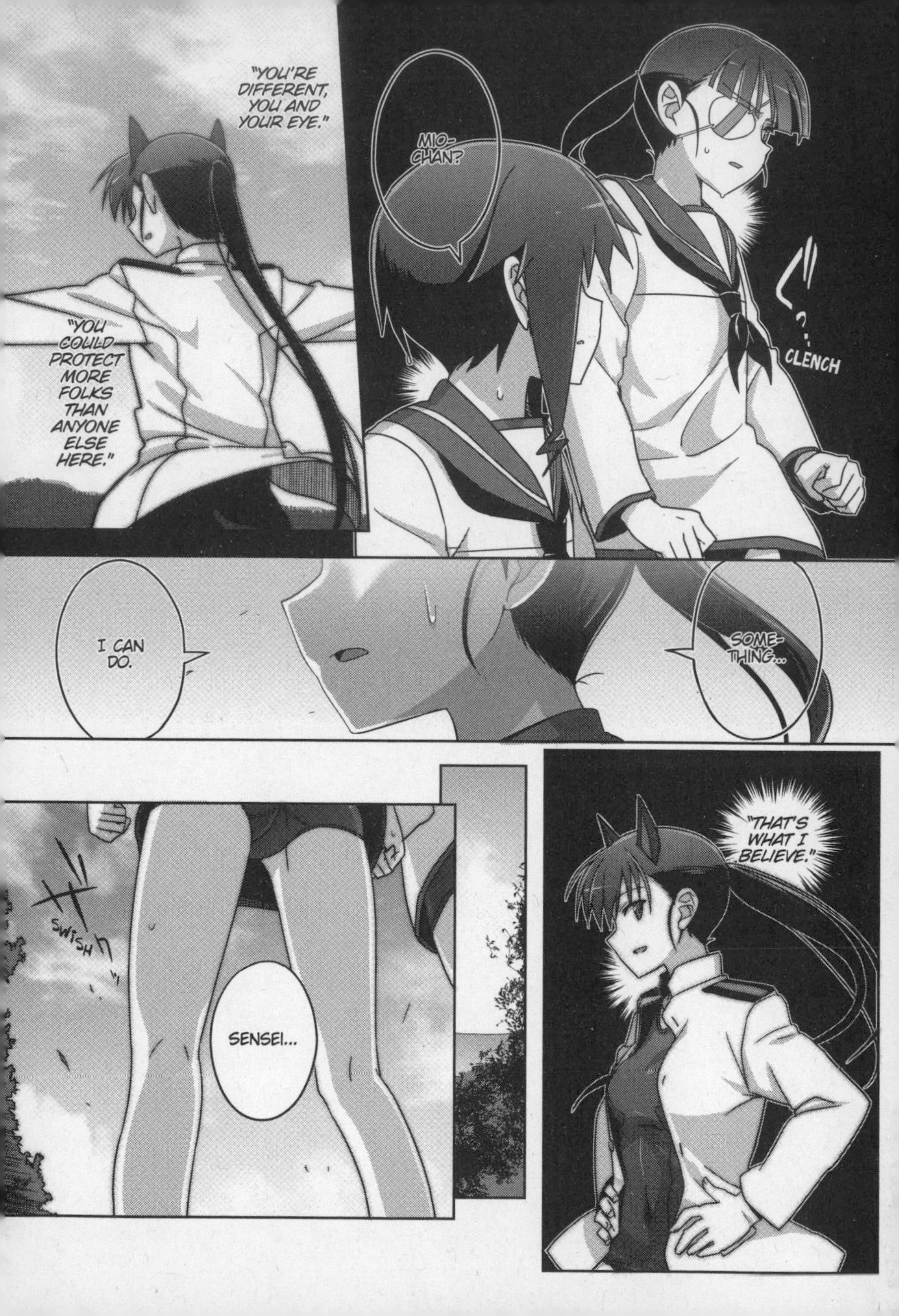
MIO-CHAN?
CLENCH
"YOU'RE DIFFERENT, YOU AND YOUR EYE."
"YOU COULD PROTECT MORE FOLKS THAN ANYONE ELSE HERE."
SOME-THING...
I CAN DO.
"THAT'S WHAT I BELIEVE."
SENSEI...
SWISH

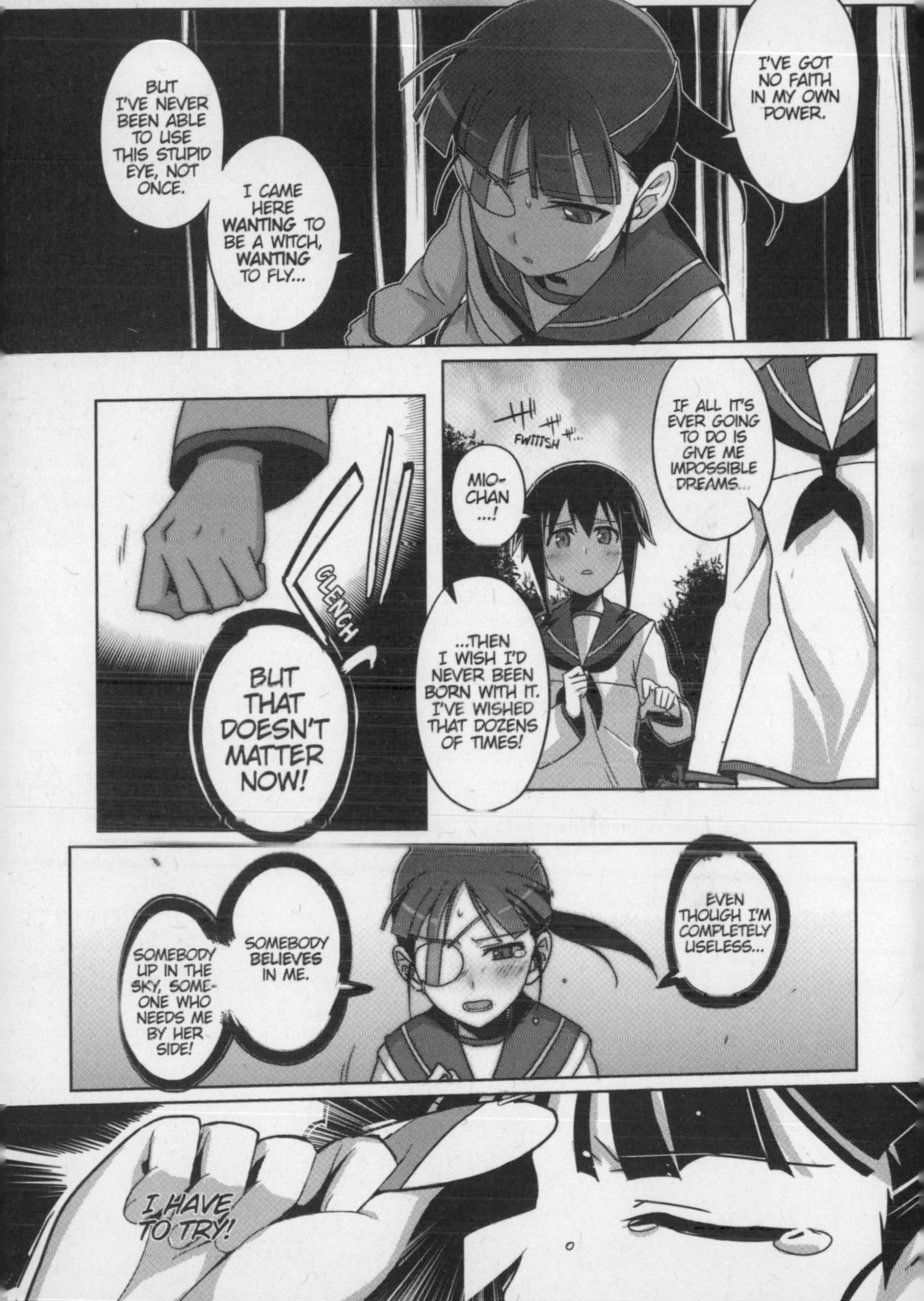
I'VE GOT NO FAITH IN MY OWN POWER.
I CAME HERE WANTING TO BE A WITCH, WANTING TO FLY...
BUT I'VE NEVER BEEN ABLE TO USE THIS STUPID EYE, NOT ONCE.
FWITISH
IF ALL IT'S EVER GOING TO DO IS GIVE ME IMPOSSIBLE DREAMS...
MIO-CHAN ...!
...THEN I WISH I'D NEVER BEEN BORN WITH IT. I'VE WISHED THAT DOZENS OF TIMES!
CLENCH
BUT THAT DOESN'T MATTER NOW!
EVEN THOUGH I'M COMPLETELY USELESS...
SOMEBODY BELIEVES IN ME.
SOMEBODY UP IN THE SKY, SOME-ONE WHO NEEDS ME BY HER SIDE!
I HAVE TO TRY!

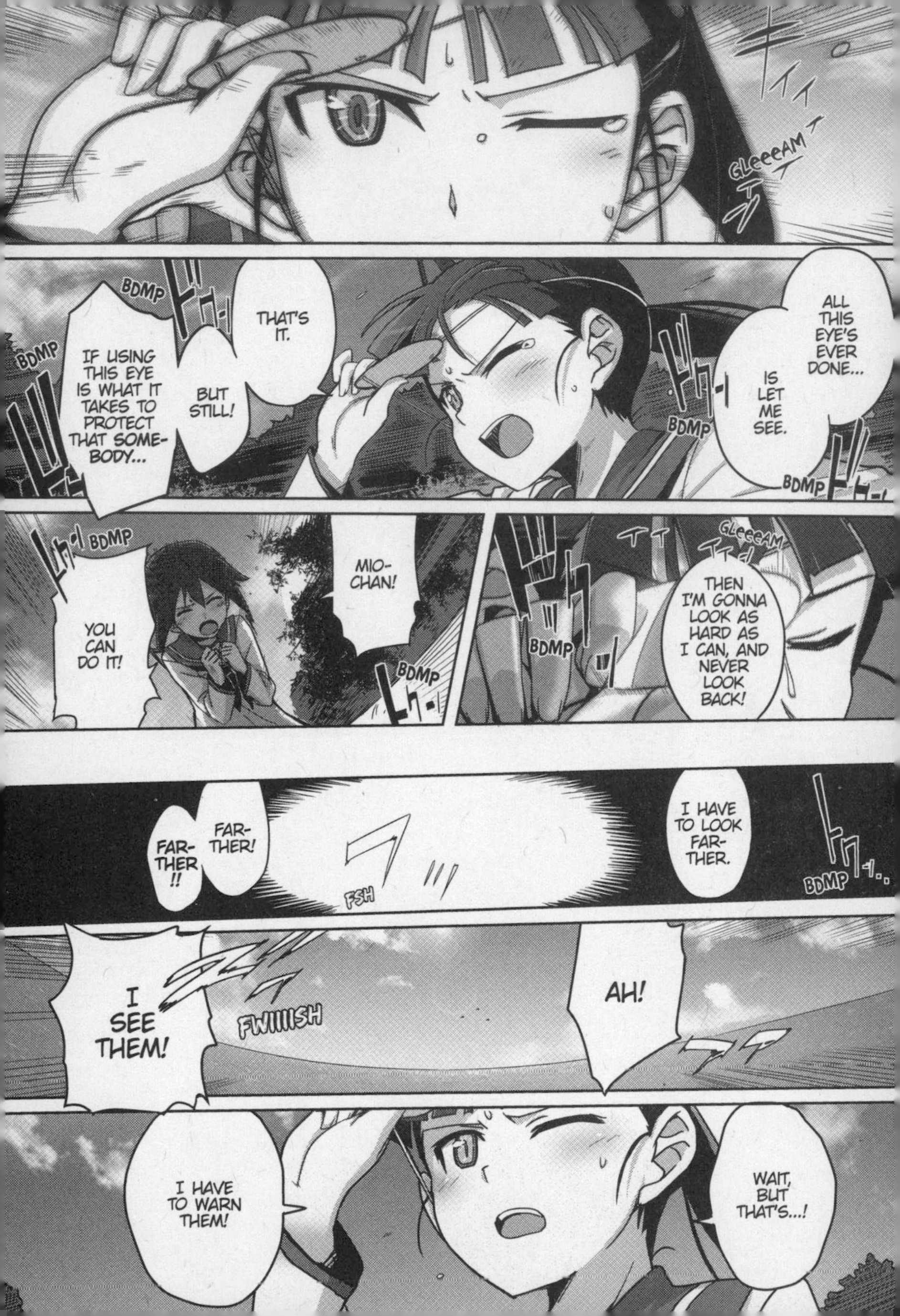
GLEEEAM
ALL THIS EYE'S EVER DONE...
IS LET ME SEE.
BDMP
BDMP
THAT'S IT.
BUT STILL!
BDMP
IF USING THIS EYE IS WHAT IT TAKES TO PROTECT THAT SOMEBODY...
BDMP
GLEEEAM
THEN I'M GONNA LOOK AS HARD AS I CAN, AND NEVER LOOK BACK!
BDMP
MIO-CHAN!
BDMP
BDMP
YOU CAN DO IT!
BDMP
I HAVE TO LOOK FARTHER.
FSH
FAR-THER!
FAR-THER!!
AH!
FWIIIISH
I SEE THEM!
WAIT, BUT THAT'S...!
I HAVE TO WARN THEM!

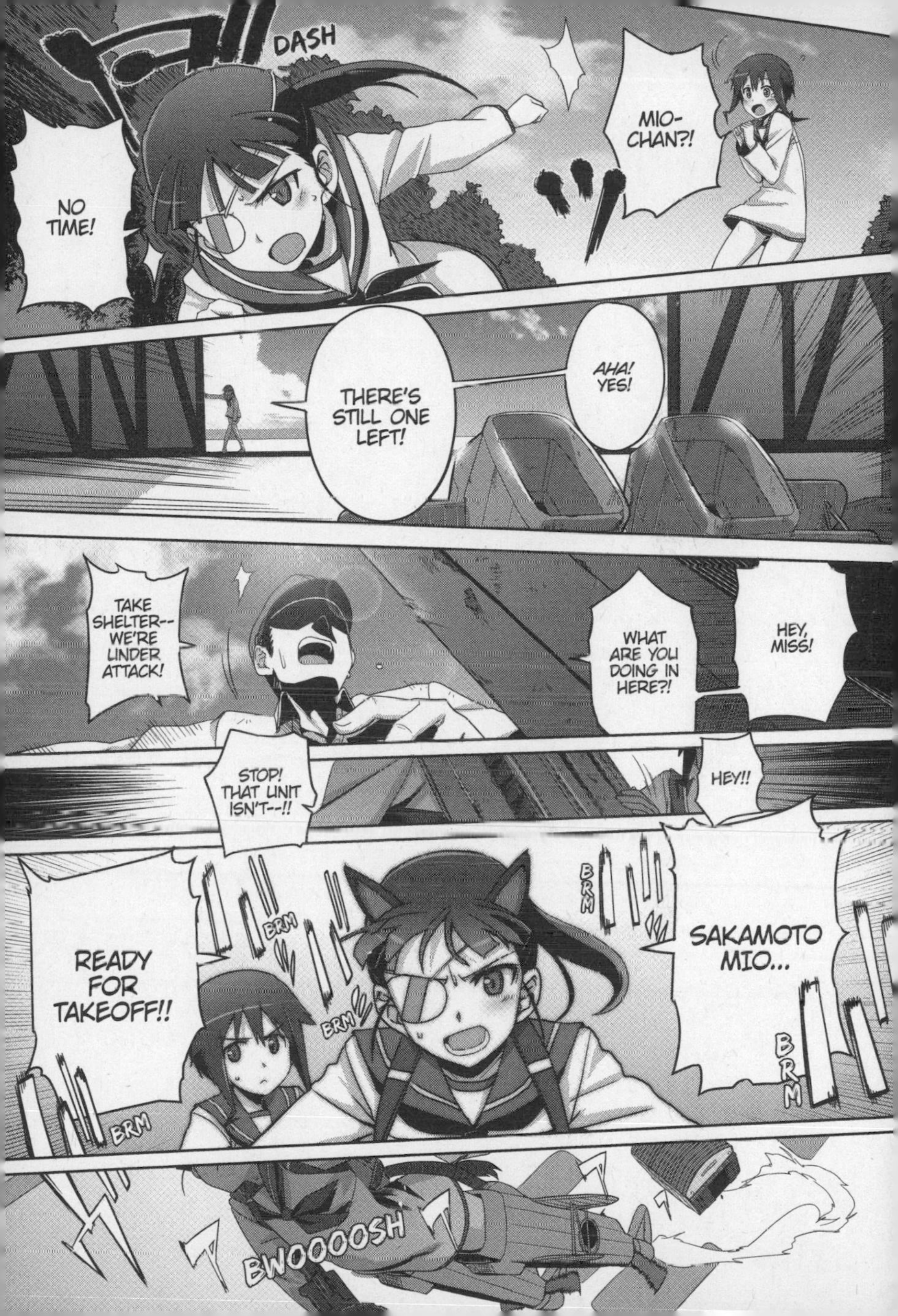
MIO-CHAN?!
DASH
NO TIME!
AHA! YES!
THERE'S STILL ONE LEFT!
HEY, MISS!
WHAT ARE YOU DOING IN HERE?!
TAKE SHELTER--WE'RE UNDER ATTACK!
HEY!!
STOP! THAT UNIT ISN'T--!!
SAKAMOTO MIO...
BRM
BRM
READY FOR TAKEOFF!!
BRM
BRM
BRM
BWOOOOSH

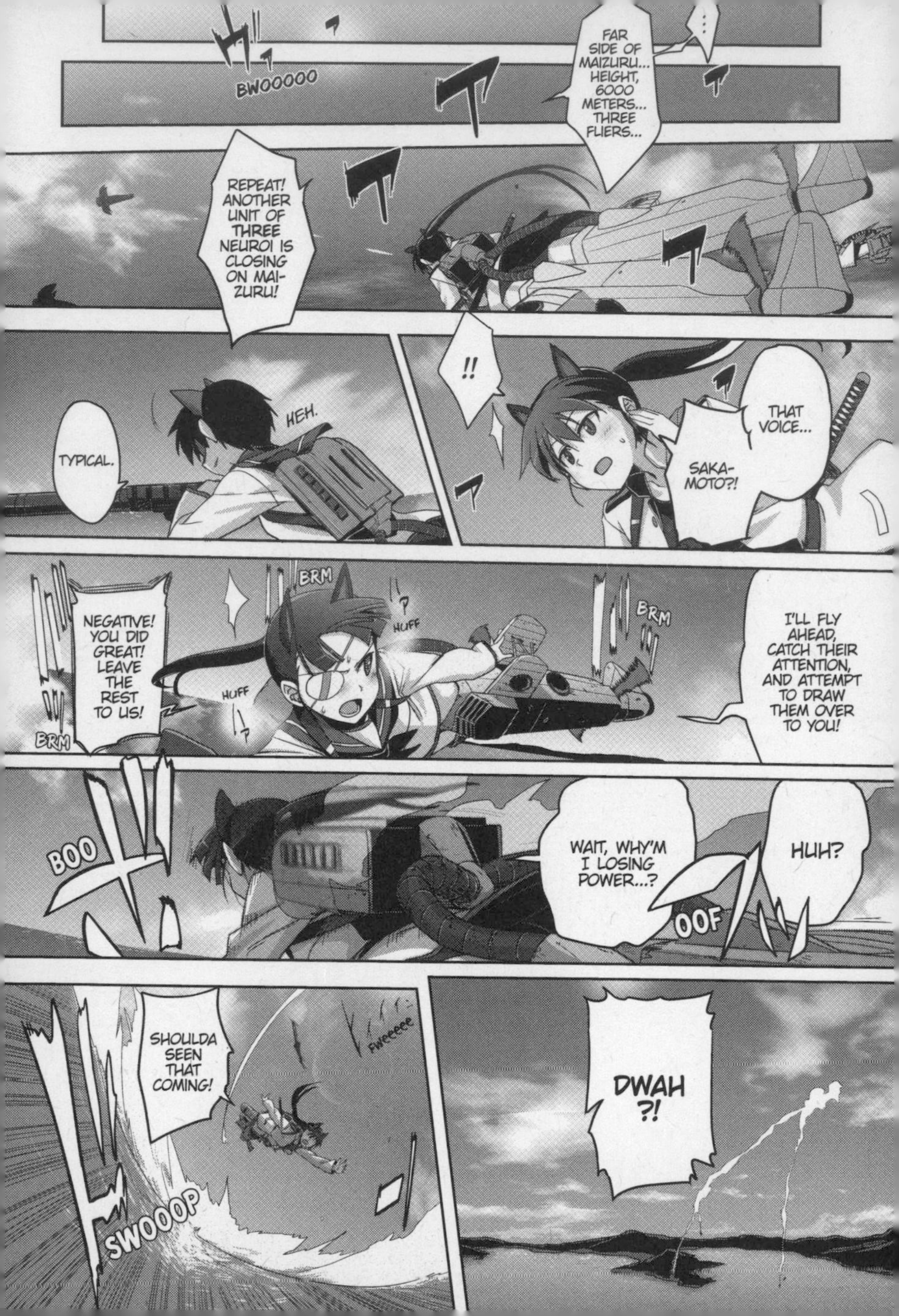
...
FAR SIDE OF MAIZURU... HEIGHT, 6000 METERS... THREE FLIERS...
BWOOOOO
REPEAT! ANOTHER UNIT OF THREE NEUROI IS CLOSING ON MAI-ZURU!
!!
THAT VOICE...
SAKA-MOTO?!
HEH.
TYPICAL.
I'LL FLY AHEAD, CATCH THEIR ATTENTION, AND ATTEMPT TO DRAW THEM OVER TO YOU!
BRM
BRM
HUFF
HUFF
NEGATIVE! YOU DID GREAT! LEAVE THE REST TO US!
BRM
HUH?
OOF
WAIT, WHY'M I LOSING POWER...?
BOO
DWAH ?!
FWEEEEE
SHOULDA SEEN THAT COMING!
SWOOOP

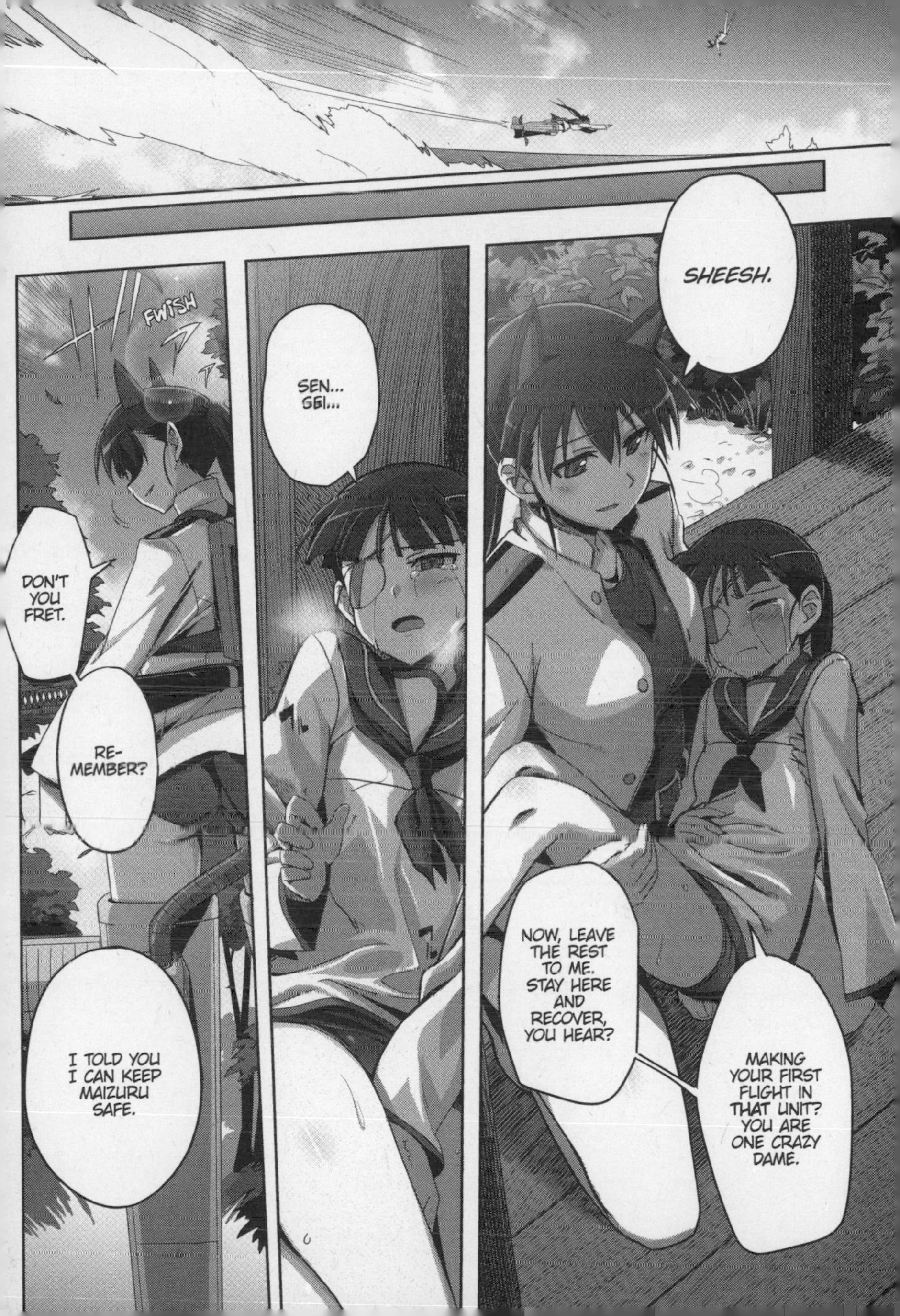
SHEESH.
MAKING YOUR FIRST FLIGHT IN THAT UNIT? YOU ARE ONE CRAZY DAME.
NOW, LEAVE THE REST TO ME. STAY HERE AND RECOVER, YOU HEAR?
SEN... SEI...
FWISH
DON'T YOU FRET.
RE-MEMBER?
I TOLD YOU I CAN KEEP MAIZURU SAFE.

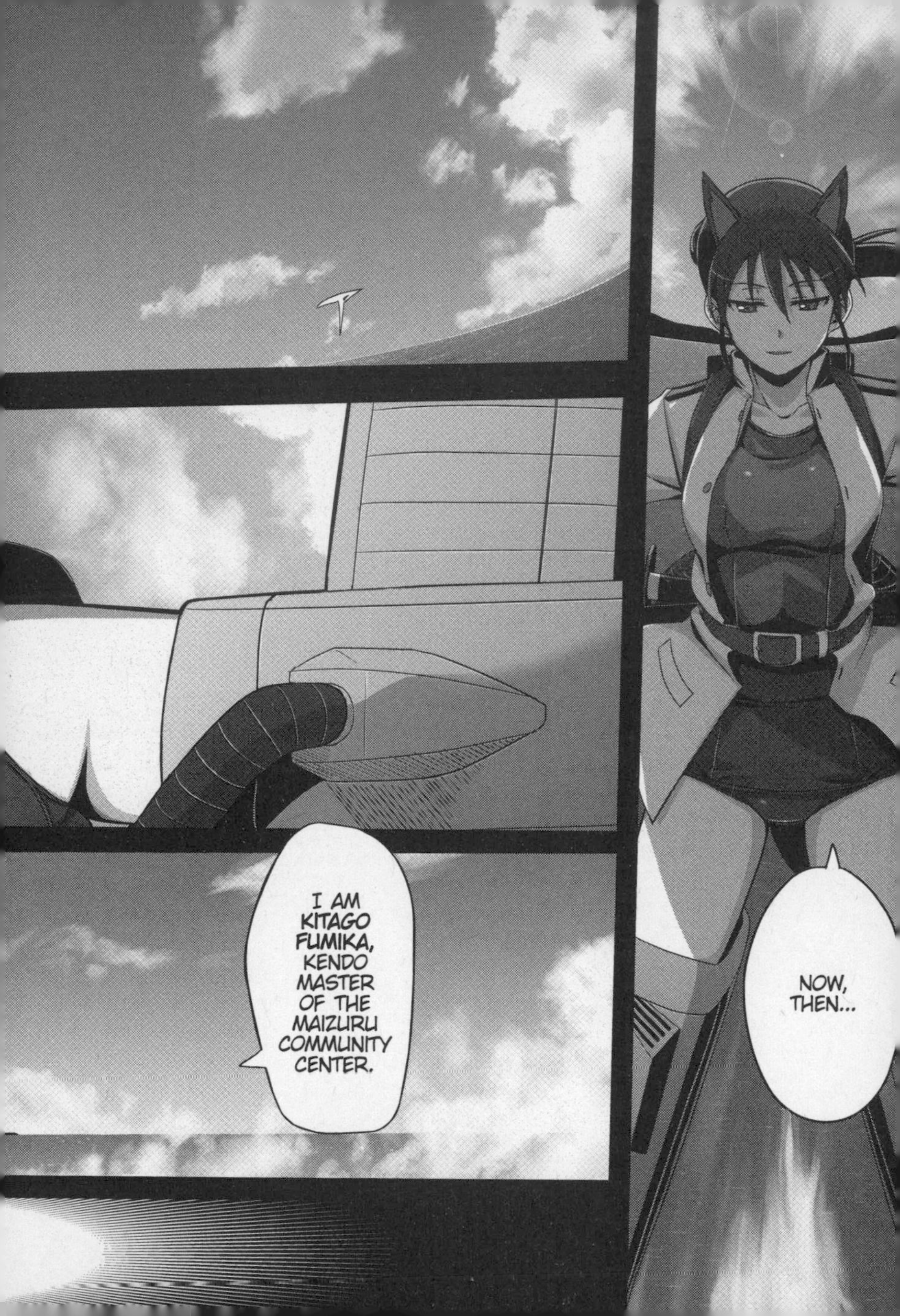
NOW, THEN...
I AM KITAGO FUMIKA, KENDO MASTER OF THE MAIZURU COMMUNITY CENTER.

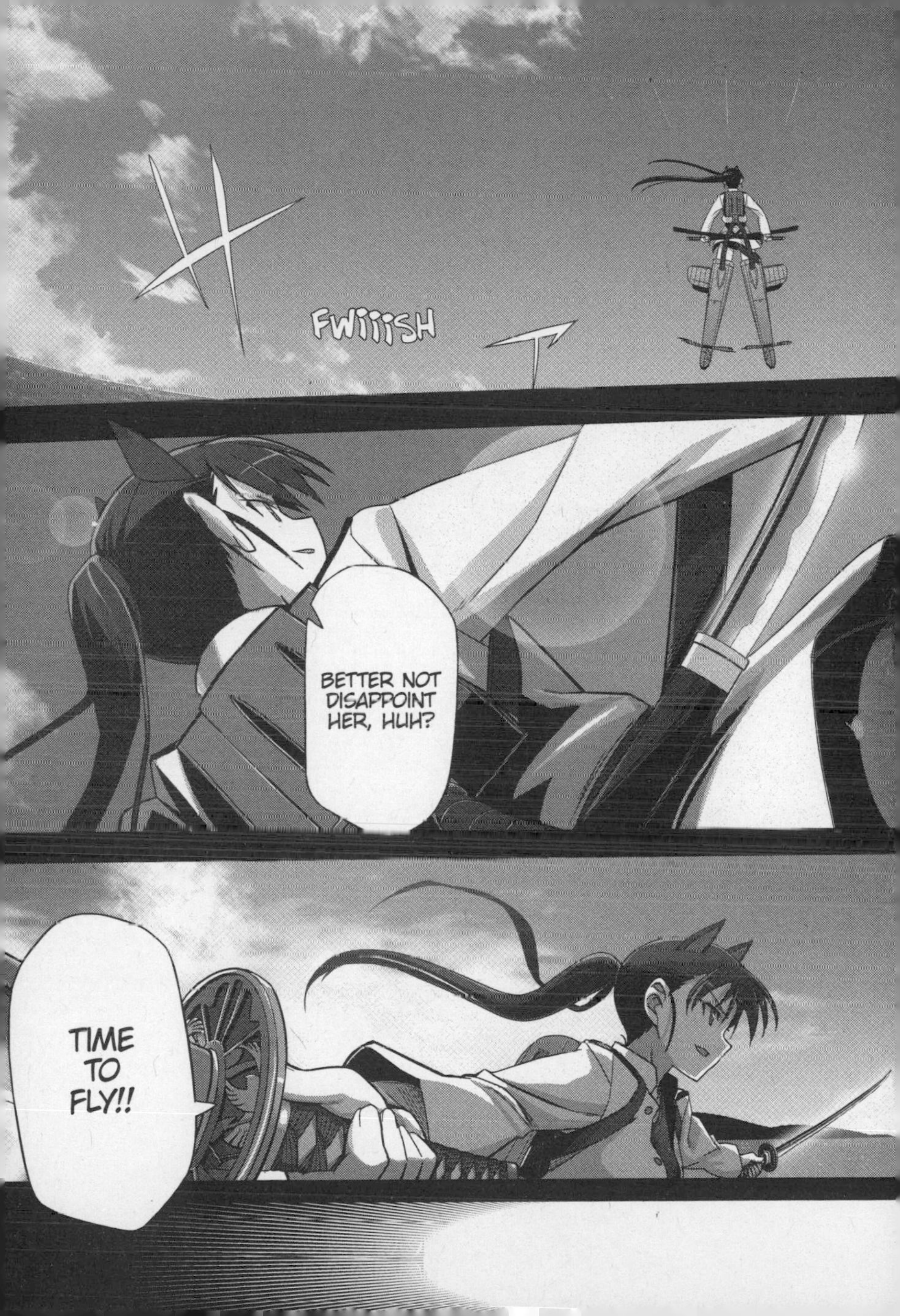
FWIIISH
BETTER NOT DISAPPOINT HER, HUH?
TIME TO FLY!!

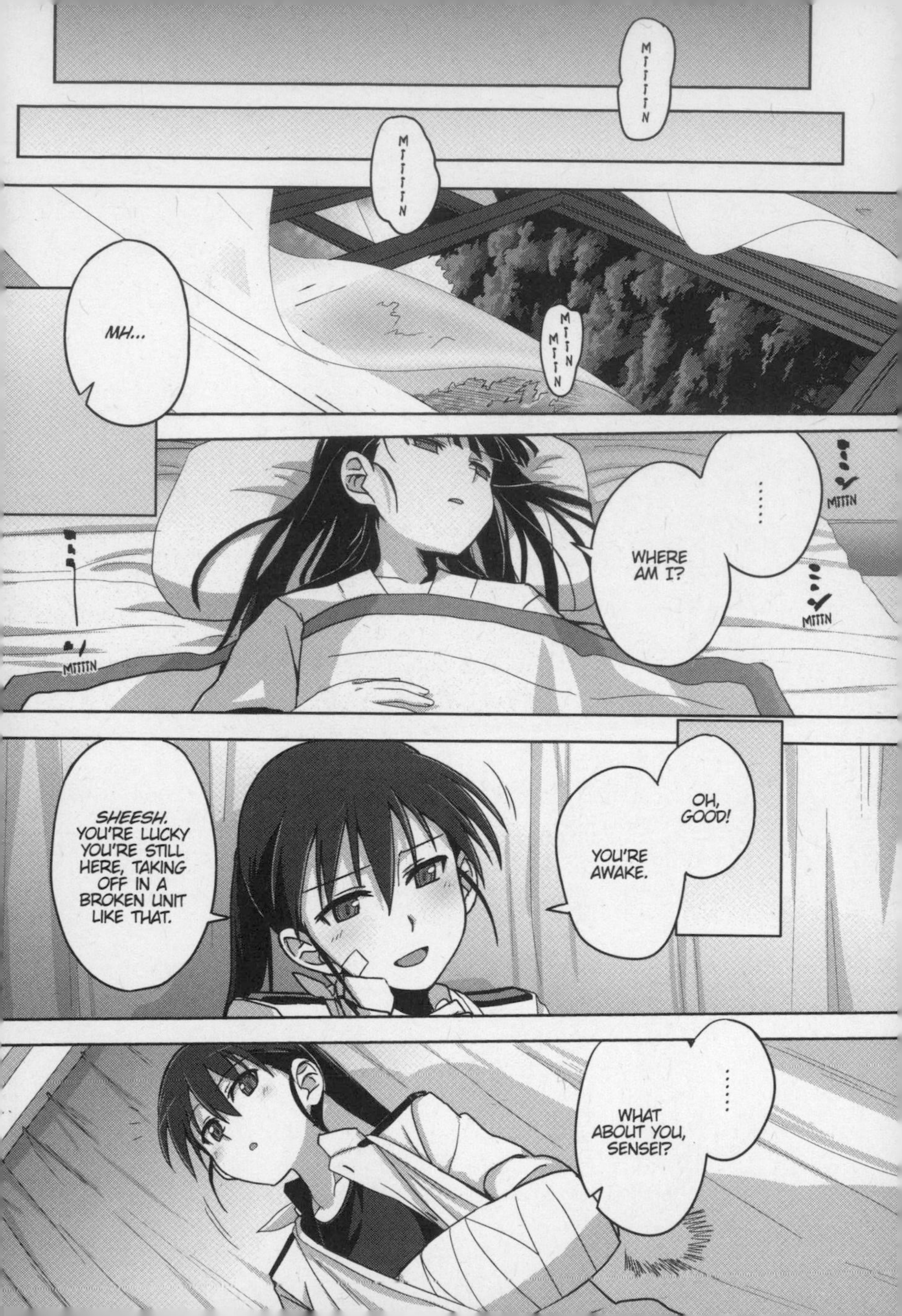
MIIIIN
MIIIIN
MIIN MIIN
MH...
......
WHERE AM I?
MIIIN
MIIIN
MIIIIN
OH, GOOD!
YOU'RE AWAKE.
SHEESH. YOU'RE LUCKY YOU'RE STILL HERE, TAKING OFF IN A BROKEN UNIT LIKE THAT.
......
WHAT ABOUT YOU, SENSEI?

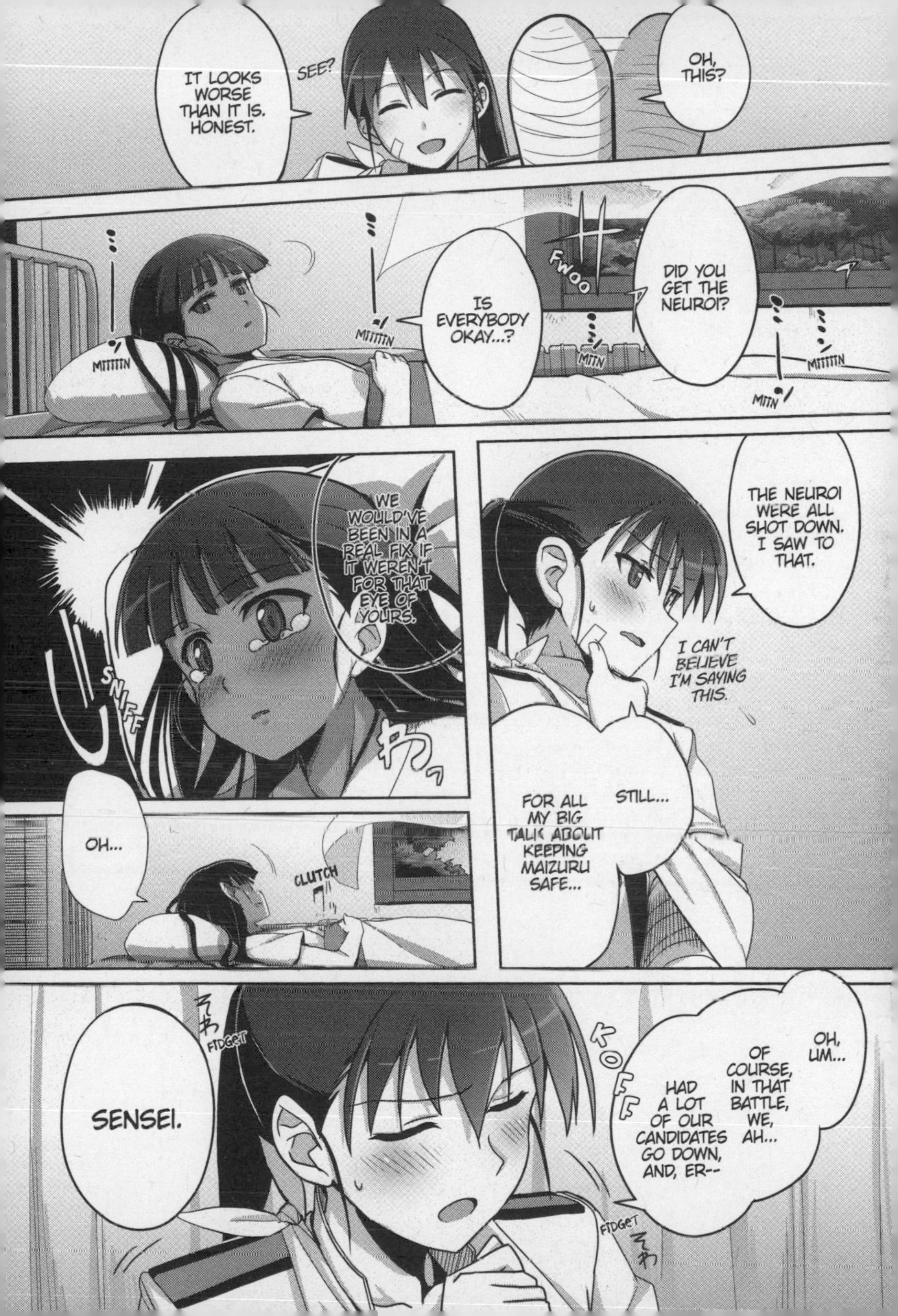
OH, THIS?
SEE?
IT LOOKS WORSE THAN IT IS. HONEST.
FWOO
DID YOU GET THE NEUROI?
MITTTN
MITN
MITN
IS EVERYBODY OKAY...?
MITTTTN
MITTTN
THE NEUROI WERE ALL SHOT DOWN. I SAW TO THAT.
I CAN'T BELIEVE I'M SAYING THIS.
STILL...
FOR ALL MY BIG TALK ABOUT KEEPING MAIZURU SAFE...
WE WOULD'VE BEEN IN A REAL FIX IF IT WEREN'T FOR THAT EYE OF YOURS.
SNIFF
わっ
CLUTCH
OH...
OH, UM...
OF COURSE, IN THAT BATTLE, WE, AH...
HAD A LOT OF OUR CANDIDATES GO DOWN, AND, ER--
KOFF
FIDGET
FIDGET
SENSEI.

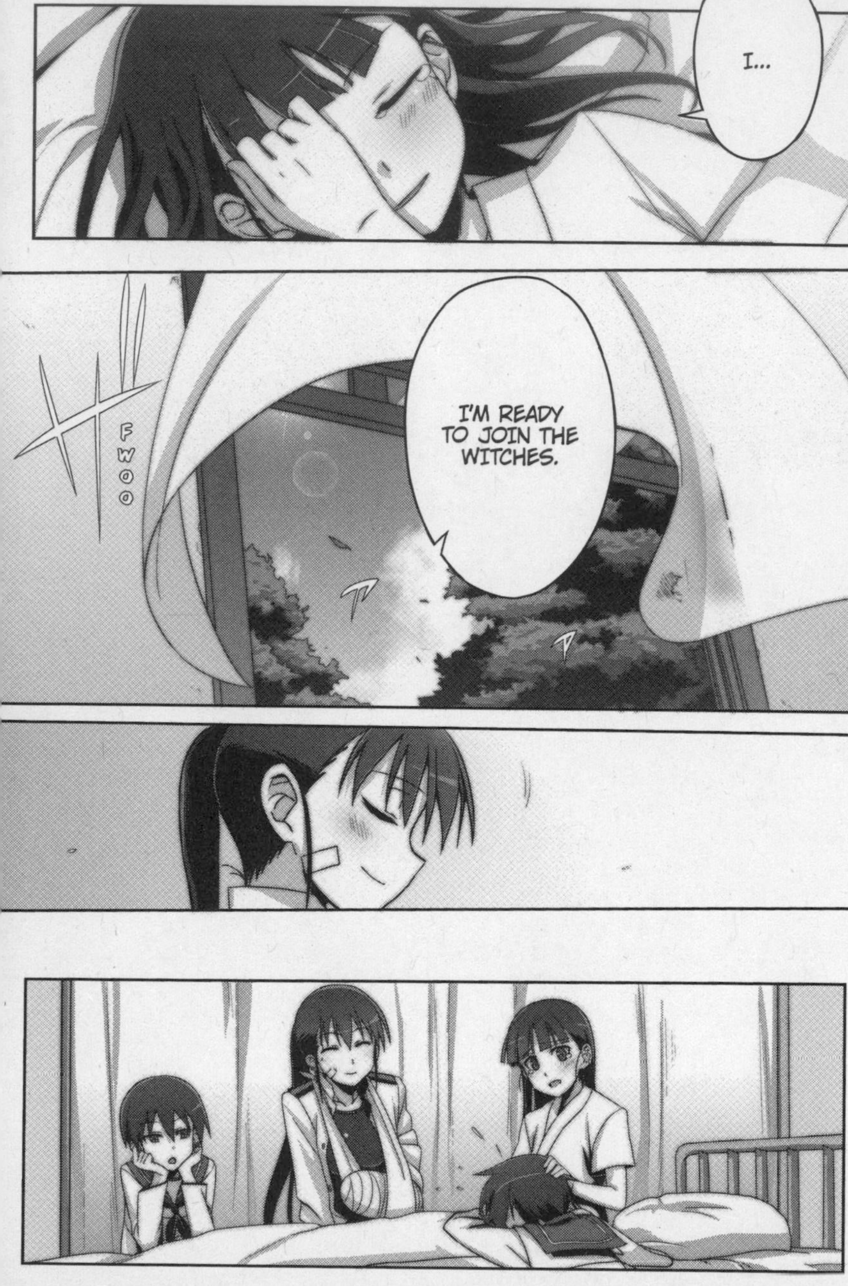
I...
FWOO
I'M READY TO JOIN THE WITCHES.

Chapter 1:
Promise in the Sky
[Mission Complete]

CHAPTER 2:
TAKING WING

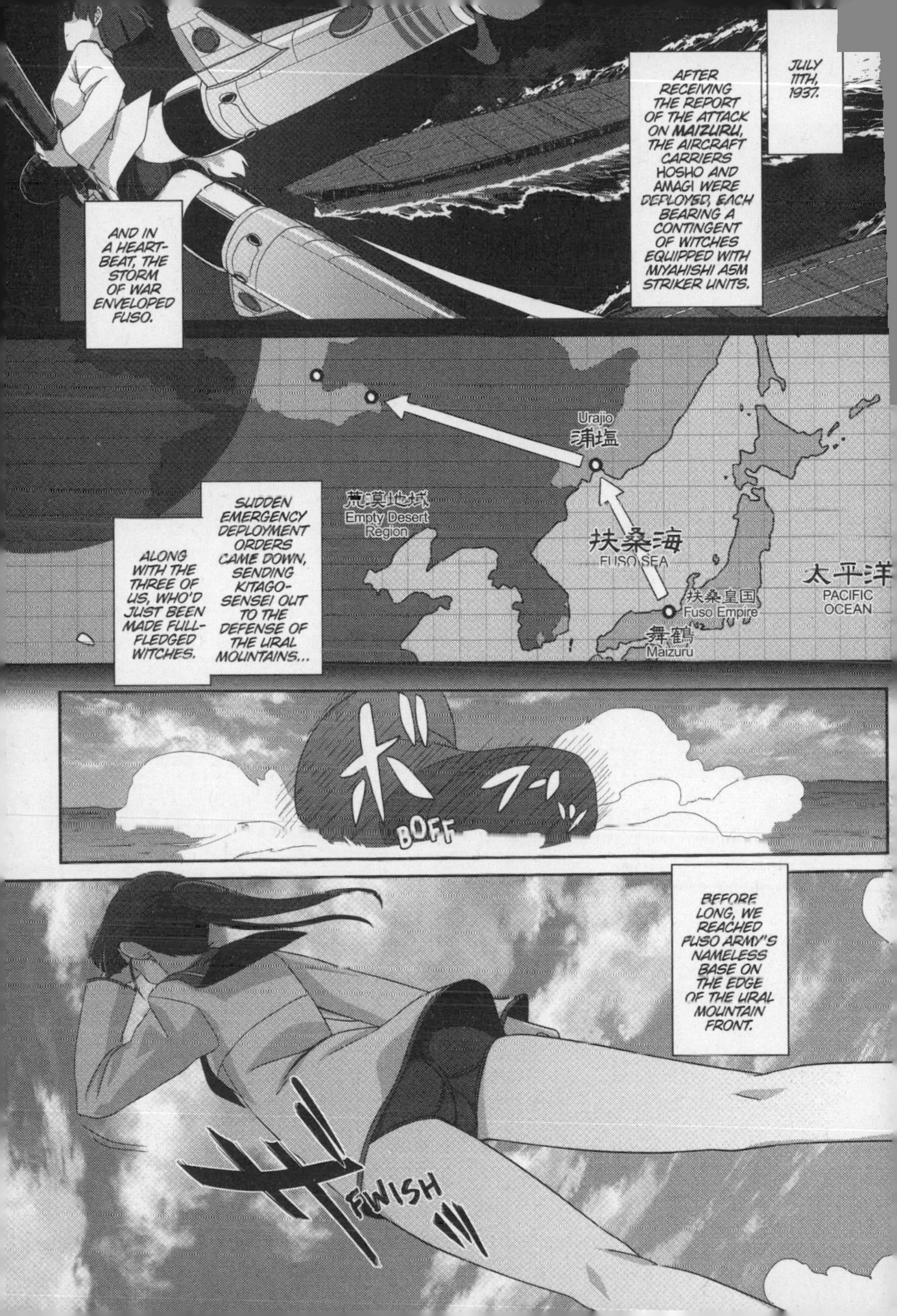
JULY 11TH, 1937.
AFTER RECEIVING THE REPORT OF THE ATTACK ON MAIZURU, THE AIRCRAFT CARRIERS HOSHO AND AMAGI WERE DEPLOYED, EACH BEARING A CONTINGENT OF WITCHES EQUIPPED WITH MIYAHISHI A5M STRIKER UNITS.
AND IN A HEART-BEAT, THE STORM OF WAR ENVELOPED FUSO.
Urajio
浦塩
荒漠地域
Empty Desert Region
扶桑海
FUSO SEA
太平洋
PACIFIC OCEAN
扶桑皇国
Fuso Empire
舞鶴
Maizuru
SUDDEN EMERGENCY DEPLOYMENT ORDERS CAME DOWN, SENDING KITAGO-SENSEI OUT TO THE DEFENSE OF THE URAL MOUNTAINS...
ALONG WITH THE THREE OF US, WHO'D JUST BEEN MADE FULL-FLEDGED WITCHES.
BOFF
BEFORE LONG, WE REACHED FUSO ARMY'S NAMELESS BASE ON THE EDGE OF THE URAL MOUNTAIN FRONT.
FWISH

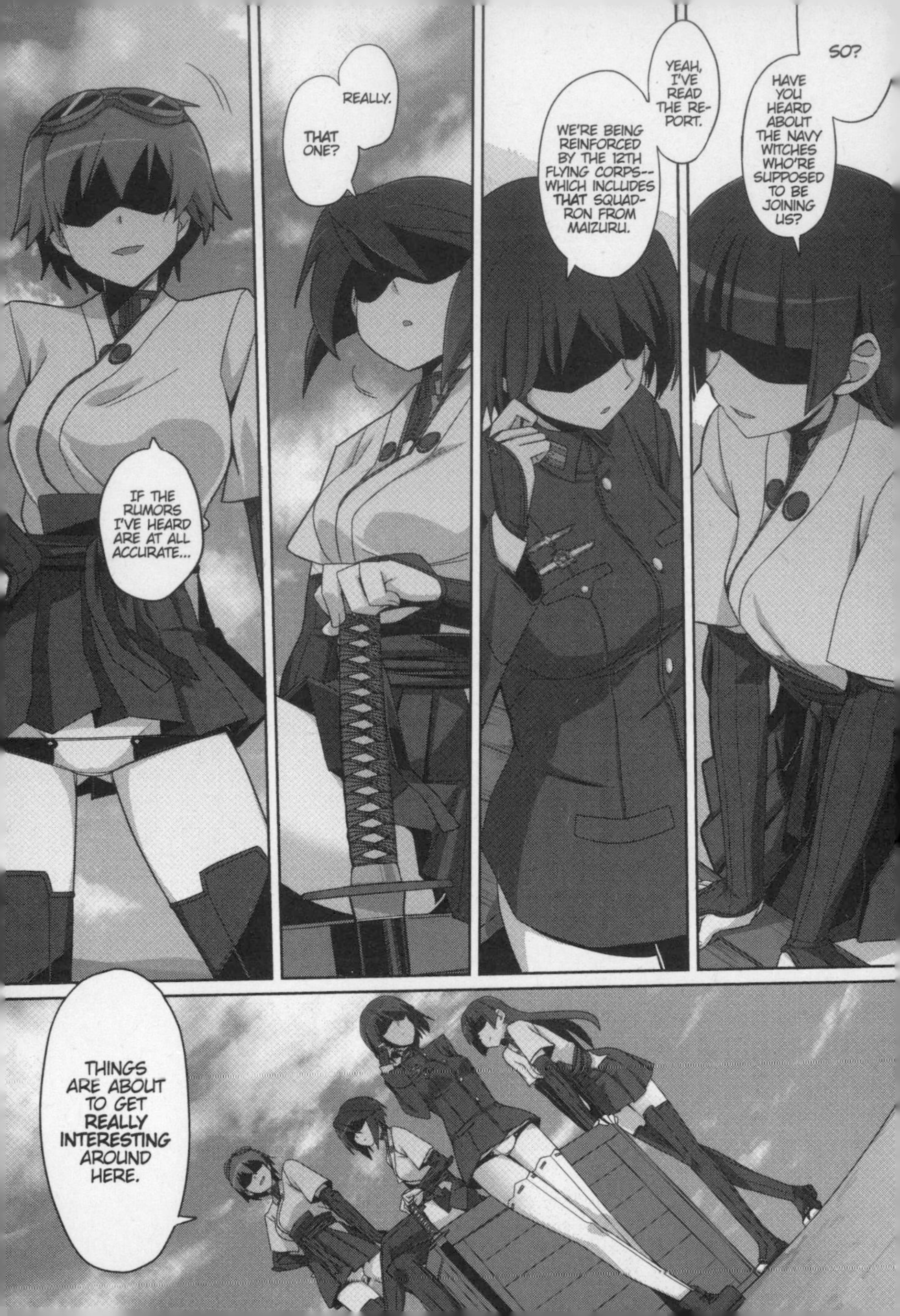
SO?
HAVE YOU HEARD ABOUT THE NAVY WITCHES WHO'RE SUPPOSED TO BE JOINING US?
YEAH, I'VE READ THE REPORT.
WE'RE BEING REINFORCED BY THE 12TH FLYING CORPS-- WHICH INCLUDES THAT SQUADRON FROM MAIZURU.
REALLY.
THAT ONE?
IF THE RUMORS I'VE HEARD ARE AT ALL ACCURATE...
THINGS ARE ABOUT TO GET REALLY INTERESTING AROUND HERE.

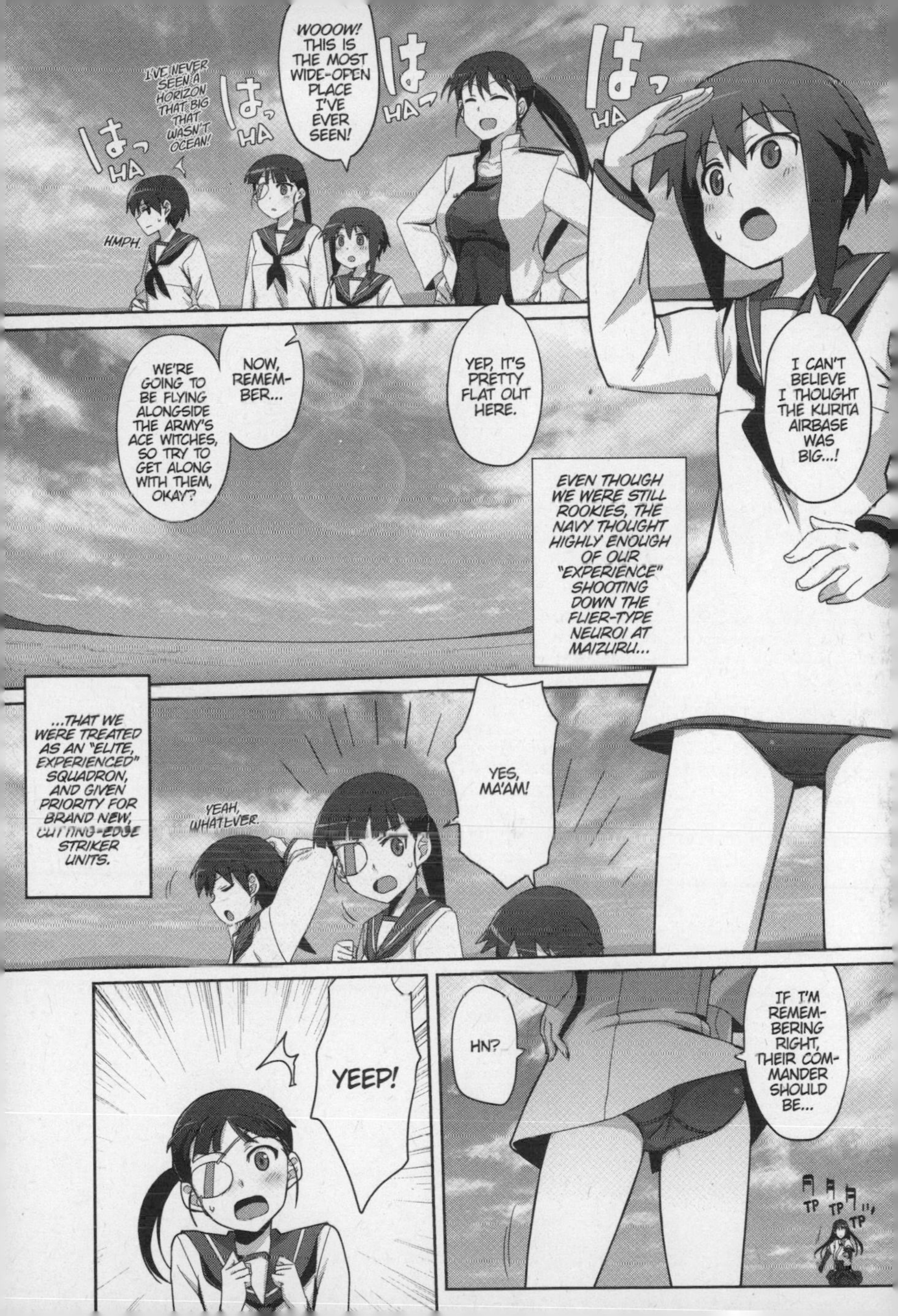

はっ HA
WOOOW! THIS IS THE MOST WIDE-OPEN PLACE I'VE EVER SEEN!
はっ HA
I'VE NEVER SEEN A HORIZON THAT BIG THAT WASN'T OCEAN!
はっ HA
はっ HA
HMPH.
I CAN'T BELIEVE I THOUGHT THE KURITA AIRBASE WAS BIG...!
YEP, IT'S PRETTY FLAT OUT HERE.
NOW, REMEMBER...
WE'RE GOING TO BE FLYING ALONGSIDE THE ARMY'S ACE WITCHES, SO TRY TO GET ALONG WITH THEM, OKAY?
EVEN THOUGH WE WERE STILL ROOKIES, THE NAVY THOUGHT HIGHLY ENOUGH OF OUR "EXPERIENCE" SHOOTING DOWN THE FLIER-TYPE NEUROI AT MAIZURU...
YES, MA'AM!
YEAH, WHATEVER.
...THAT WE WERE TREATED AS AN "ELITE, EXPERIENCED" SQUADRON, AND GIVEN PRIORITY FOR BRAND NEW, CUTTING-EDGE STRIKER UNITS.
IF I'M REMEMBERING RIGHT, THEIR COMMANDER SHOULD BE...
HN?
TP TP TP
YEEP!

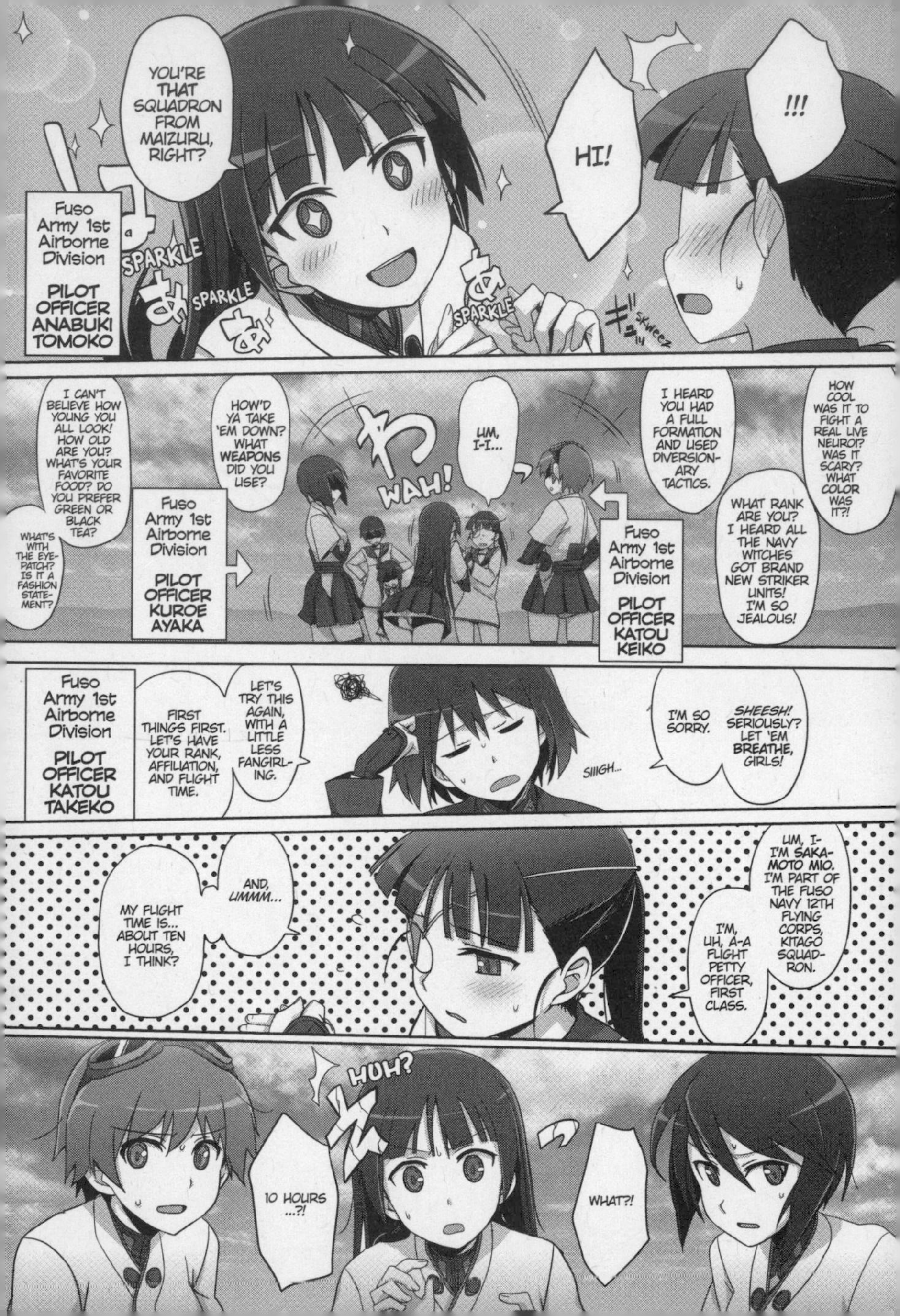
!!!
HI!
YOU'RE THAT SQUADRON FROM MAIZURU, RIGHT?
Fuso Army 1st Airborne Division
PILOT OFFICER ANABUKI TOMOKO
SPARKLE
SPARKLE
SPARKLE
SKWEEZ
HOW COOL WAS IT TO FIGHT A REAL LIVE NEUROI? WAS IT SCARY? WHAT COLOR WAS IT?!
WHAT RANK ARE YOU? I HEARD ALL THE NAVY WITCHES GOT BRAND NEW STRIKER UNITS! I'M SO JEALOUS!
I HEARD YOU HAD A FULL FORMATION AND USED DIVERSIONARY TACTICS.
Fuso Army 1st Airborne Division
PILOT OFFICER KATOU KEIKO
UM, I-I...
WAH!
HOW'D YA TAKE 'EM DOWN? WHAT WEAPONS DID YOU USE?
Fuso Army 1st Airborne Division
PILOT OFFICER KUROE AYAKA
I CAN'T BELIEVE HOW YOUNG YOU ALL LOOK! HOW OLD ARE YOU? WHAT'S YOUR FAVORITE FOOD? DO YOU PREFER GREEN OR BLACK TEA?
WHAT'S WITH THE EYE-PATCH? IS IT A FASHION STATEMENT?
SHEESH! SERIOUSLY? LET 'EM BREATHE, GIRLS!
I'M SO SORRY.
SIIIGH...
LET'S TRY THIS AGAIN, WITH A LITTLE LESS FANGIRLING.
FIRST THINGS FIRST. LET'S HAVE YOUR RANK, AFFILIATION, AND FLIGHT TIME.
Fuso Army 1st Airborne Division
PILOT OFFICER KATOU TAKEKO
UM, I- I'M SAKAMOTO MIO. I'M PART OF THE FUSO NAVY 12TH FLYING CORPS, KITAGO SQUADRON.
I'M, UH, A-A FLIGHT PETTY OFFICER, FIRST CLASS.
AND, UMMM...
MY FLIGHT TIME IS... ABOUT TEN HOURS, I THINK?
WHAT?!
HUH?
10 HOURS ...?!

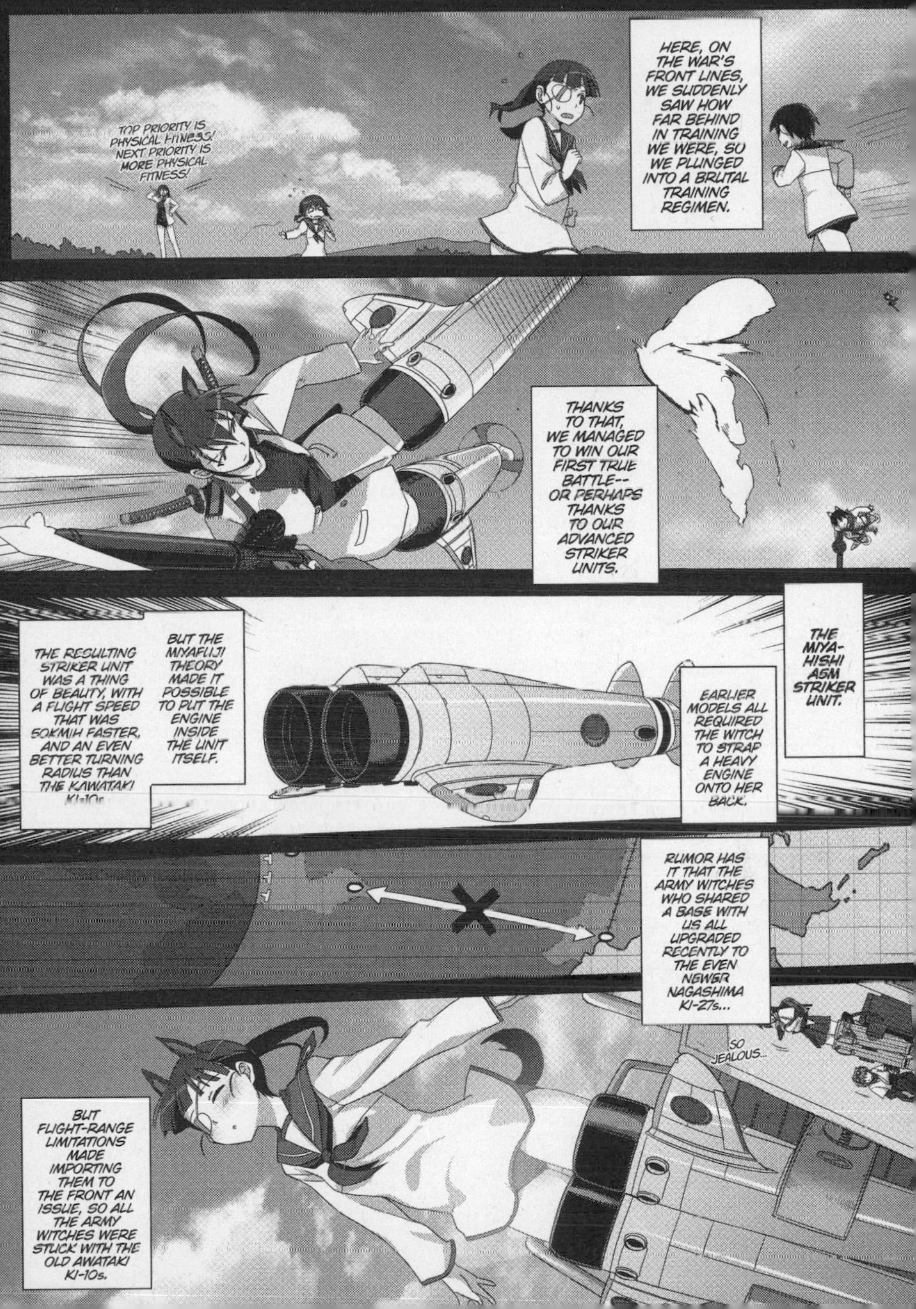
HERE, ON THE WAR'S FRONT LINES, WE SUDDENLY SAW HOW FAR BEHIND IN TRAINING WE WERE, SO WE PLUNGED INTO A BRUTAL TRAINING REGIMEN.
TOP PRIORITY IS PHYSICAL FITNESS! NEXT PRIORITY IS MORE PHYSICAL FITNESS!
THANKS TO THAT, WE MANAGED TO WIN OUR FIRST TRUE BATTLE-- OR PERHAPS THANKS TO OUR ADVANCED STRIKER UNITS.
THE MIYAHISHI A5M STRIKER UNIT.
EARLIER MODELS ALL REQUIRED THE WITCH TO STRAP A HEAVY ENGINE ONTO HER BACK.
BUT THE MIYAFUJI THEORY MADE IT POSSIBLE TO PUT THE ENGINE INSIDE THE UNIT ITSELF.
THE RESULTING STRIKER UNIT WAS A THING OF BEAUTY, WITH A FLIGHT SPEED THAT WAS 50KM/H FASTER, AND AN EVEN BETTER TURNING RADIUS THAN THE KAWATAKI KI-10s.
RUMOR HAS IT THAT THE ARMY WITCHES WHO SHARED A BASE WITH US ALL UPGRADED RECENTLY TO THE EVEN NEWER NAGASHIMA KI-27s...
SO JEALOUS...
BUT FLIGHT-RANGE LIMITATIONS MADE IMPORTING THEM TO THE FRONT AN ISSUE, SO ALL THE ARMY WITCHES WERE STUCK WITH THE OLD AWATAKI KI-10s.

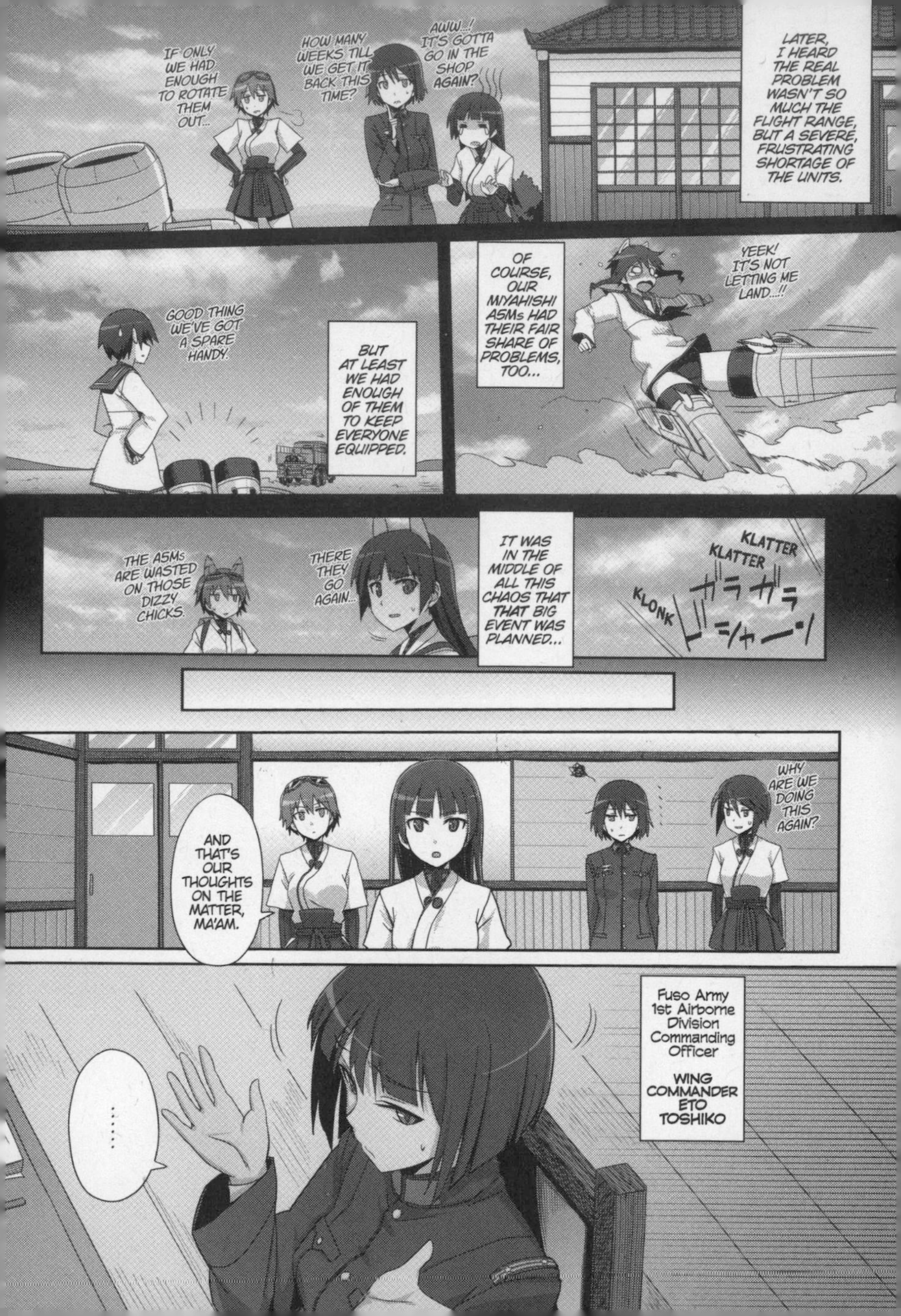
LATER, I HEARD THE REAL PROBLEM WASN'T SO MUCH THE FLIGHT RANGE, BUT A SEVERE, FRUSTRATING SHORTAGE OF THE UNITS.
AWW...! IT'S GOTTA GO IN THE SHOP AGAIN?
HOW MANY WEEKS TILL WE GET IT BACK THIS TIME?
IF ONLY WE HAD ENOUGH TO ROTATE THEM OUT...
OF COURSE, OUR MIYAHISHI ASMs HAD THEIR FAIR SHARE OF PROBLEMS, TOO...
YEEK! IT'S NOT LETTING ME LAND...!!
BUT AT LEAST WE HAD ENOUGH OF THEM TO KEEP EVERYONE EQUIPPED.
GOOD THING WE'VE GOT A SPARE HANDY.
KLATTER
KLATTER
KLONK
IT WAS IN THE MIDDLE OF ALL THIS CHAOS THAT THAT BIG EVENT WAS PLANNED...
THERE THEY GO AGAIN...
THE ASMs ARE WASTED ON THOSE DIZZY CHICKS.
WHY ARE WE DOING THIS AGAIN?
AND THAT'S OUR THOUGHTS ON THE MATTER, MA'AM.
Fuso Army 1st Airborne Division Commanding Officer
WING COMMANDER ETO TOSHIKO
......

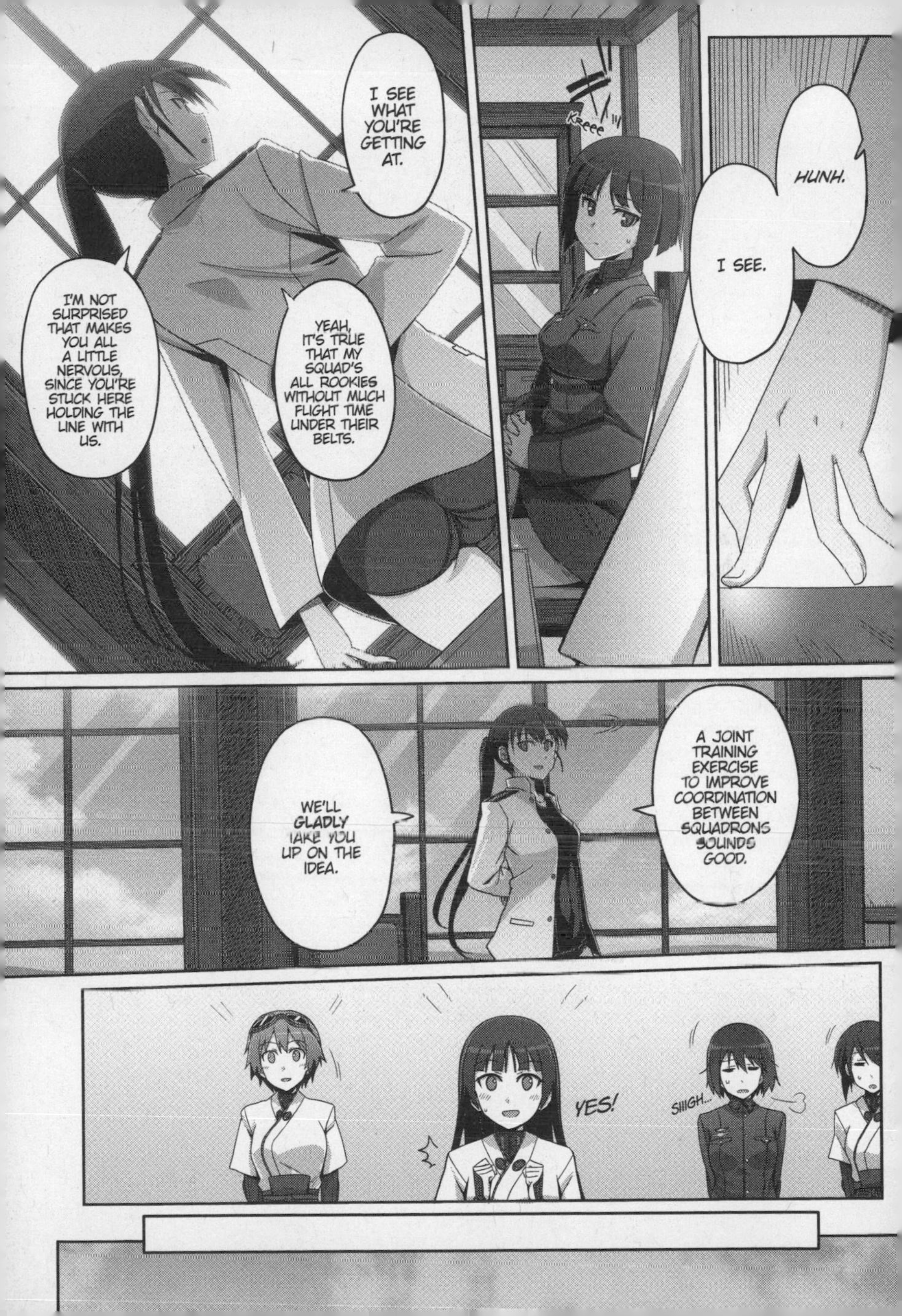
HUNH.
I SEE.
Kreee
I SEE WHAT YOU'RE GETTING AT.
YEAH, IT'S TRUE THAT MY SQUAD'S ALL ROOKIES WITHOUT MUCH FLIGHT TIME UNDER THEIR BELTS.
I'M NOT SURPRISED THAT MAKES YOU ALL A LITTLE NERVOUS, SINCE YOU'RE STUCK HERE HOLDING THE LINE WITH US.
A JOINT TRAINING EXERCISE TO IMPROVE COORDINATION BETWEEN SQUADRONS SOUNDS GOOD.
WE'LL GLADLY TAKE YOU UP ON THE IDEA.
SIIGH...
YES!

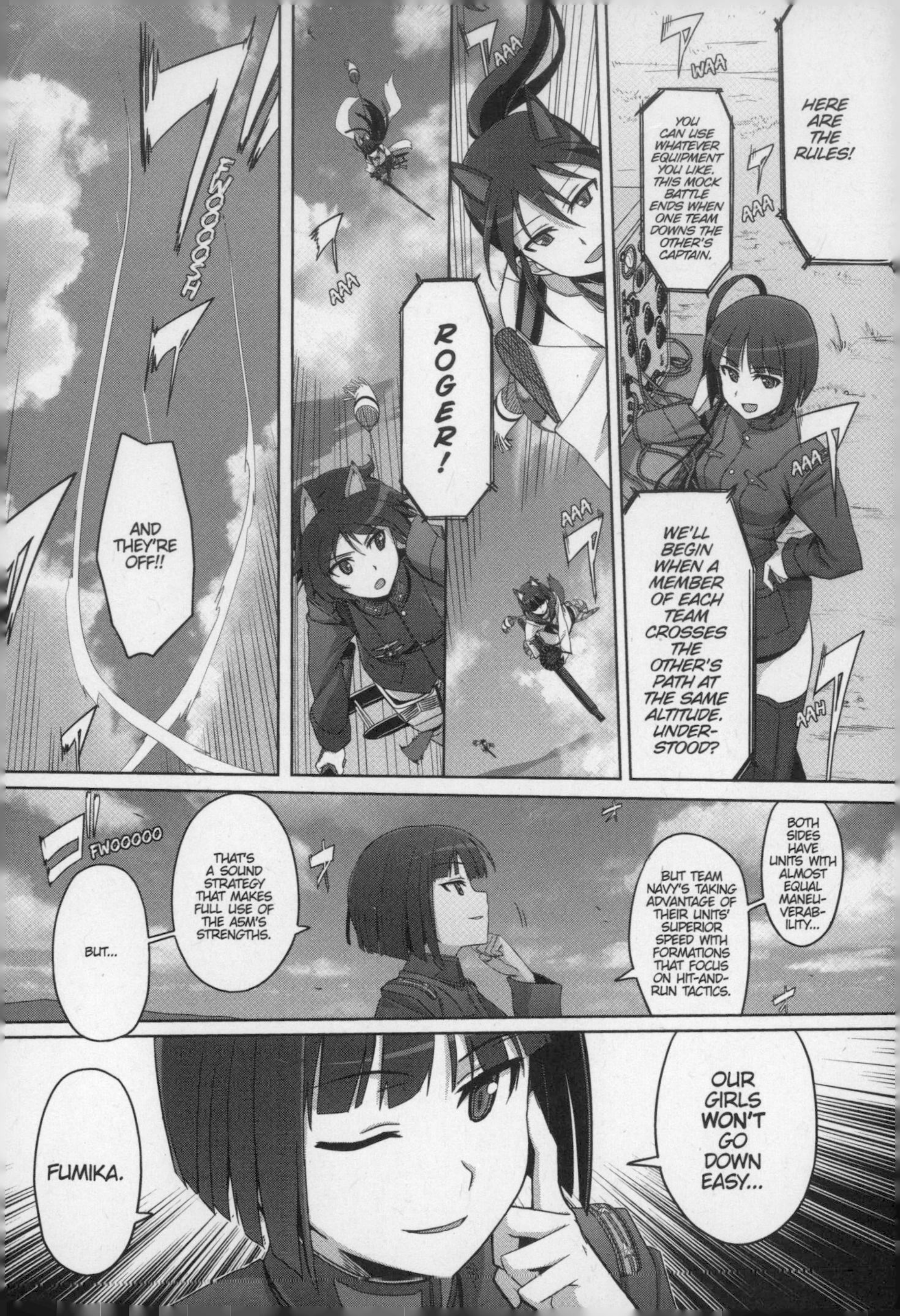

HERE ARE THE RULES!
WAA
YOU CAN USE WHATEVER EQUIPMENT YOU LIKE. THIS MOCK BATTLE ENDS WHEN ONE TEAM DOWNS THE OTHER'S CAPTAIN.
AAA
AAA
WE'LL BEGIN WHEN A MEMBER OF EACH TEAM CROSSES THE OTHER'S PATH AT THE SAME ALTITUDE. UNDERSTOOD?
AAH
AAA
ROGER!
AAA
AAA
FWOOOOSH
AND THEY'RE OFF!!
BOTH SIDES HAVE UNITS WITH ALMOST EQUAL MANEUVERABILITY...
BUT TEAM NAVY'S TAKING ADVANTAGE OF THEIR UNITS' SUPERIOR SPEED WITH FORMATIONS THAT FOCUS ON HIT-AND-RUN TACTICS.
THAT'S A SOUND STRATEGY THAT MAKES FULL USE OF THE ASM'S STRENGTHS.
BUT...
FWOOOOO
OUR GIRLS WON'T GO DOWN EASY...
FUMIKA.

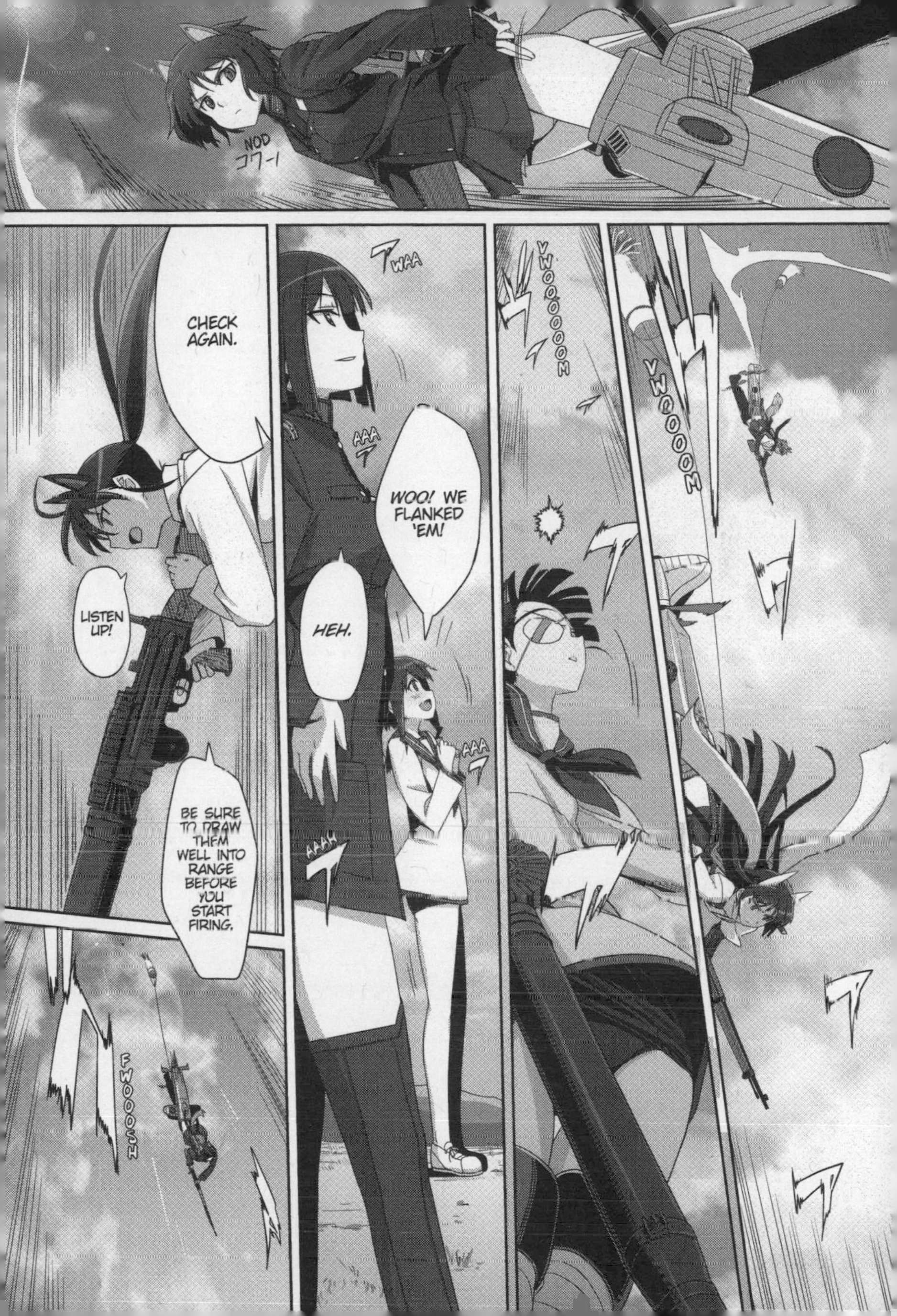
NOD
VWOOOOOM
VWOOOOOOOOM
WAA
AAA
WOO! WE FLANKED 'EM!
HEH.
AAA
AAAH
CHECK AGAIN.
LISTEN UP!
BE SURE TO DRAW THEM WELL INTO RANGE BEFORE YOU START FIRING.
FWOOOSH

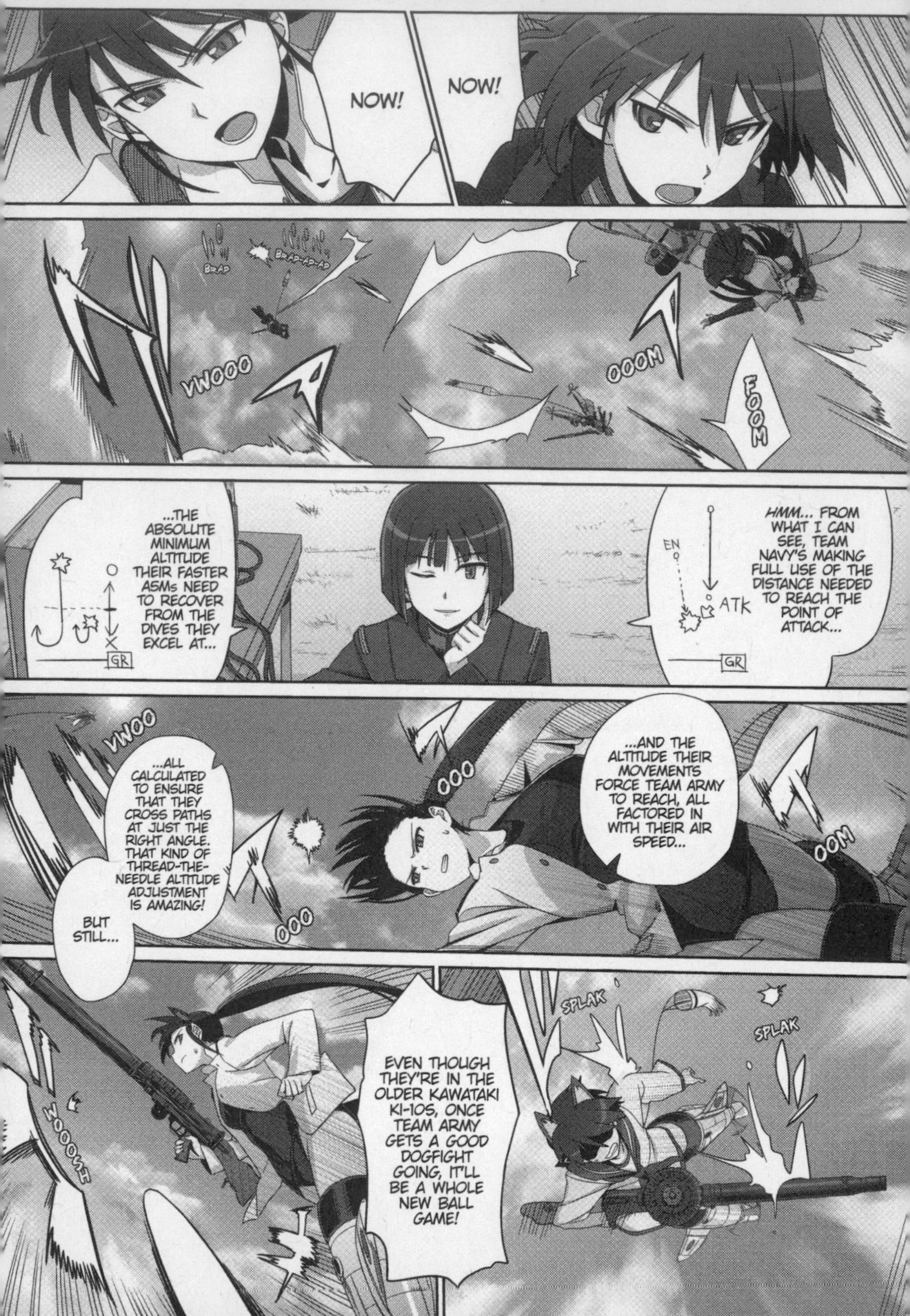
NOW!
NOW!
FOOM
OOOM
BRAP-AP-AP
BRAP
VWOOO
HMM... FROM WHAT I CAN SEE, TEAM NAVY'S MAKING FULL USE OF THE DISTANCE NEEDED TO REACH THE POINT OF ATTACK...
EN
ATK
GR
...THE ABSOLUTE MINIMUM ALTITUDE THEIR FASTER ASMs NEED TO RECOVER FROM THE DIVES THEY EXCEL AT...
GR
OOM
...AND THE ALTITUDE THEIR MOVEMENTS FORCE TEAM ARMY TO REACH, ALL FACTORED IN WITH THEIR AIR SPEED...
OOO
VWOO
...ALL CALCULATED TO ENSURE THAT THEY CROSS PATHS AT JUST THE RIGHT ANGLE. THAT KIND OF THREAD-THE-NEEDLE ALTITUDE ADJUSTMENT IS AMAZING!
OOO
BUT STILL...
SPLAK
SPLAK
EVEN THOUGH THEY'RE IN THE OLDER KAWATAKI KI-10S, ONCE TEAM ARMY GETS A GOOD DOGFIGHT GOING, IT'LL BE A WHOLE NEW BALL GAME!
WOOOSH

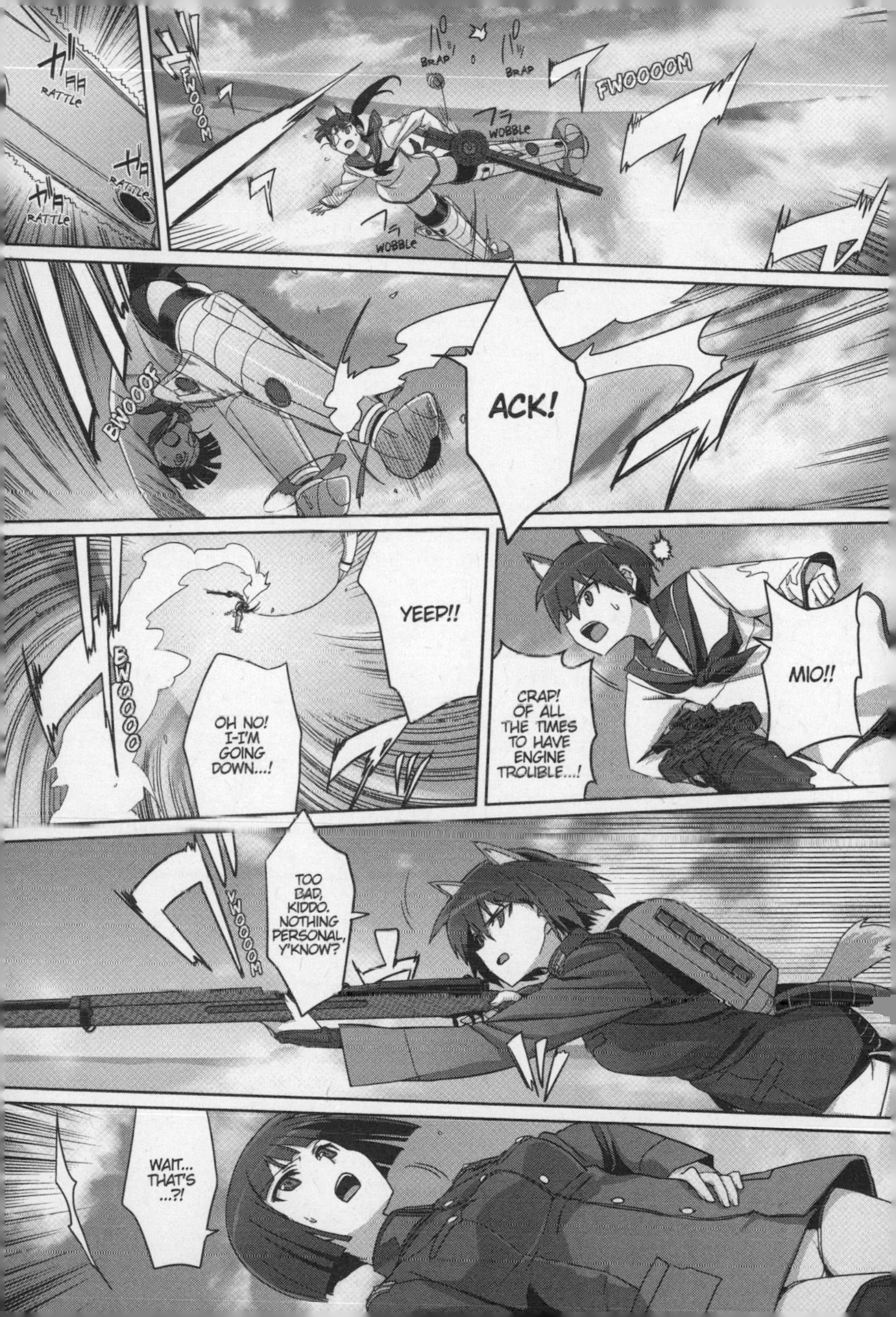
BRAP
BRAP
FWOOOOM
FWOOOM
WOBBLE
WOBBLE
RATTLE
RATTLE
RATTLE
ACK!
BWOOOF
MIO!!
CRAP! OF ALL THE TIMES TO HAVE ENGINE TROUBLE...!
YEEP!!
BWOOOO
OH NO! I-I'M GOING DOWN...!
TOO BAD, KIDDO. NOTHING PERSONAL, Y'KNOW?
VWOOOOM
WAIT... THAT'S ...?!

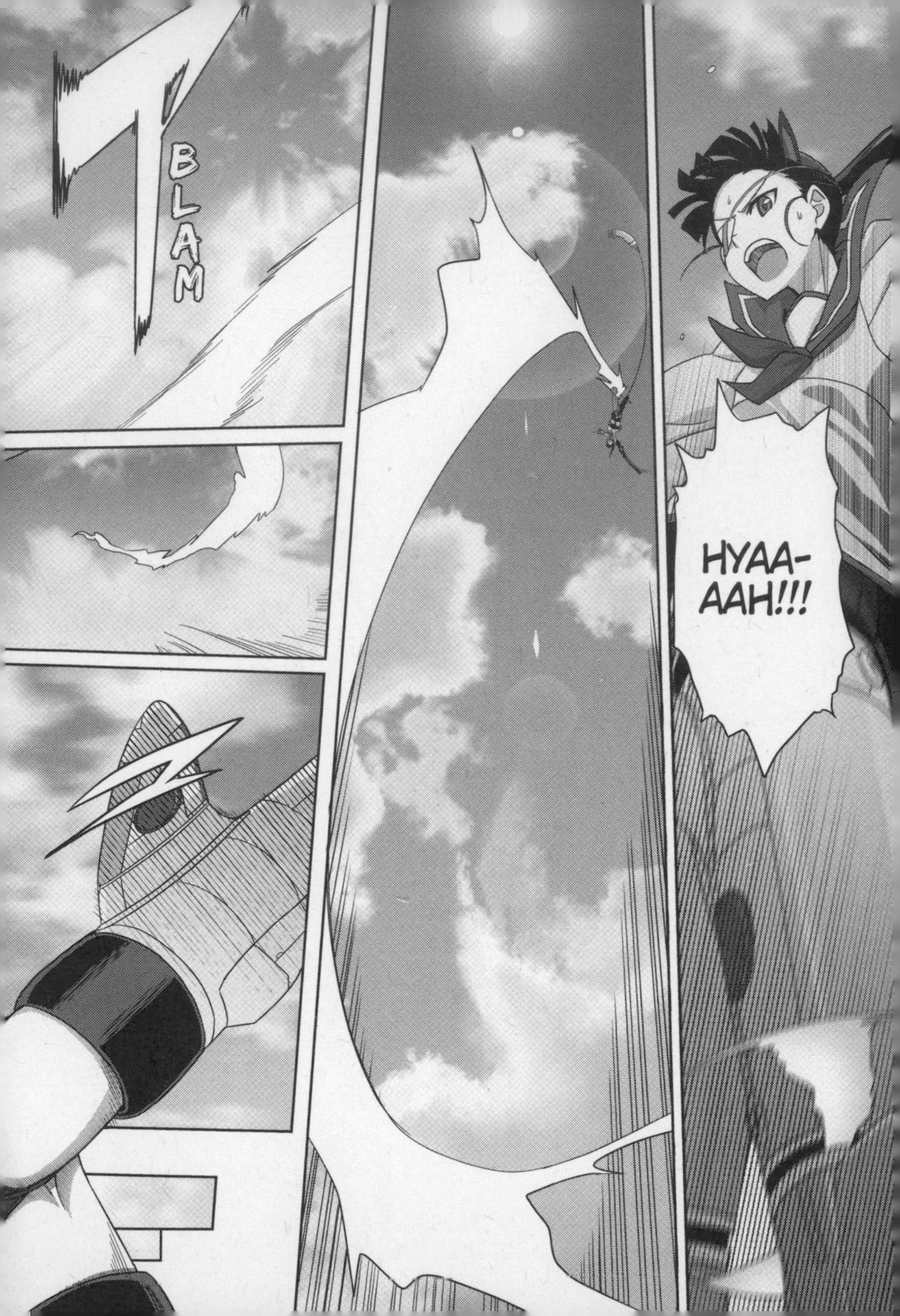
HYAA-
AAH!!!
BLAM

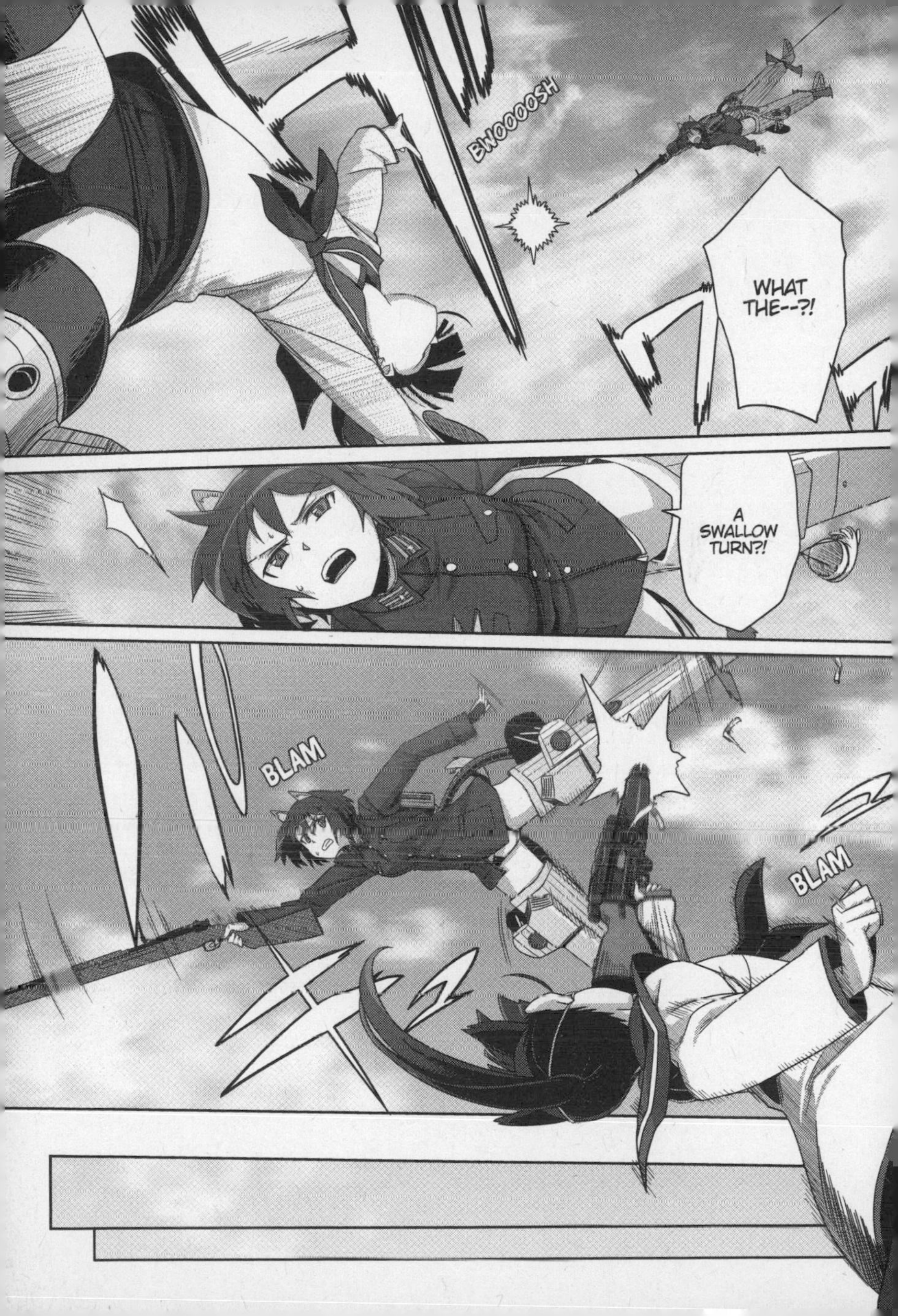
WHAT THE--?!
BWOOOOSH
A SWALLOW TURN?!
BLAM
BLAM

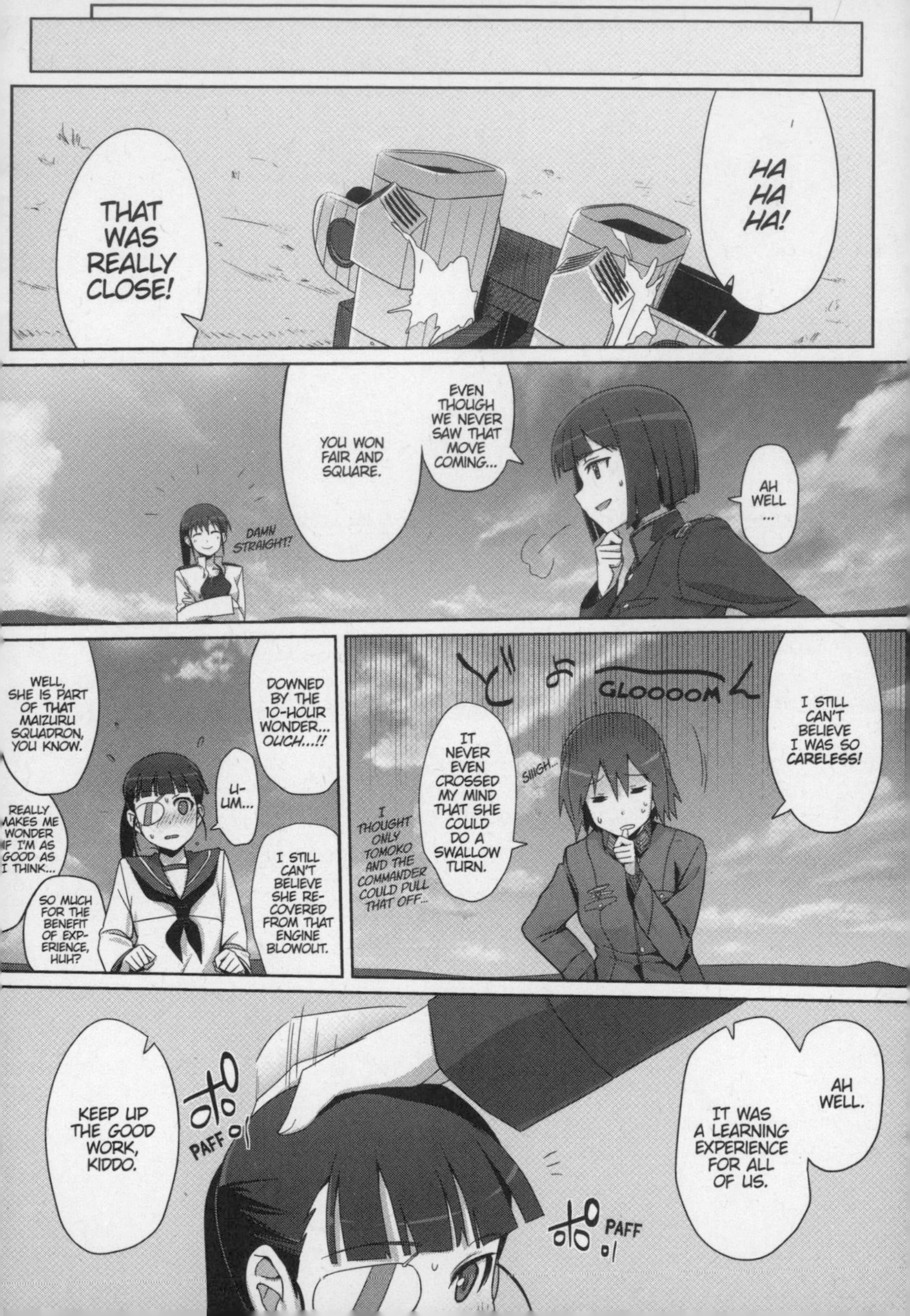
HA HA HA!
THAT WAS REALLY CLOSE!
AH WELL ...
EVEN THOUGH WE NEVER SAW THAT MOVE COMING...
YOU WON FAIR AND SQUARE.
DAMN STRAIGHT!
I STILL CAN'T BELIEVE I WAS SO CARELESS!
GLOOOOM
SIIIGH...
IT NEVER EVEN CROSSED MY MIND THAT SHE COULD DO A SWALLOW TURN.
I THOUGHT ONLY TOMOKO AND THE COMMANDER COULD PULL THAT OFF...
DOWNED BY THE 10-HOUR WONDER... OUCH...!!
WELL, SHE IS PART OF THAT MAIZURU SQUADRON, YOU KNOW.
U-UM...
I STILL CAN'T BELIEVE SHE RE-COVERED FROM THAT ENGINE BLOWOUT.
REALLY AKES ME WONDER F I'M AS GOOD AS I THINK...
SO MUCH FOR THE BENEFIT OF EXP-ERIENCE, HUH?
AH WELL.
IT WAS A LEARNING EXPERIENCE FOR ALL OF US.
PAFF
KEEP UP THE GOOD WORK, KIDDO.
PAFF

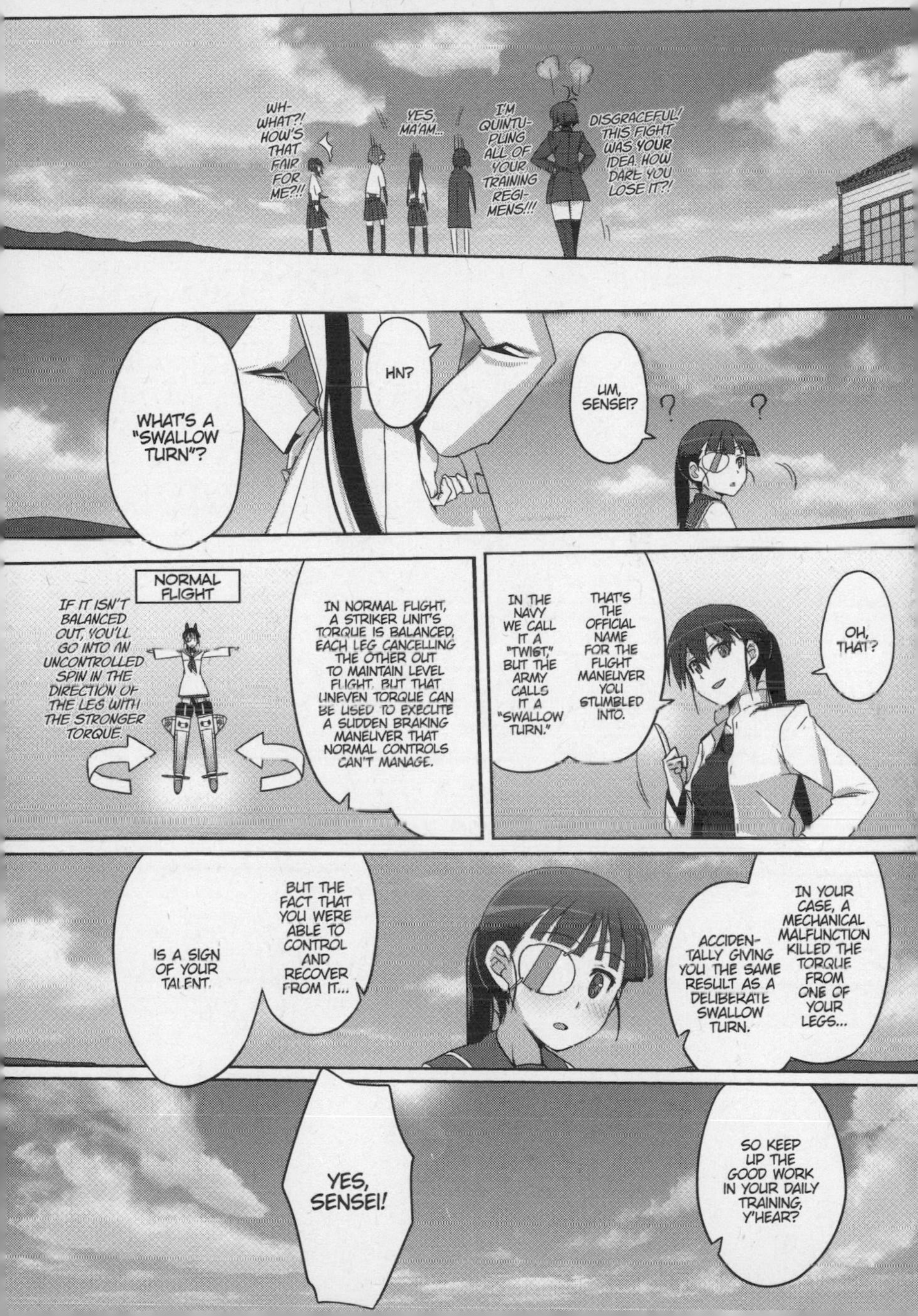
DISGRACEFUL! THIS FIGHT WAS YOUR IDEA. HOW DARE YOU LOSE IT?!
I'M QUINTUPLING ALL OF YOUR TRAINING REGIMENS!!!
YES, MA'AM...
WH-WHAT?! HOW'S THAT FAIR FOR ME?!!
UM, SENSEI?
HN?
WHAT'S A "SWALLOW TURN"?
OH, THAT?
THAT'S THE OFFICIAL NAME FOR THE FLIGHT MANEUVER YOU STUMBLED INTO.
IN THE NAVY WE CALL IT A "TWIST," BUT THE ARMY CALLS IT A "SWALLOW TURN."
IN NORMAL FLIGHT, A STRIKER UNIT'S TORQUE IS BALANCED, EACH LEG CANCELLING THE OTHER OUT TO MAINTAIN LEVEL FLIGHT. BUT THAT UNEVEN TORQUE CAN BE USED TO EXECUTE A SUDDEN BRAKING MANEUVER THAT NORMAL CONTROLS CAN'T MANAGE.
NORMAL FLIGHT
IF IT ISN'T BALANCED OUT, YOU'LL GO INTO AN UNCONTROLLED SPIN IN THE DIRECTION OF THE LEG WITH THE STRONGER TORQUE.
IN YOUR CASE, A MECHANICAL MALFUNCTION KILLED THE TORQUE FROM ONE OF YOUR LEGS...
ACCIDENTALLY GIVING YOU THE SAME RESULT AS A DELIBERATE SWALLOW TURN.
BUT THE FACT THAT YOU WERE ABLE TO CONTROL AND RECOVER FROM IT...
IS A SIGN OF YOUR TALENT.
SO KEEP UP THE GOOD WORK IN YOUR DAILY TRAINING, Y'HEAR?
YES, SENSEI!

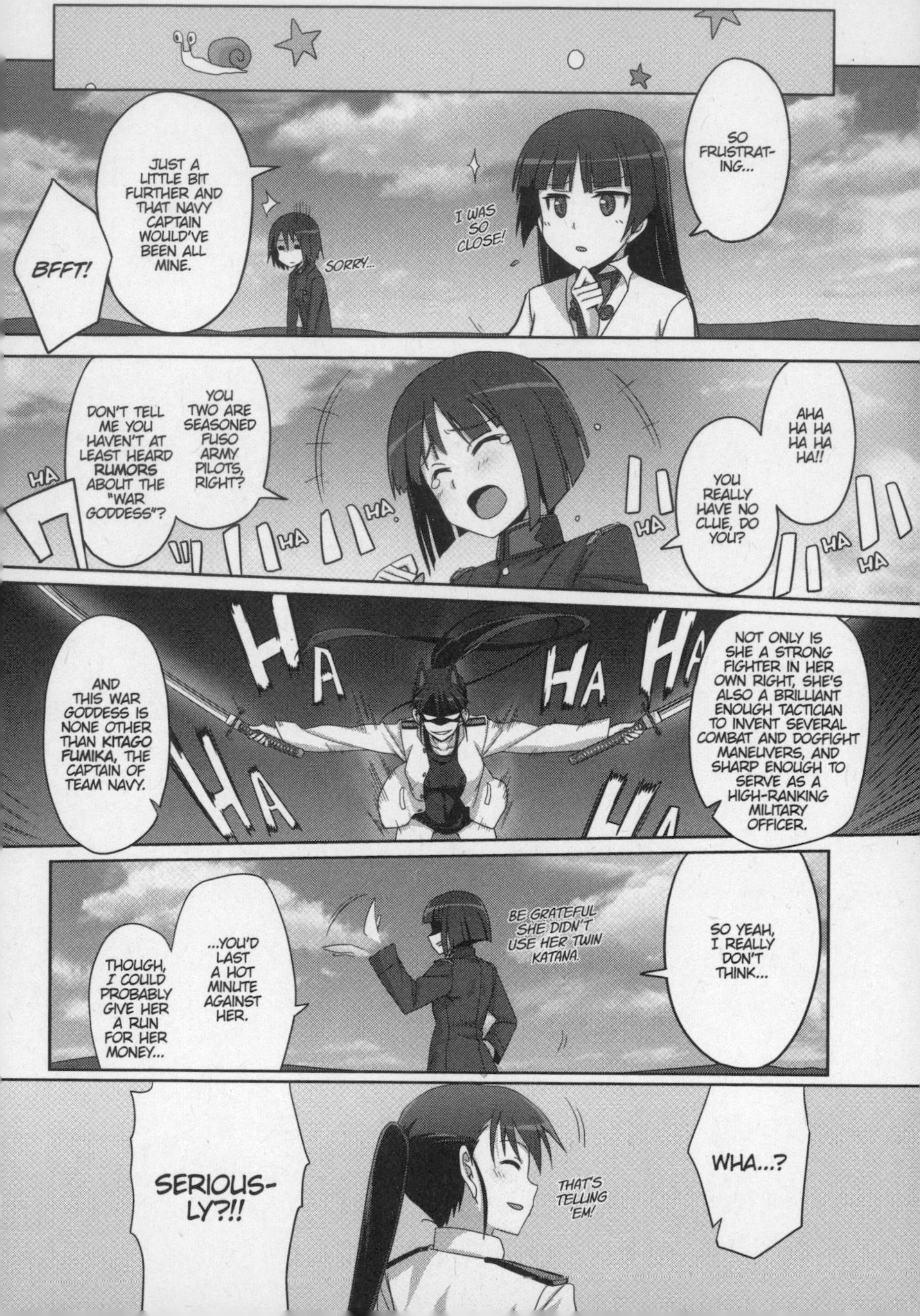
SO FRUSTRATING...
I WAS SO CLOSE!
JUST A LITTLE BIT FURTHER AND THAT NAVY CAPTAIN WOULD'VE BEEN ALL MINE.
SORRY...
BFFT!
AHA HA HA HA HA!!
YOU REALLY HAVE NO CLUE, DO YOU?
HA HA HA
YOU TWO ARE SEASONED FUSO ARMY PILOTS, RIGHT?
DON'T TELL ME YOU HAVEN'T AT LEAST HEARD RUMORS ABOUT THE "WAR GODDESS"?
HA HA HA
NOT ONLY IS SHE A STRONG FIGHTER IN HER OWN RIGHT, SHE'S ALSO A BRILLIANT ENOUGH TACTICIAN TO INVENT SEVERAL COMBAT AND DOGFIGHT MANEUVERS, AND SHARP ENOUGH TO SERVE AS A HIGH-RANKING MILITARY OFFICER.
HA HA HA
AND THIS WAR GODDESS IS NONE OTHER THAN KITAGO FUMIKA, THE CAPTAIN OF TEAM NAVY.
HA HA
SO YEAH, I REALLY DON'T THINK...
BE GRATEFUL SHE DIDN'T USE HER TWIN KATANA.
...YOU'D LAST A HOT MINUTE AGAINST HER.
THOUGH, I COULD PROBABLY GIVE HER A RUN FOR HER MONEY...
WHA...?
THAT'S TELLING 'EM!
SERIOUS-LY?!!

Chapter 2:
Taking Wing
[Mission Complete]

CHAPTER 3:
THE THREE CROWS
OF THE FUSO SEA

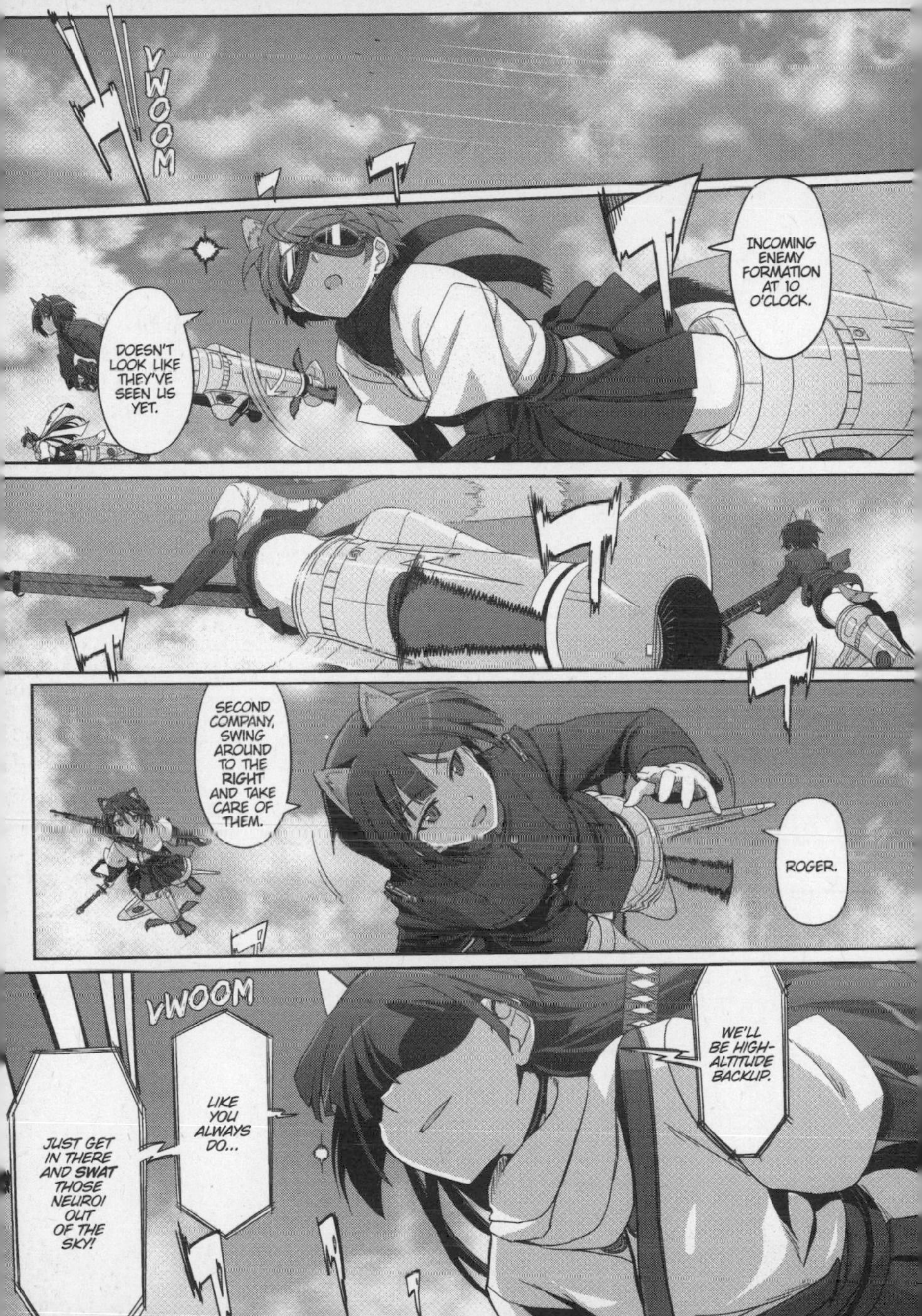
VWOOM
INCOMING ENEMY FORMATION AT 10 O'CLOCK.
DOESN'T LOOK LIKE THEY'VE SEEN US YET.
SECOND COMPANY, SWING AROUND TO THE RIGHT AND TAKE CARE OF THEM.
ROGER.
WE'LL BE HIGH-ALTITUDE BACKUP.
VWOOM
LIKE YOU ALWAYS DO...
JUST GET IN THERE AND SWAT THOSE NEUROI OUT OF THE SKY!

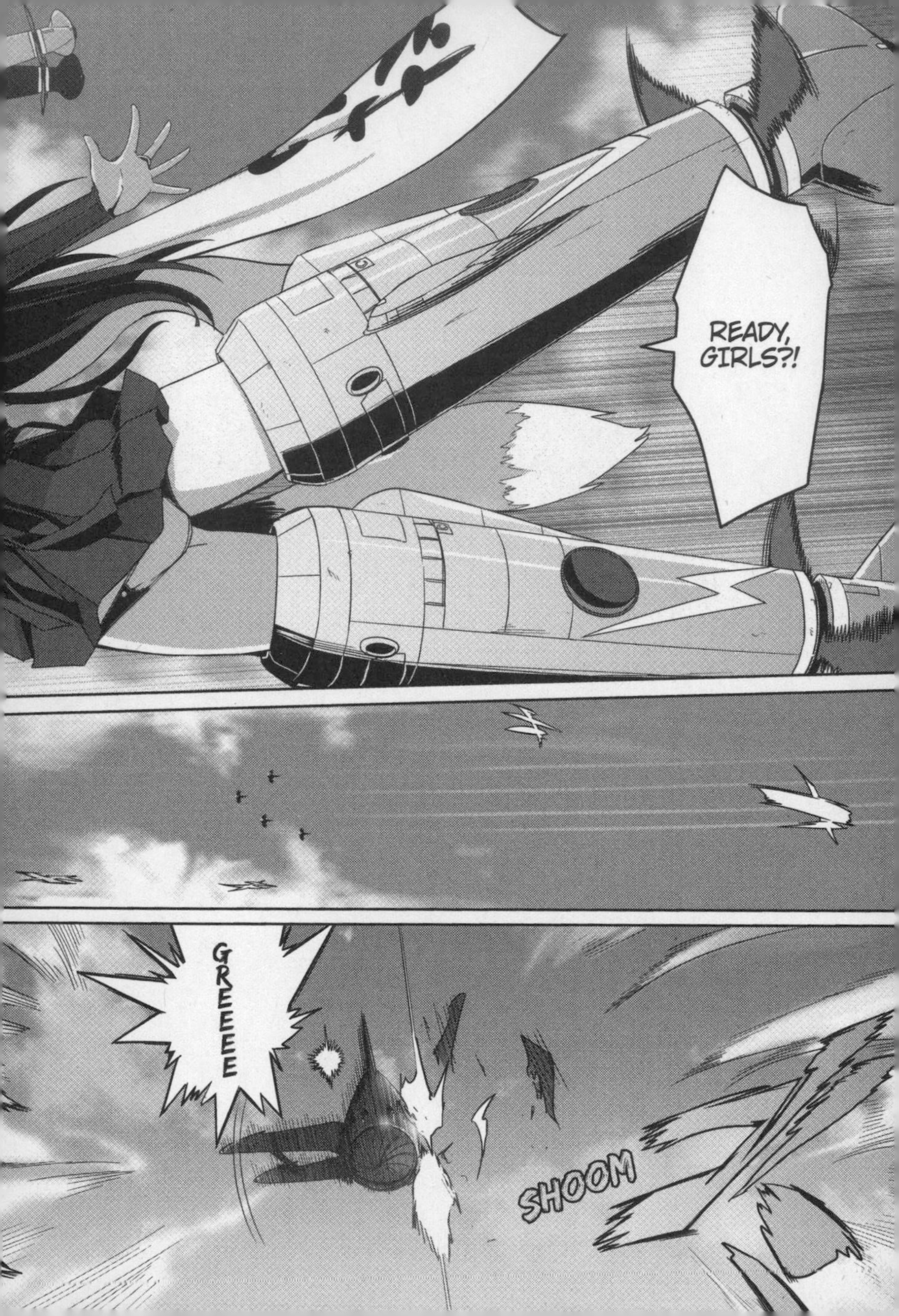
READY, GIRLS?!
GREEEE
SHOOM

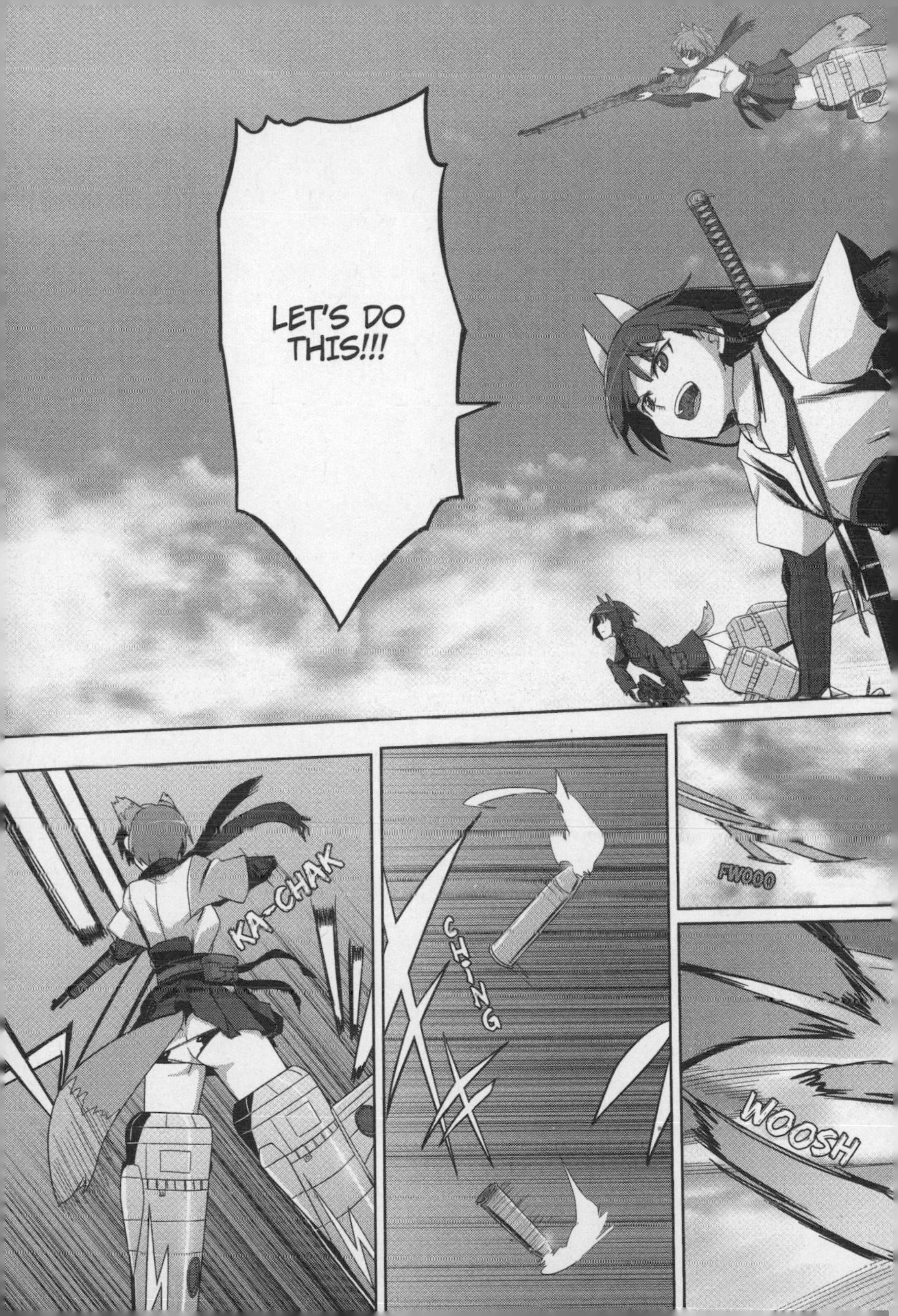
LET'S DO THIS!!!
FWOOO
WOOSH
CHING
KA-CHAK

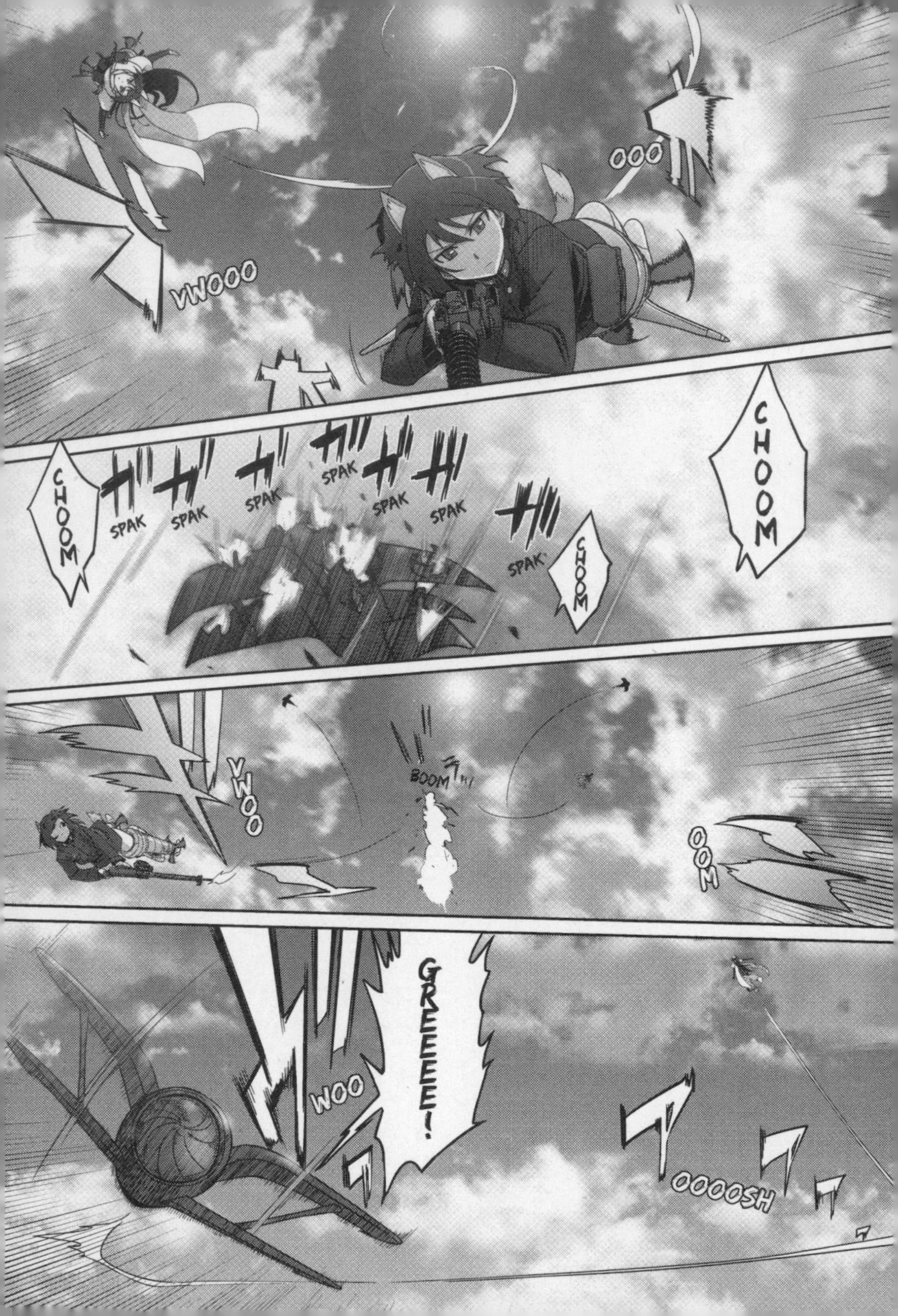
OOO
VWOOO
CHOOM
SPAK
SPAK
SPAK
SPAK
SPAK
SPAK
SPAK
CHOOM
CHOOM
OOM
BOOM
VWOO
OOOOSH
GREEEEE!
WOO

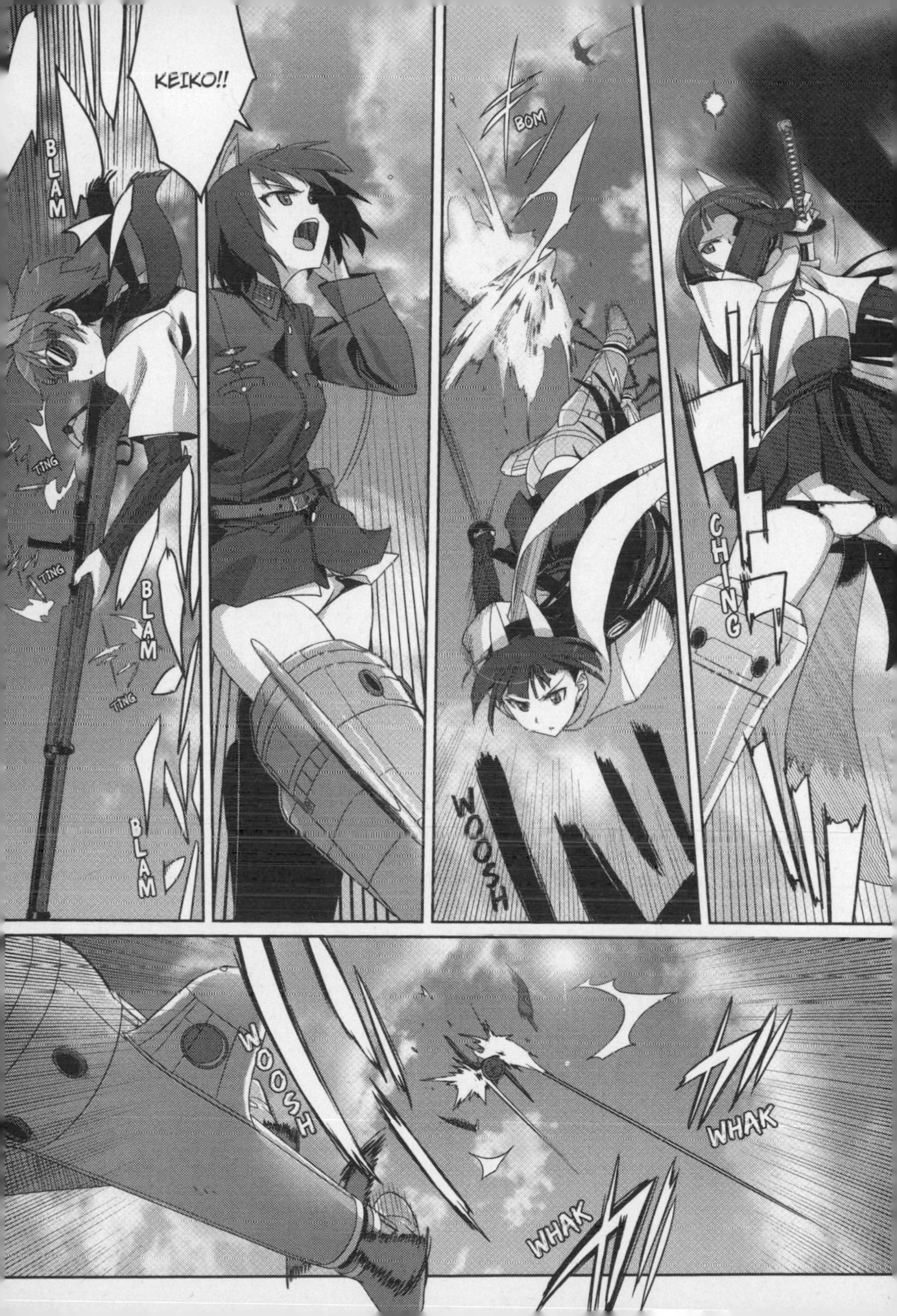
CHING
BOM
WOOSH
KEIKO!!
BLAM
TING
TING
BLAM
TING
BLAM
WHAK
WOOSH
WHAK

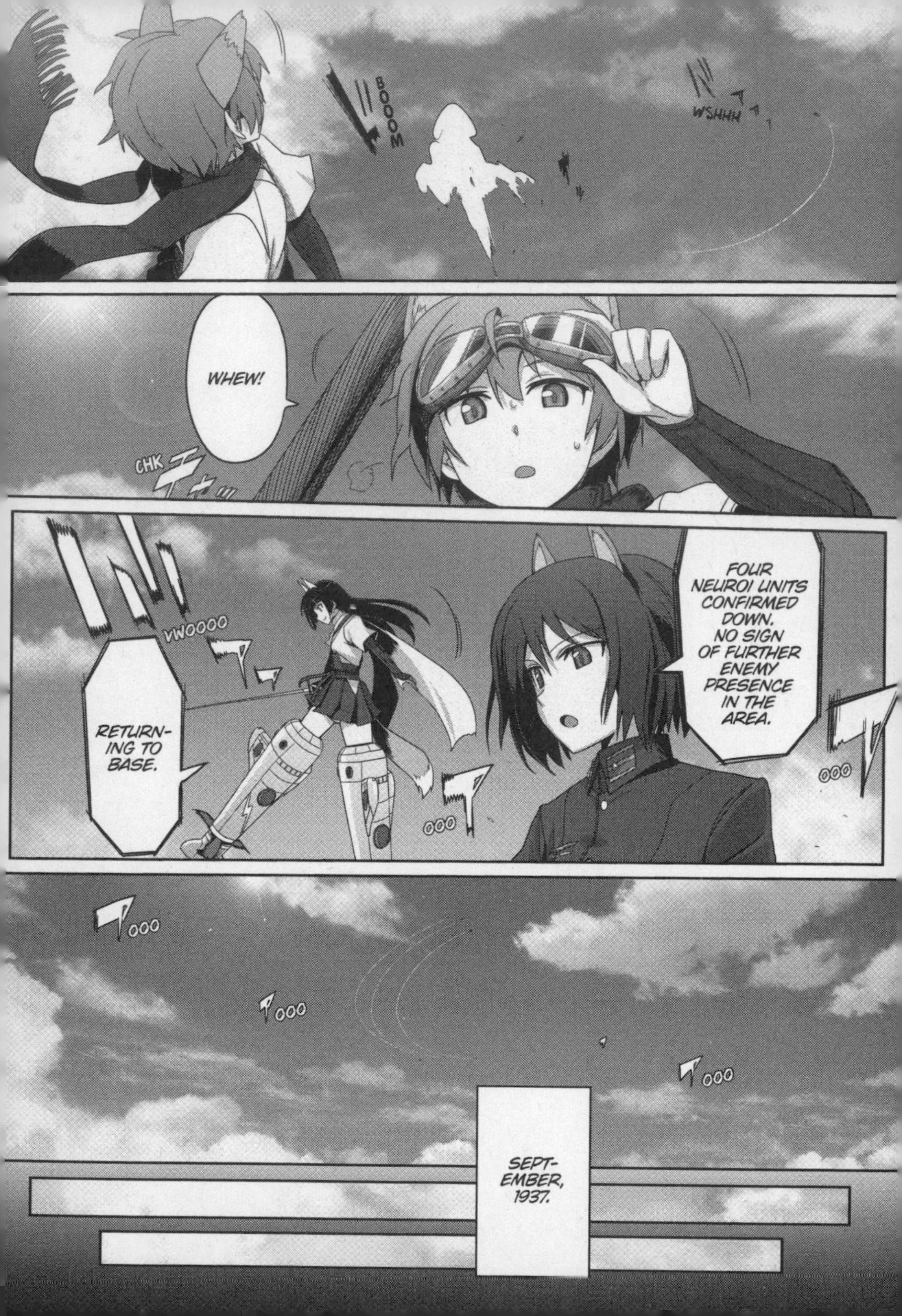
WSHHH
BOOOM
WHEW!
CHK
FOUR NEUROI UNITS CONFIRMED DOWN. NO SIGN OF FURTHER ENEMY PRESENCE IN THE AREA.
OOO
VWOOOO
RETURNING TO BASE.
OOO
OOO
OOO
OOO
SEPTEMBER, 1937.

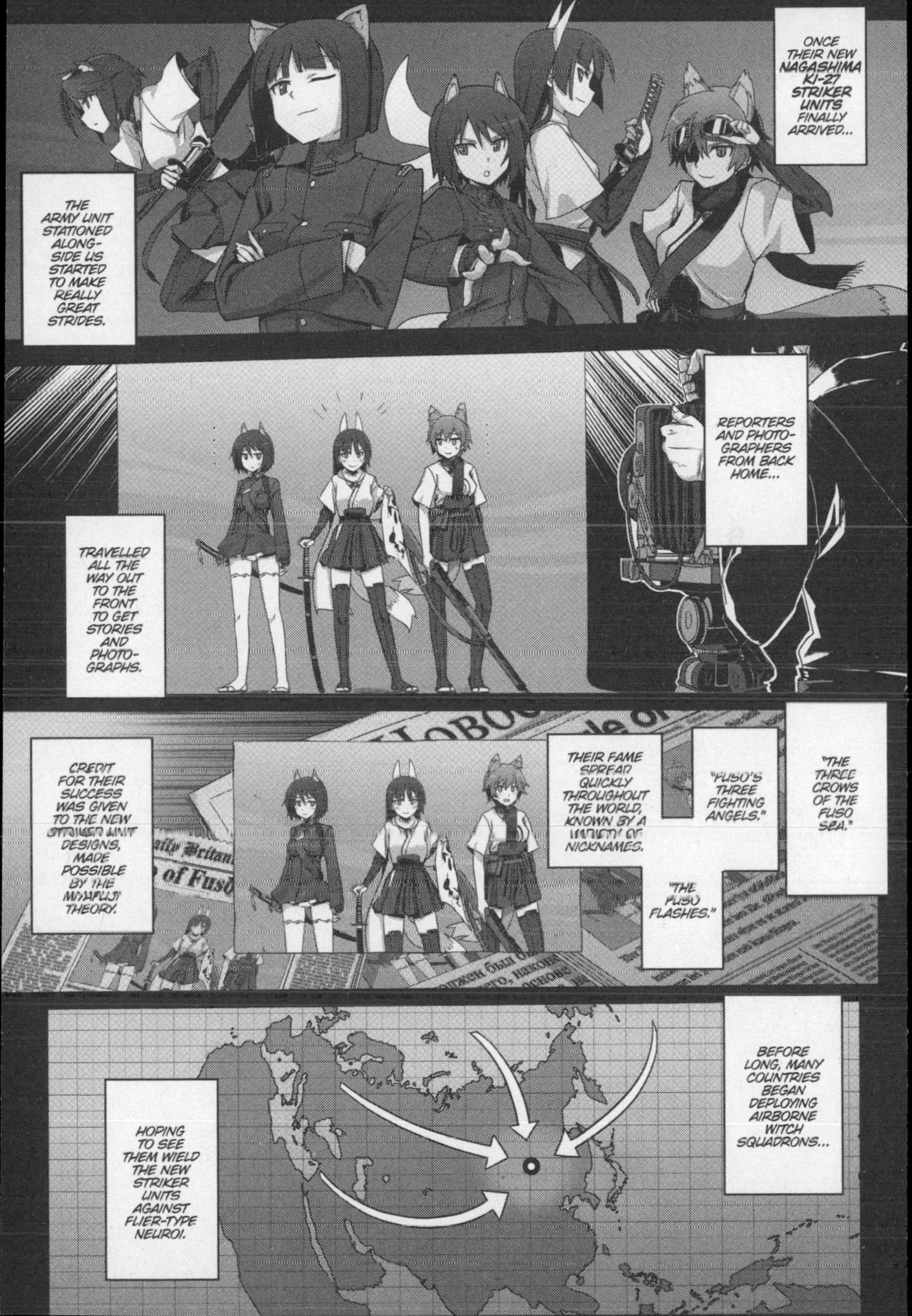
ONCE THEIR NEW NAGASHIMA KI-27 STRIKER UNITS FINALLY ARRIVED...
THE ARMY UNIT STATIONED ALONGSIDE US STARTED TO MAKE REALLY GREAT STRIDES.
REPORTERS AND PHOTOGRAPHERS FROM BACK HOME...
TRAVELLED ALL THE WAY OUT TO THE FRONT TO GET STORIES AND PHOTOGRAPHS.
"THE THREE CROWS OF THE FUSO SEA."
"FUSO'S THREE FIGHTING ANGELS."
THEIR FAME SPREAD QUICKLY THROUGHOUT THE WORLD, KNOWN BY A VARIETY OF NICKNAMES.
"THE FUSO FLASHES."
CREDIT FOR THEIR SUCCESS WAS GIVEN TO THE NEW STRIKER UNIT DESIGNS, MADE POSSIBLE BY THE MIYAFUJI THEORY.
BEFORE LONG, MANY COUNTRIES BEGAN DEPLOYING AIRBORNE WITCH SQUADRONS...
HOPING TO SEE THEM WIELD THE NEW STRIKER UNITS AGAINST FLIER-TYPE NEUROI.

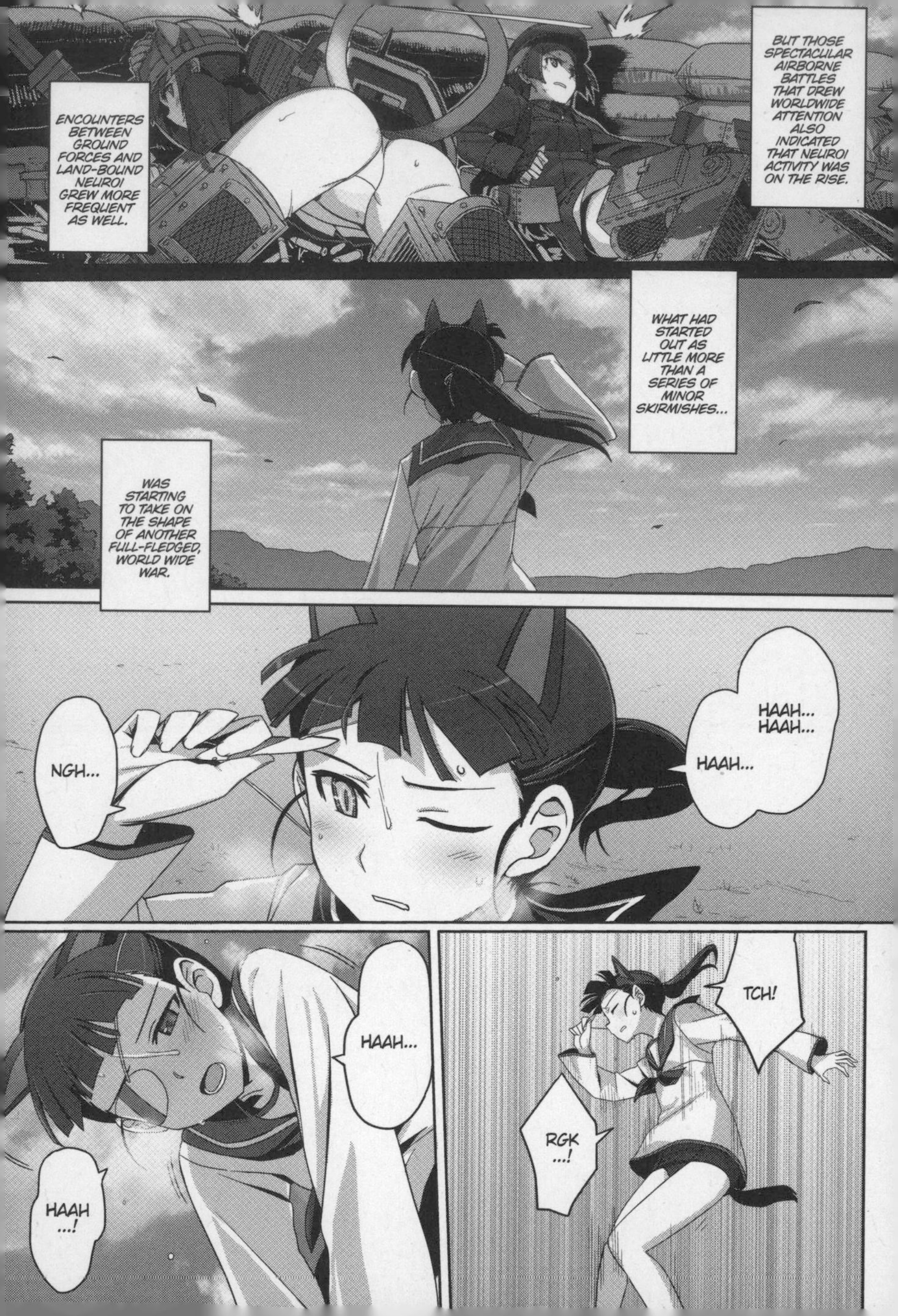
BUT THOSE SPECTACULAR AIRBORNE BATTLES THAT DREW WORLDWIDE ATTENTION ALSO INDICATED THAT NEUROI ACTIVITY WAS ON THE RISE.
ENCOUNTERS BETWEEN GROUND FORCES AND LAND-BOUND NEUROI GREW MORE FREQUENT AS WELL.
WHAT HAD STARTED OUT AS LITTLE MORE THAN A SERIES OF MINOR SKIRMISHES...
WAS STARTING TO TAKE ON THE SHAPE OF ANOTHER FULL-FLEDGED, WORLD WIDE WAR.
HAAH... HAAH...
HAAH...
NGH...
TCH!
RGK ...!
HAAH...
HAAH ...!

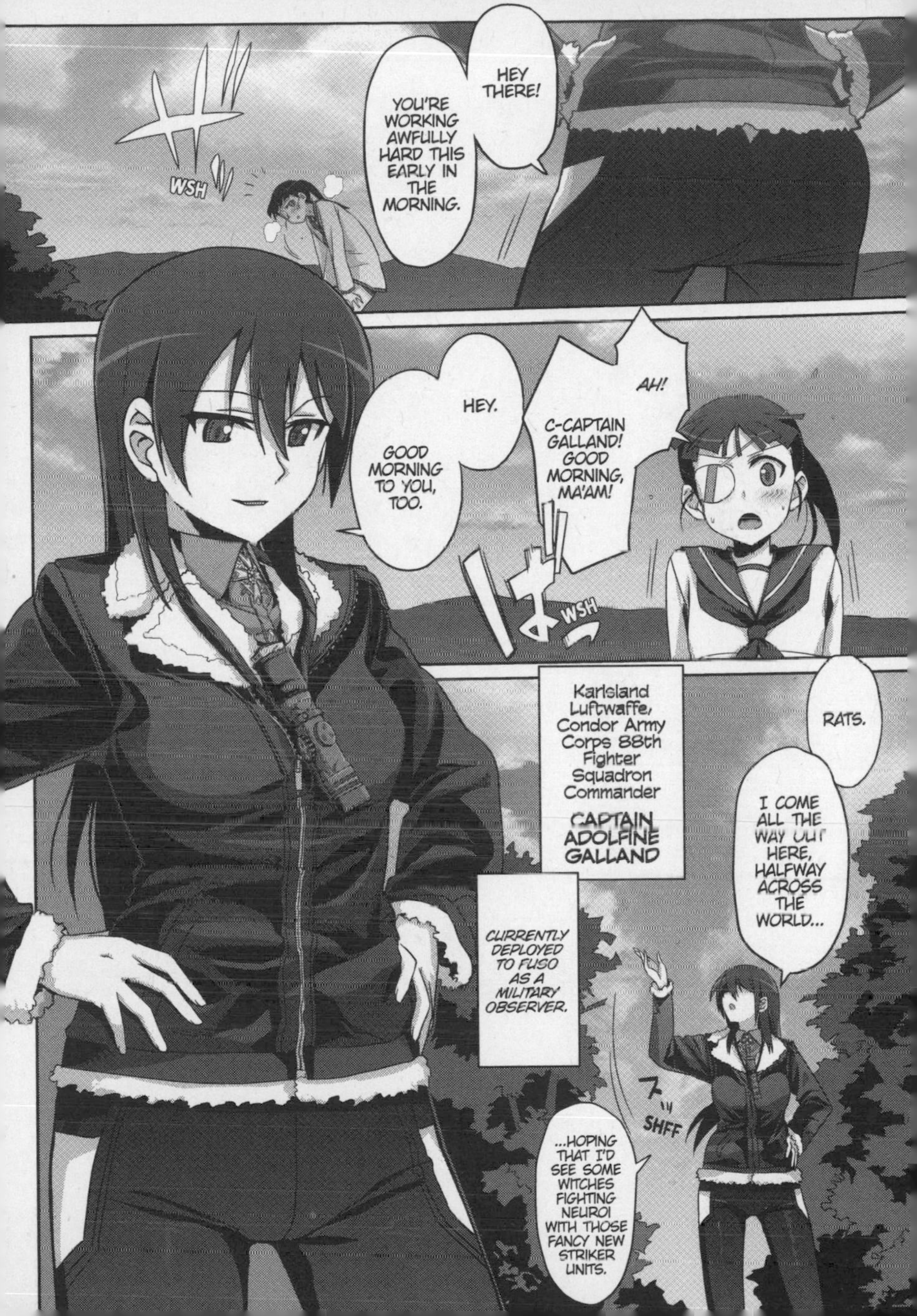
HEY THERE!
YOU'RE WORKING AWFULLY HARD THIS EARLY IN THE MORNING.
WSH
AH!
C-CAPTAIN GALLAND! GOOD MORNING, MA'AM!
HEY.
GOOD MORNING TO YOU, TOO.
WSH
RATS.
I COME ALL THE WAY OUT HERE, HALFWAY ACROSS THE WORLD...
Karlsland Luftwaffe, Condor Army Corps 88th Fighter Squadron Commander
CAPTAIN ADOLFINE GALLAND
CURRENTLY DEPLOYED TO FUSO AS A MILITARY OBSERVER.
SHFF
...HOPING THAT I'D SEE SOME WITCHES FIGHTING NEUROI WITH THOSE FANCY NEW STRIKER UNITS.

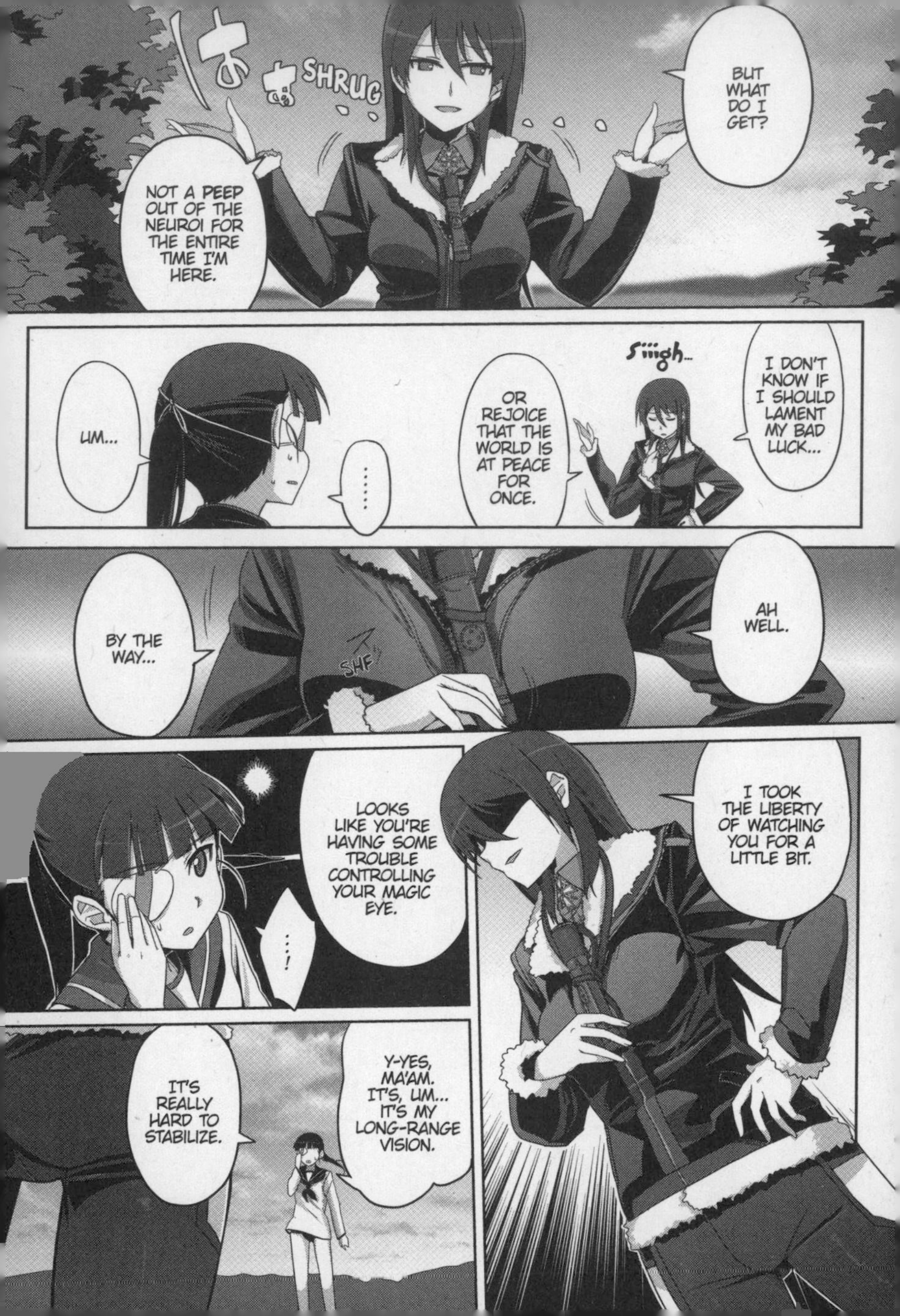
BUT WHAT DO I GET?
SHRUG
NOT A PEEP OUT OF THE NEUROI FOR THE ENTIRE TIME I'M HERE.
I DON'T KNOW IF I SHOULD LAMENT MY BAD LUCK...
Siiigh...
OR REJOICE THAT THE WORLD IS AT PEACE FOR ONCE.
......
UM...
AH WELL.
SHF
BY THE WAY...
I TOOK THE LIBERTY OF WATCHING YOU FOR A LITTLE BIT.
LOOKS LIKE YOU'RE HAVING SOME TROUBLE CONTROLLING YOUR MAGIC EYE.
...!
Y-YES, MA'AM. IT'S, UM... IT'S MY LONG-RANGE VISION.
IT'S REALLY HARD TO STABILIZE.

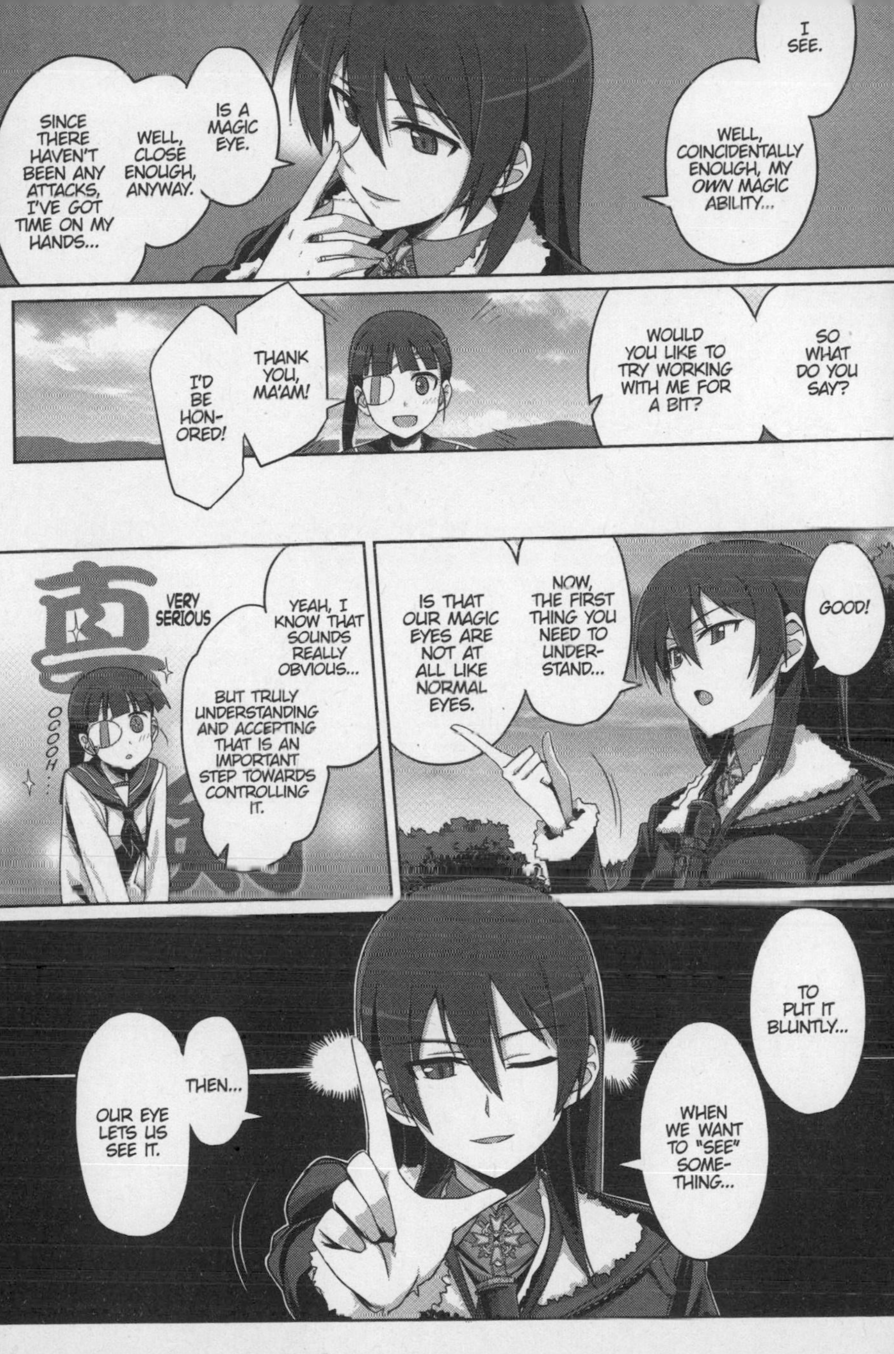
I SEE.
WELL, COINCIDENTALLY ENOUGH, MY OWN MAGIC ABILITY...
IS A MAGIC EYE.
WELL, CLOSE ENOUGH, ANYWAY.
SINCE THERE HAVEN'T BEEN ANY ATTACKS, I'VE GOT TIME ON MY HANDS...
SO WHAT DO YOU SAY?
WOULD YOU LIKE TO TRY WORKING WITH ME FOR A BIT?
THANK YOU, MA'AM!
I'D BE HON-ORED!
GOOD!
NOW, THE FIRST THING YOU NEED TO UNDER-STAND...
IS THAT OUR MAGIC EYES ARE NOT AT ALL LIKE NORMAL EYES.
YEAH, I KNOW THAT SOUNDS REALLY OBVIOUS...
BUT TRULY UNDERSTANDING AND ACCEPTING THAT IS AN IMPORTANT STEP TOWARDS CONTROLLING IT.
VERY SERIOUS
OOOOH...
TO PUT IT BLUNTLY...
WHEN WE WANT TO "SEE" SOME-THING...
THEN...
OUR EYE LETS US SEE IT.

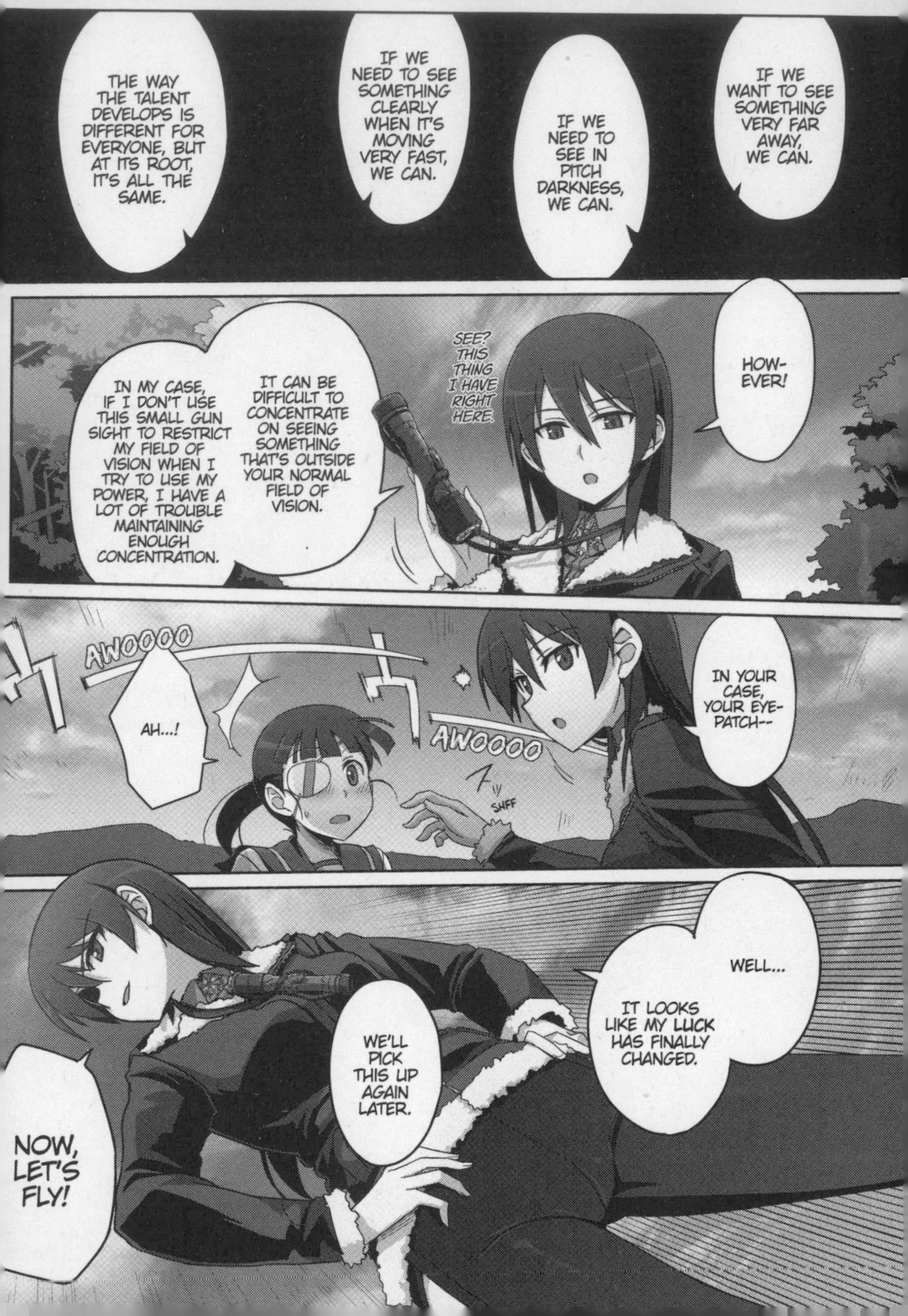
IF WE WANT TO SEE SOMETHING VERY FAR AWAY, WE CAN.
IF WE NEED TO SEE IN PITCH DARKNESS, WE CAN.
IF WE NEED TO SEE SOMETHING CLEARLY WHEN IT'S MOVING VERY FAST, WE CAN.
THE WAY THE TALENT DEVELOPS IS DIFFERENT FOR EVERYONE, BUT AT ITS ROOT, IT'S ALL THE SAME.
HOW-EVER!
SEE? THIS THING I HAVE RIGHT HERE.
IT CAN BE DIFFICULT TO CONCENTRATE ON SEEING SOMETHING THAT'S OUTSIDE YOUR NORMAL FIELD OF VISION.
IN MY CASE, IF I DON'T USE THIS SMALL GUN SIGHT TO RESTRICT MY FIELD OF VISION WHEN I TRY TO USE MY POWER, I HAVE A LOT OF TROUBLE MAINTAINING ENOUGH CONCENTRATION.
IN YOUR CASE, YOUR EYE-PATCH--
AWOOOO
SHFF
AH...!
AWOOOO
WELL...
IT LOOKS LIKE MY LUCK HAS FINALLY CHANGED.
WE'LL PICK THIS UP AGAIN LATER.
NOW, LET'S FLY!

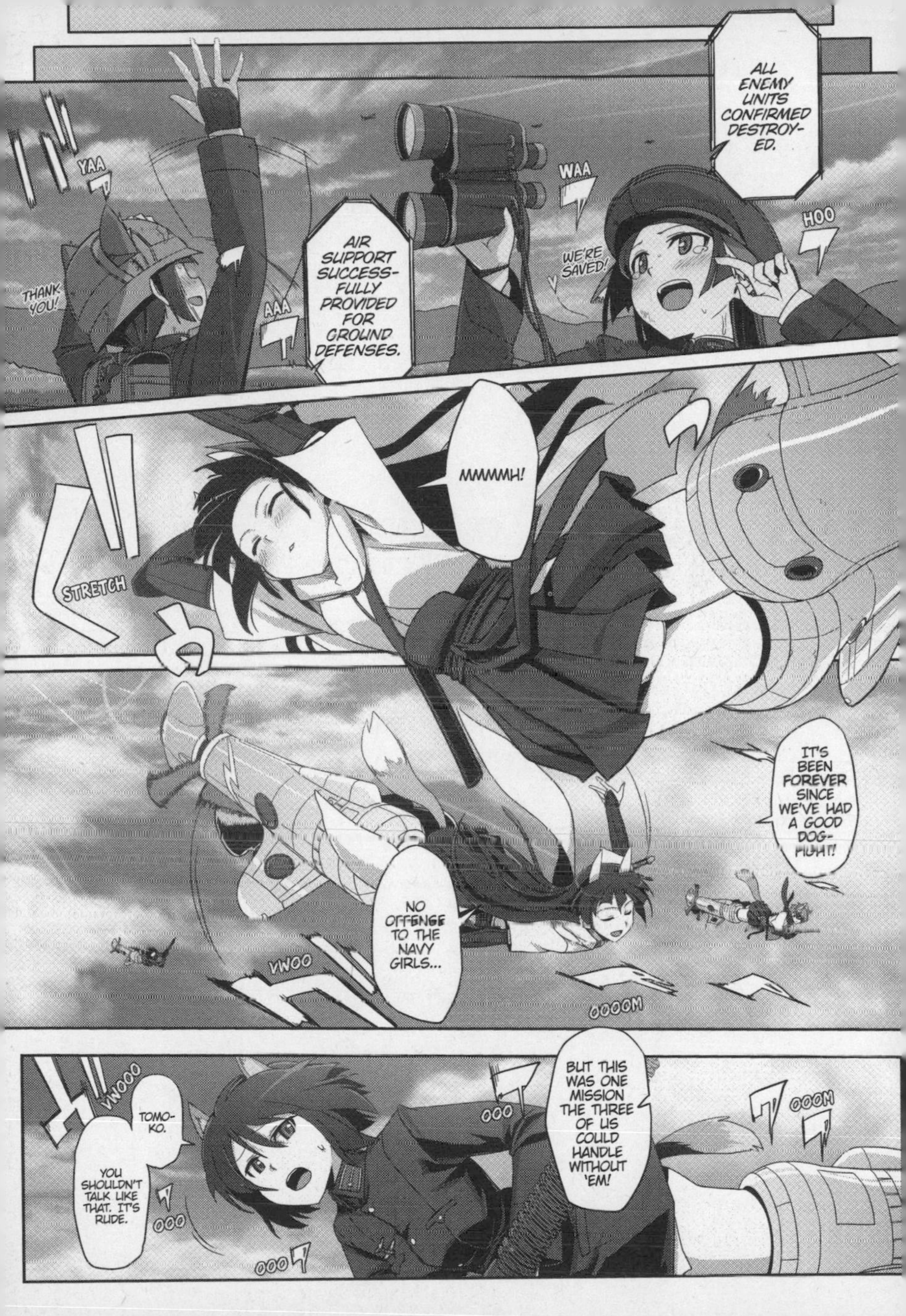
ALL ENEMY UNITS CONFIRMED DESTROYED.
HOO
WE'RE SAVED!
WAA
AIR SUPPORT SUCCESSFULLY PROVIDED FOR GROUND DEFENSES.
AAA
YAA
THANK YOU!
MMMMH!
STRETCH
IT'S BEEN FOREVER SINCE WE'VE HAD A GOOD DOGFIGHT!
NO OFFENSE TO THE NAVY GIRLS...
VWOO
OOOOM
OOOM
BUT THIS WAS ONE MISSION THE THREE OF US COULD HANDLE WITHOUT 'EM!
OOO
TOMOKO.
VWOOO
YOU SHOULDN'T TALK LIKE THAT. IT'S RUDE.
OOO
OOO

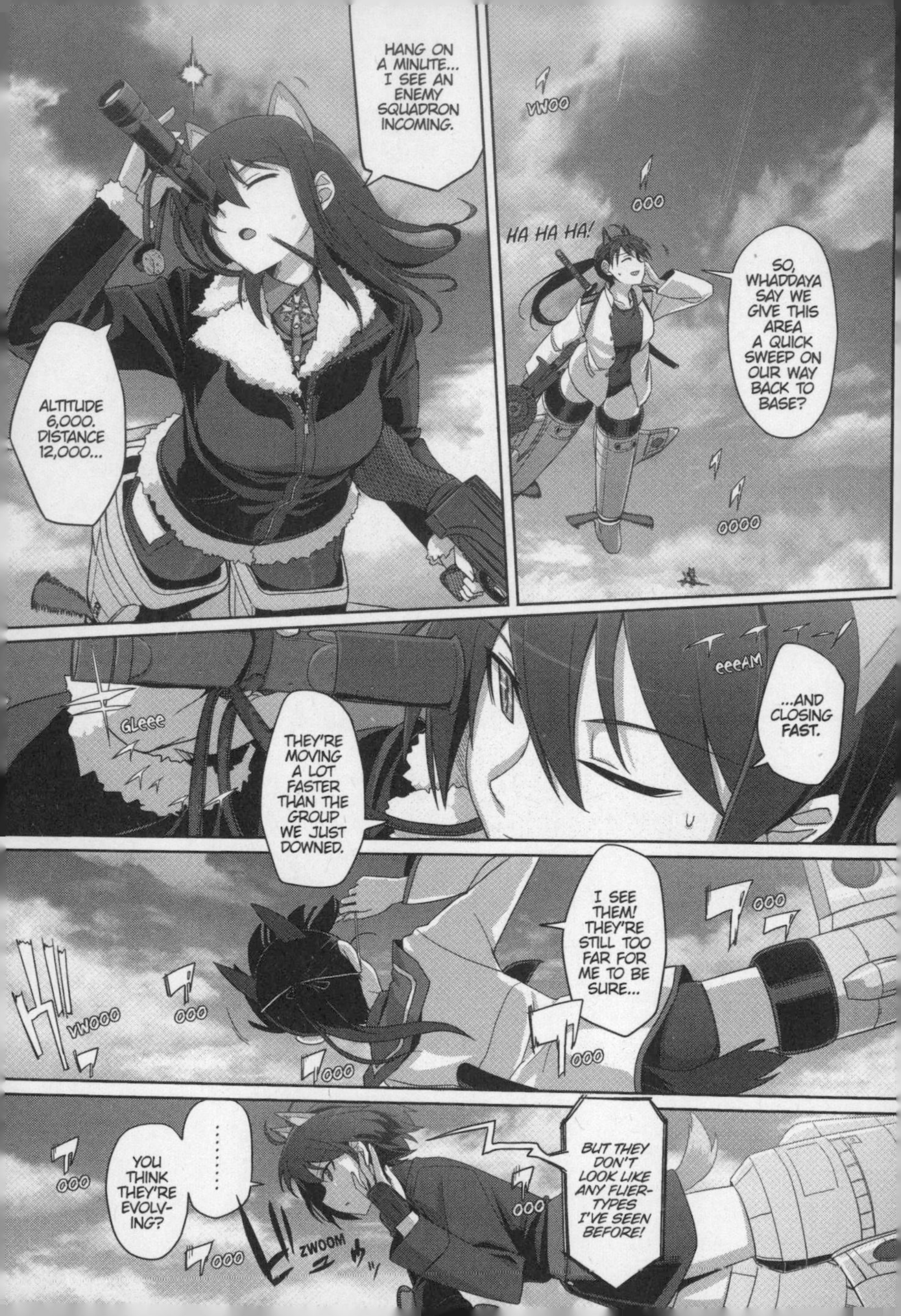
VWOO
OOO
HA HA HA!
SO, WHADDAYA SAY WE GIVE THIS AREA A QUICK SWEEP ON OUR WAY BACK TO BASE?
OOOO
HANG ON A MINUTE... I SEE AN ENEMY SQUADRON INCOMING.
ALTITUDE 6,000. DISTANCE 12,000...
eeeAM
...AND CLOSING FAST.
THEY'RE MOVING A LOT FASTER THAN THE GROUP WE JUST DOWNED.
GLeee
OOO
I SEE THEM! THEY'RE STILL TOO FAR FOR ME TO BE SURE...
OOO
OOO
VWOOO
OOO
BUT THEY DON'T LOOK LIKE ANY FLIER-TYPES I'VE SEEN BEFORE!
OOO
......
YOU THINK THEY'RE EVOLV-ING?
OOO
ZWOOM
OOO

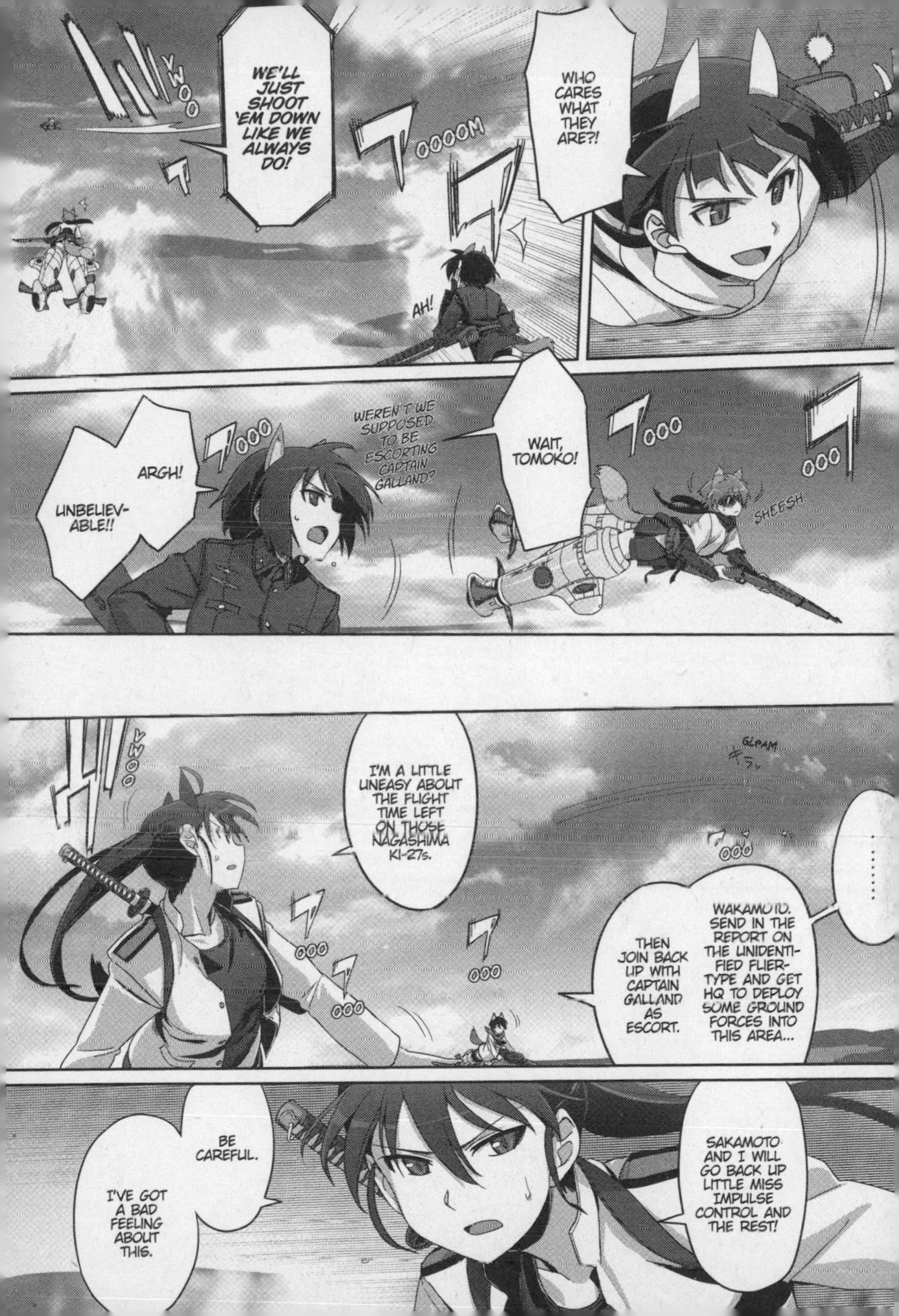
WHO CARES WHAT THEY ARE?!
OOOOM
WE'LL JUST SHOOT 'EM DOWN LIKE WE ALWAYS DO!
VWOO
AH!
OOO
WAIT, TOMOKO!
SHEESH
WEREN'T WE SUPPOSED TO BE ESCORTING CAPTAIN GALLAND?
ARGH!
UNBELIEV-ABLE!!
......
GLPAM
WAKAMOTO. SEND IN THE REPORT ON THE UNIDENTI-FIED FLIER-TYPE AND GET HQ TO DEPLOY SOME GROUND FORCES INTO THIS AREA...
THEN JOIN BACK UP WITH CAPTAIN GALLAND AS ESCORT.
I'M A LITTLE UNEASY ABOUT THE FLIGHT TIME LEFT ON THOSE NAGASHIMA KI-27s.
VWOO
SAKAMOTO AND I WILL GO BACK UP LITTLE MISS IMPULSE CONTROL AND THE REST!
BE CAREFUL.
I'VE GOT A BAD FEELING ABOUT THIS.

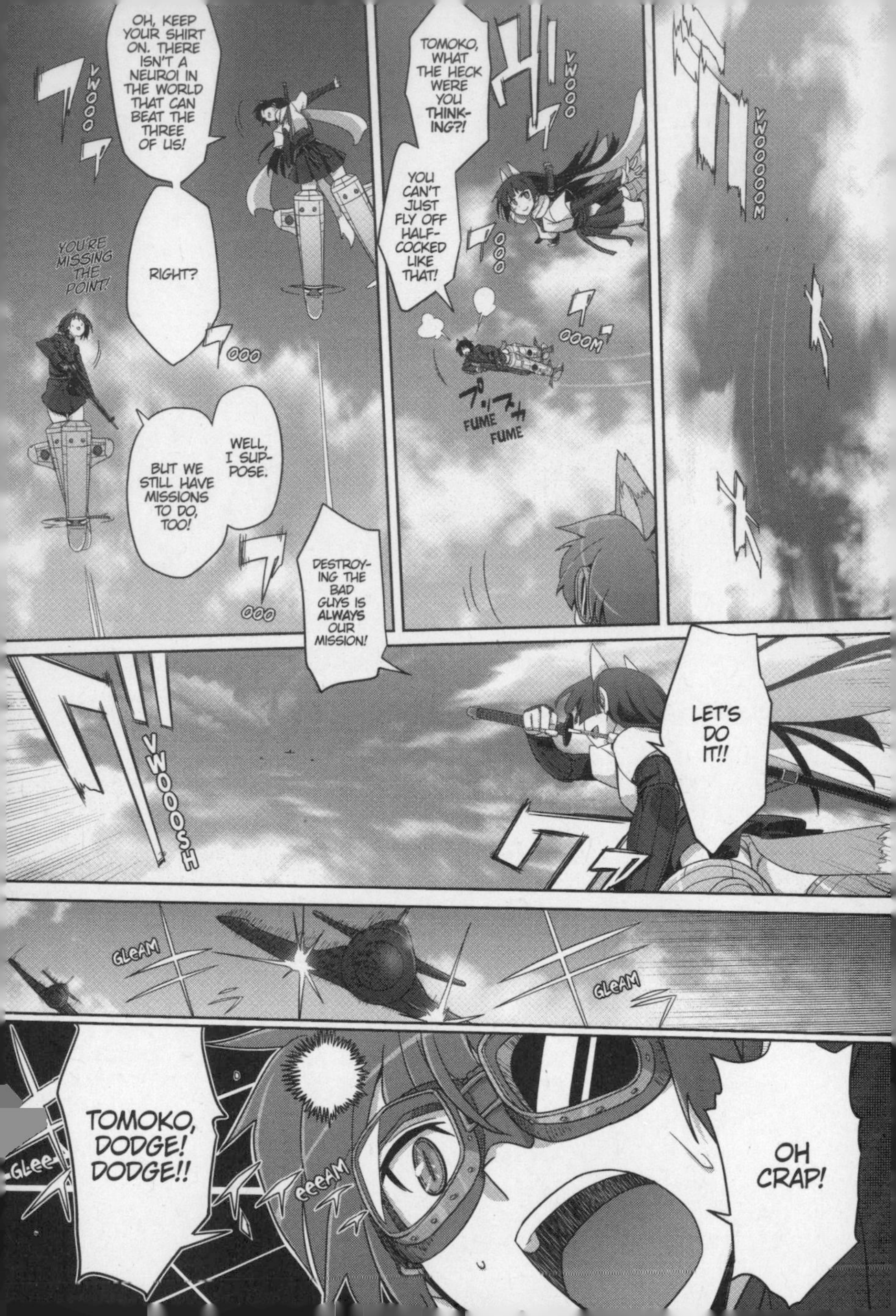
VWOOOOOOM
TOMOKO, WHAT THE HECK WERE YOU THINKING?!
VWOOOO
YOU CAN'T JUST FLY OFF HALF-COCKED LIKE THAT!
OOO
OOOM
FUME FUME
OH, KEEP YOUR SHIRT ON. THERE ISN'T A NEUROI IN THE WORLD THAT CAN BEAT THE THREE OF US!
VWOOOO
RIGHT?
YOU'RE MISSING THE POINT!
OOO
WELL, I SUP-POSE.
BUT WE STILL HAVE MISSIONS TO DO, TOO!
OOO
DESTROYING THE BAD GUYS IS ALWAYS OUR MISSION!
LET'S DO IT!!
VWOOOSH
GLEAM
GLEAM
OH CRAP!
TOMOKO, DODGE! DODGE!!
GLEE
eeeAM

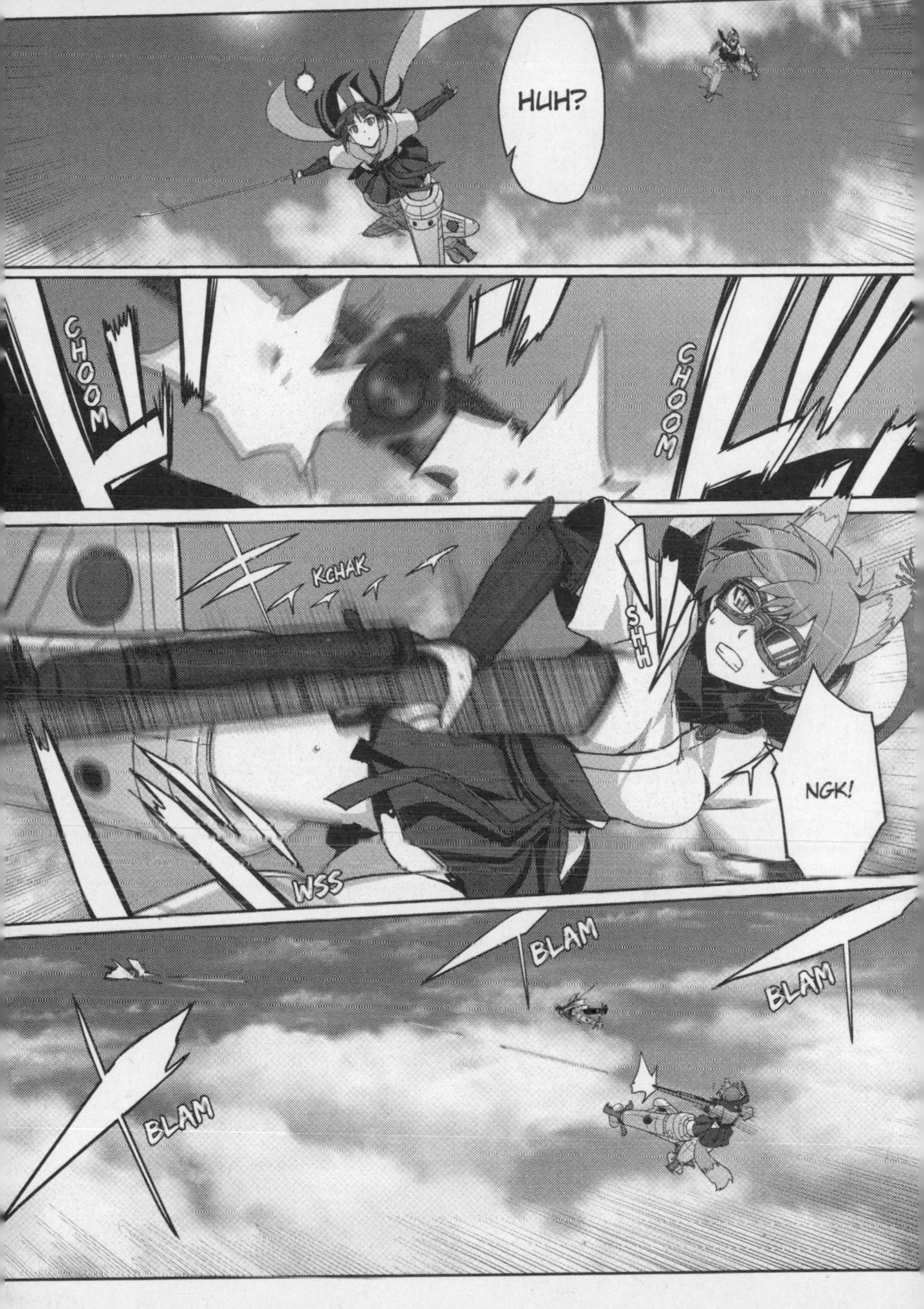
HUH?
CHOOM
CHOOM
KCHAK
SHHH
NGK!
WSS
BLAM
BLAM
BLAM

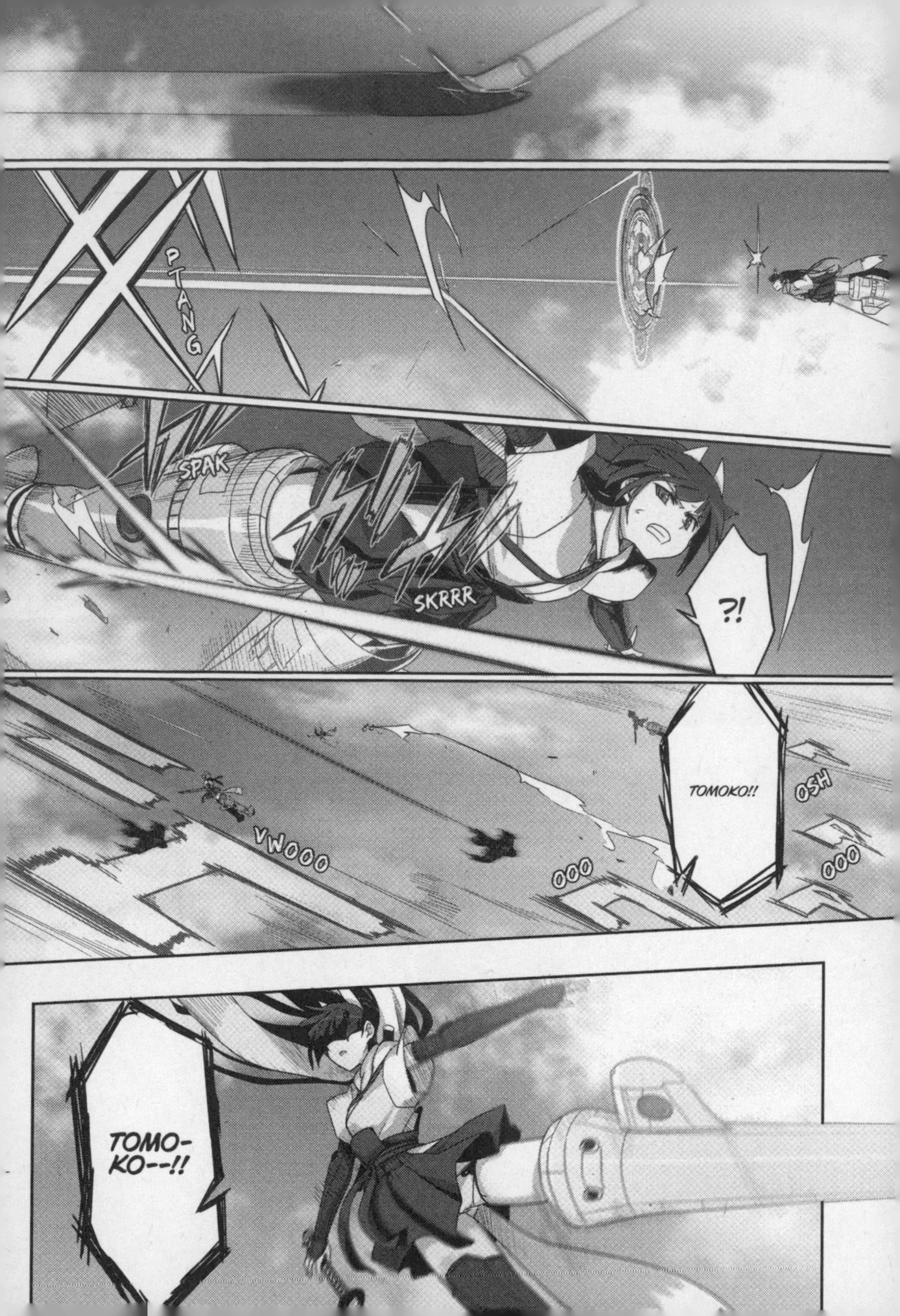
PTANG
?!
SKRRR
SPAK
TOMOKO!!
OSH
OOO
OOO
VWOOO
TOMO-
KO--!!

Chapter 3:
The Three Crows
of the Fuso Sea
[Mission Complete]

CHAPTER 4:
OPERATION FIRST STRIKE

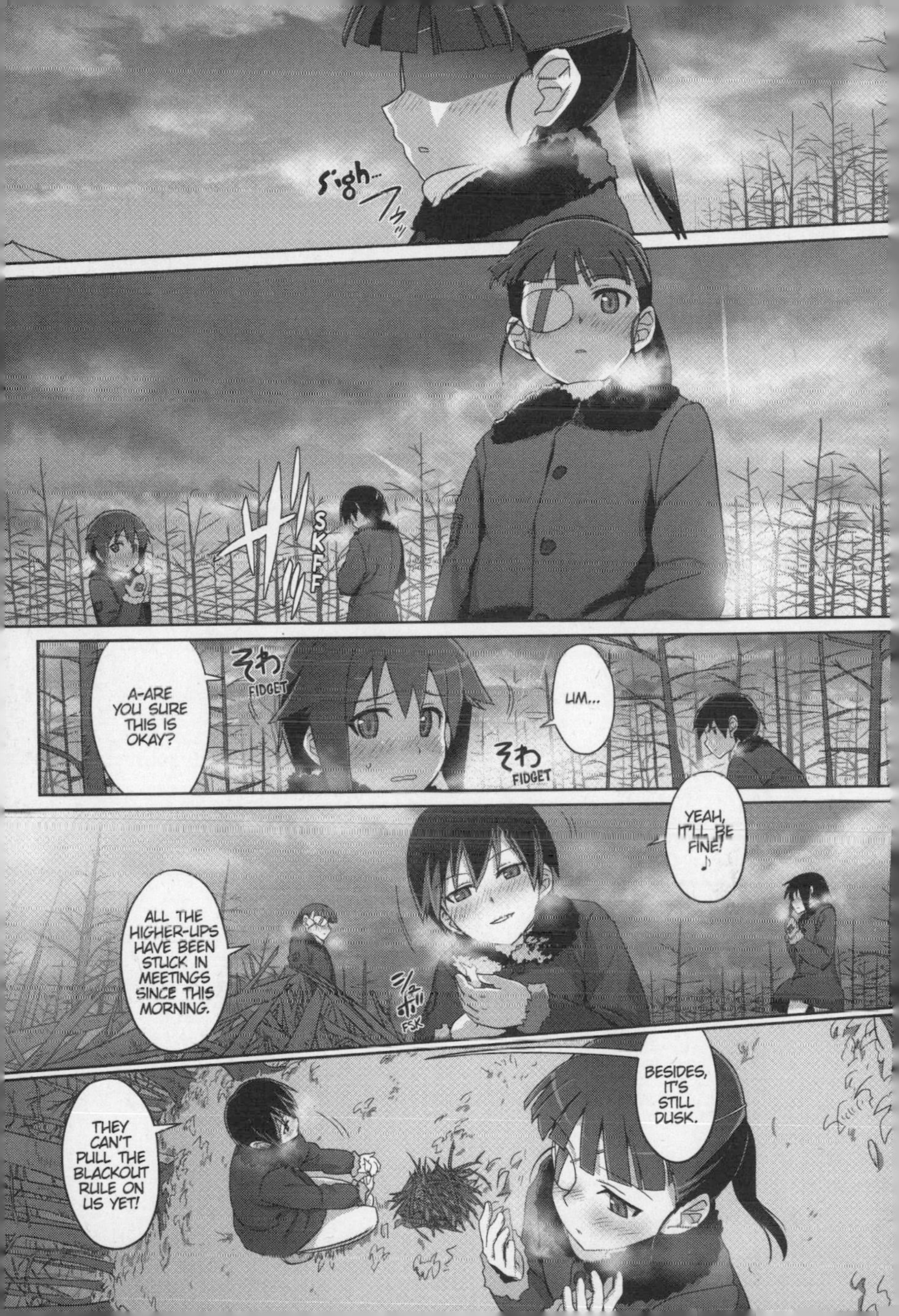
sigh...
SKFF
UM...
そわ FIDGET
そわ FIDGET
A-ARE YOU SURE THIS IS OKAY?
YEAH, IT'LL BE FINE! ♪
ALL THE HIGHER-UPS HAVE BEEN STUCK IN MEETINGS SINCE THIS MORNING.
FSK
BESIDES, IT'S STILL DUSK.
THEY CAN'T PULL THE BLACKOUT RULE ON US YET!

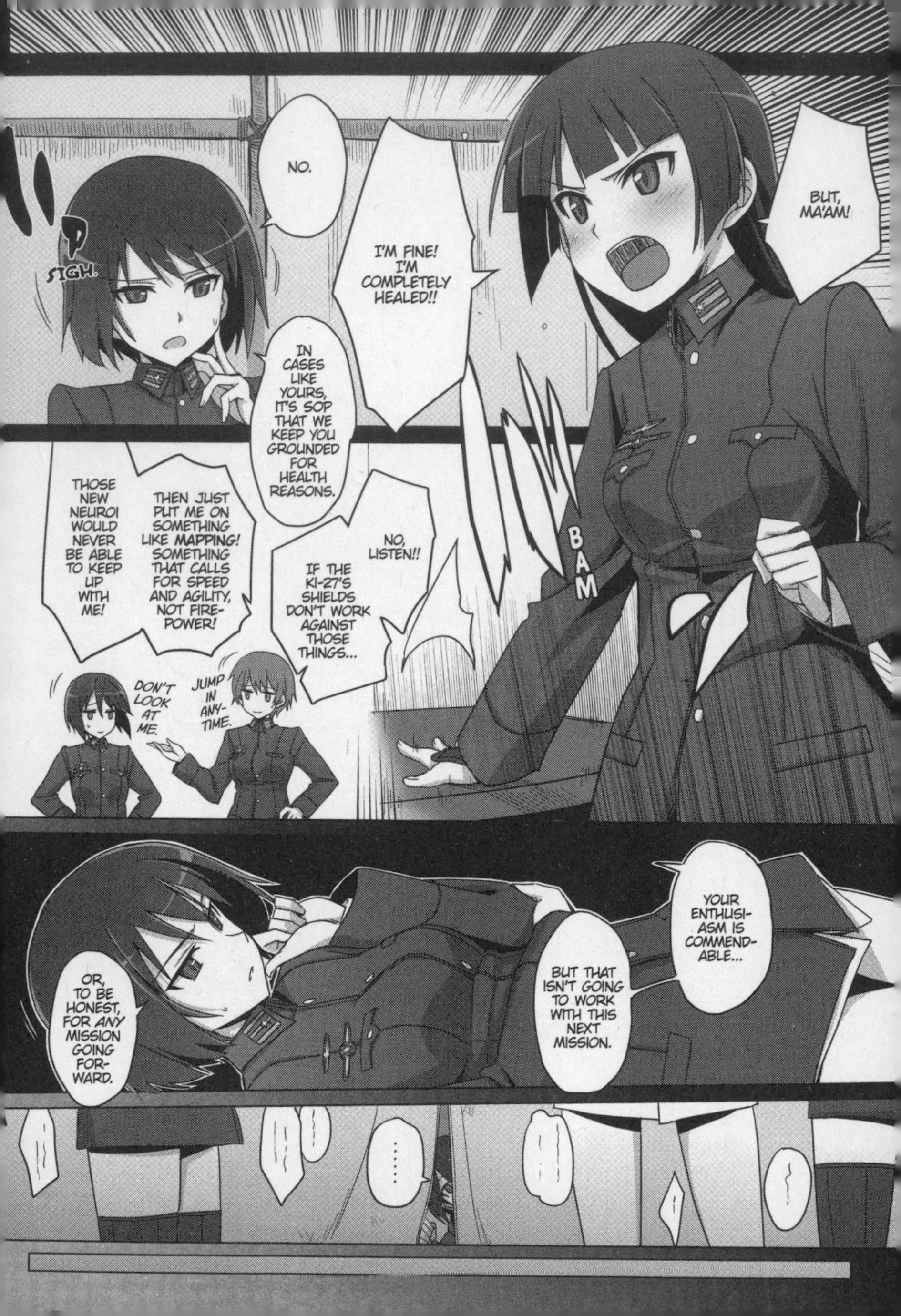
BUT, MA'AM!
NO.
I'M FINE! I'M COMPLETELY HEALED!!
SIGH.
IN CASES LIKE YOURS, IT'S SOP THAT WE KEEP YOU GROUNDED FOR HEALTH REASONS.
BAM
NO, LISTEN!!
IF THE KI-27'S SHIELDS DON'T WORK AGAINST THOSE THINGS...
THEN JUST PUT ME ON SOMETHING LIKE MAPPING! SOMETHING THAT CALLS FOR SPEED AND AGILITY, NOT FIRE-POWER!
THOSE NEW NEUROI WOULD NEVER BE ABLE TO KEEP UP WITH ME!
JUMP IN ANY-TIME.
DON'T LOOK AT ME.
YOUR ENTHUSI-ASM IS COMMEND-ABLE...
BUT THAT ISN'T GOING TO WORK WITH THIS NEXT MISSION.
OR, TO BE HONEST, FOR ANY MISSION GOING FOR-WARD.
......

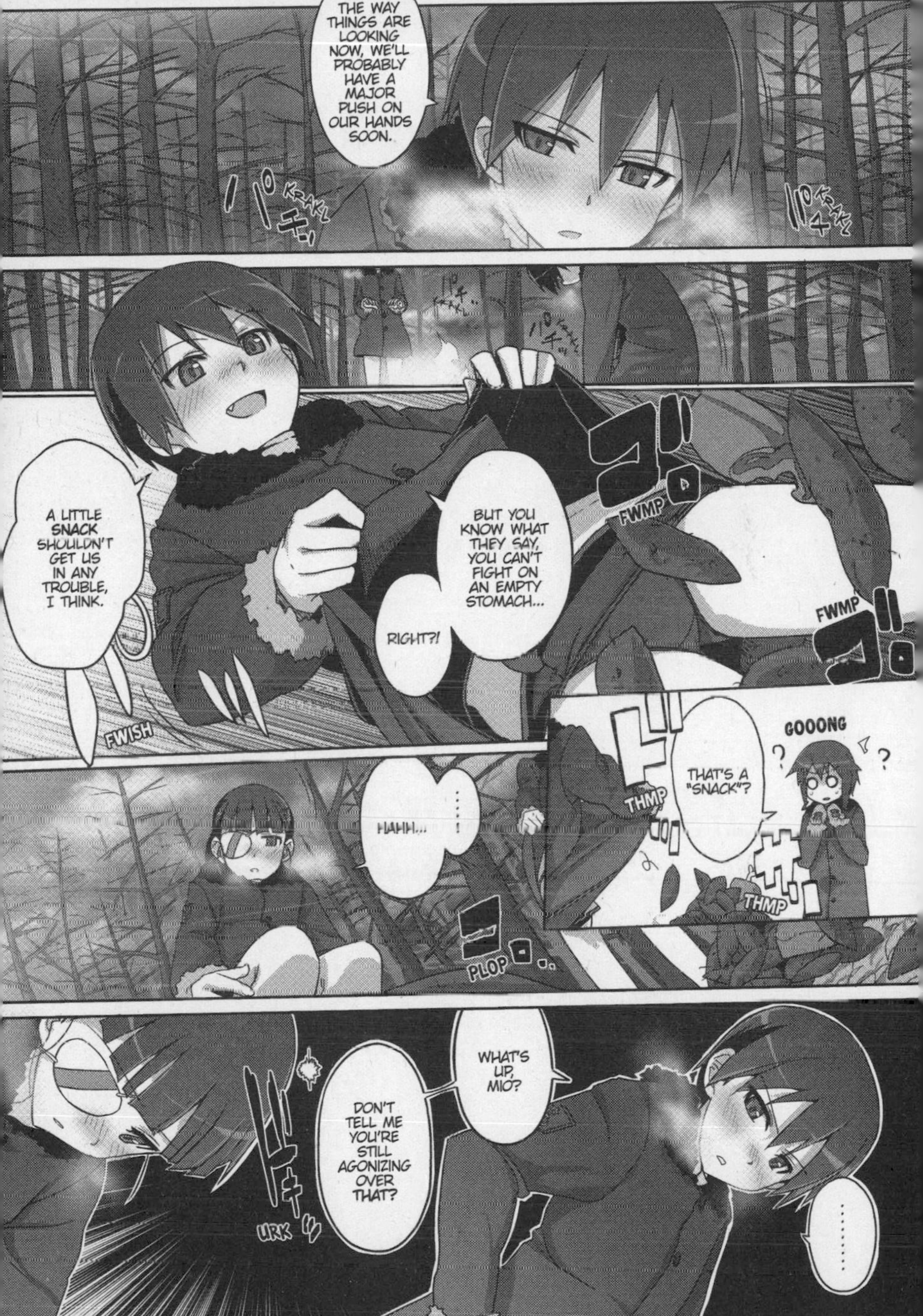
THE WAY THINGS ARE LOOKING NOW, WE'LL PROBABLY HAVE A MAJOR PUSH ON OUR HANDS SOON.
KRAKL
KRAKL
FWMP
FWMP
BUT YOU KNOW WHAT THEY SAY, YOU CAN'T FIGHT ON AN EMPTY STOMACH...
RIGHT?!
A LITTLE SNACK SHOULDN'T GET US IN ANY TROUBLE, I THINK.
FWISH
GOOONG
THAT'S A "SNACK"?
THMP
THMP
......!
HAHH...
PLOP
WHAT'S UP, MIO?
DON'T TELL ME YOU'RE STILL AGONIZING OVER THAT?
......
URK

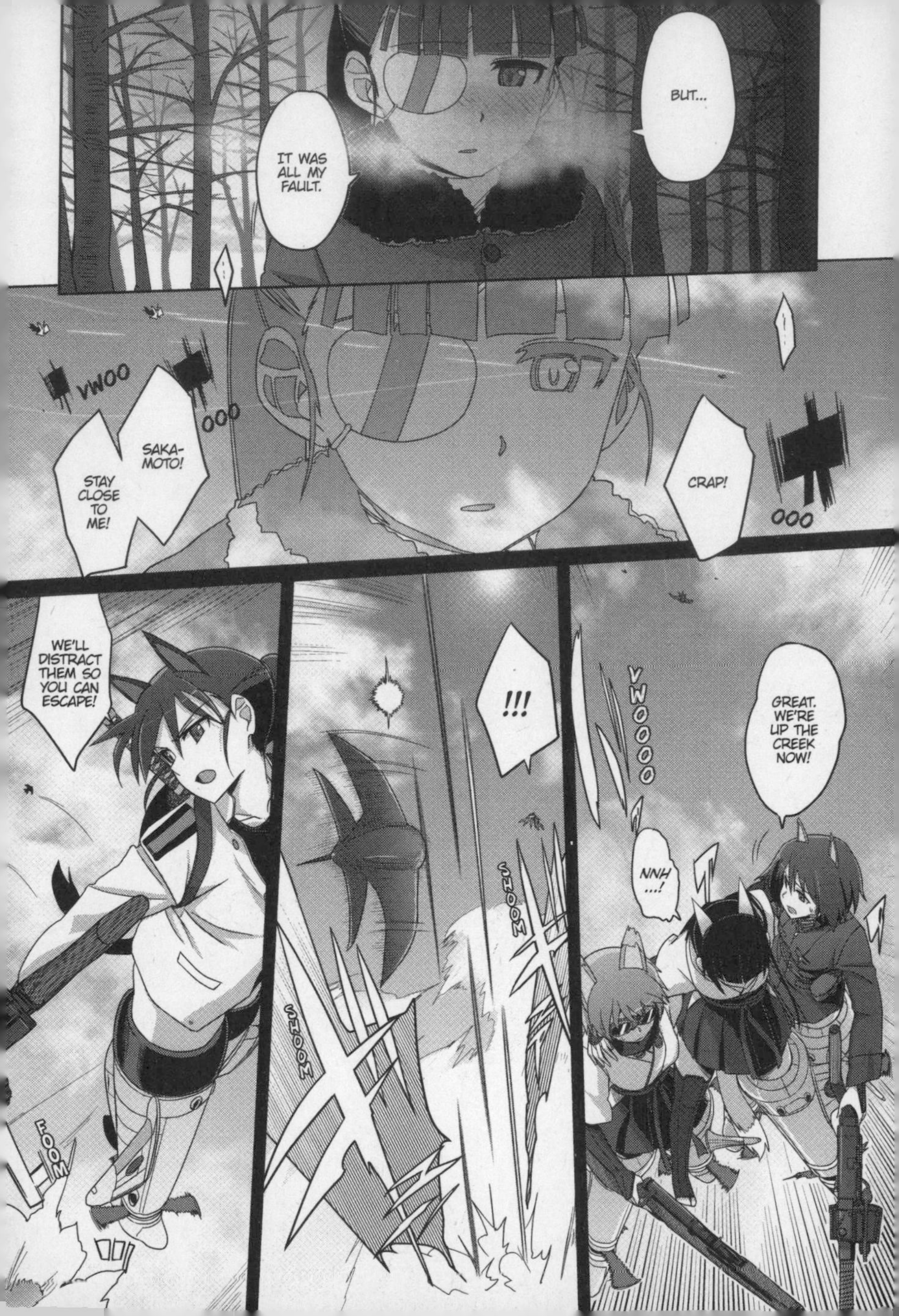
BUT...
IT WAS ALL MY FAULT.
!
!
CRAP!
OOO
SAKA-MOTO!
STAY CLOSE TO ME!
VWOO
OOO
GREAT. WE'RE UP THE CREEK NOW!
VWOOOOO
NNH ...!
!!!
SHOOM
SHOOM
WE'LL DISTRACT THEM SO YOU CAN ESCAPE!
FOOM

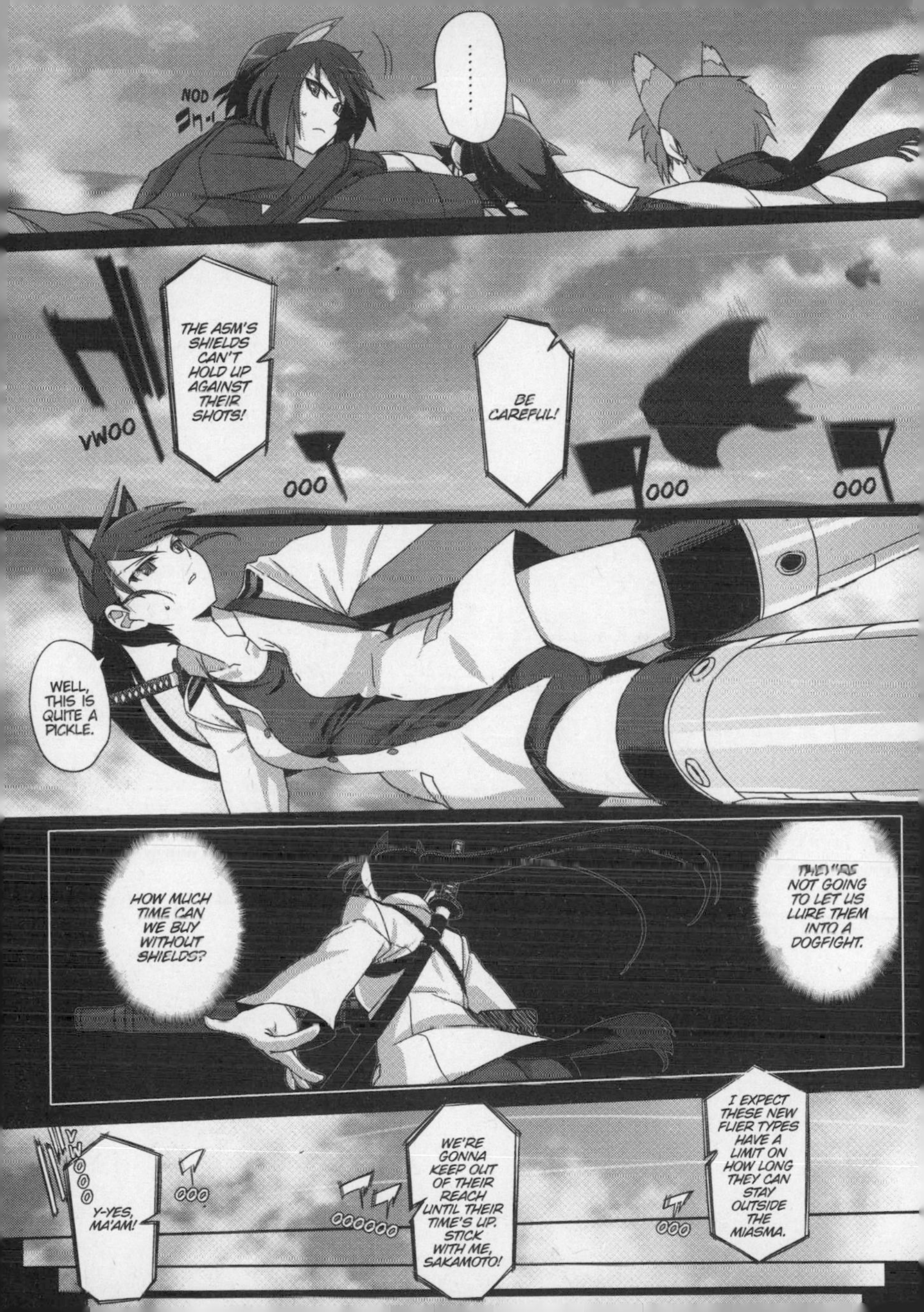
......
NOD
THE ASM'S SHIELDS CAN'T HOLD UP AGAINST THEIR SHOTS!
BE CAREFUL!
OOO
OOO
OOO
VWOO
WELL, THIS IS QUITE A PICKLE.
THEY'RE NOT GOING TO LET US LURE THEM INTO A DOGFIGHT.
HOW MUCH TIME CAN WE BUY WITHOUT SHIELDS?
I EXPECT THESE NEW FLIER TYPES HAVE A LIMIT ON HOW LONG THEY CAN STAY OUTSIDE THE MIASMA.
OOO
WE'RE GONNA KEEP OUT OF THEIR REACH UNTIL THEIR TIME'S UP. STICK WITH ME, SAKAMOTO!
OOOOOO
OOO
Y-YES, MA'AM!
VWOOO

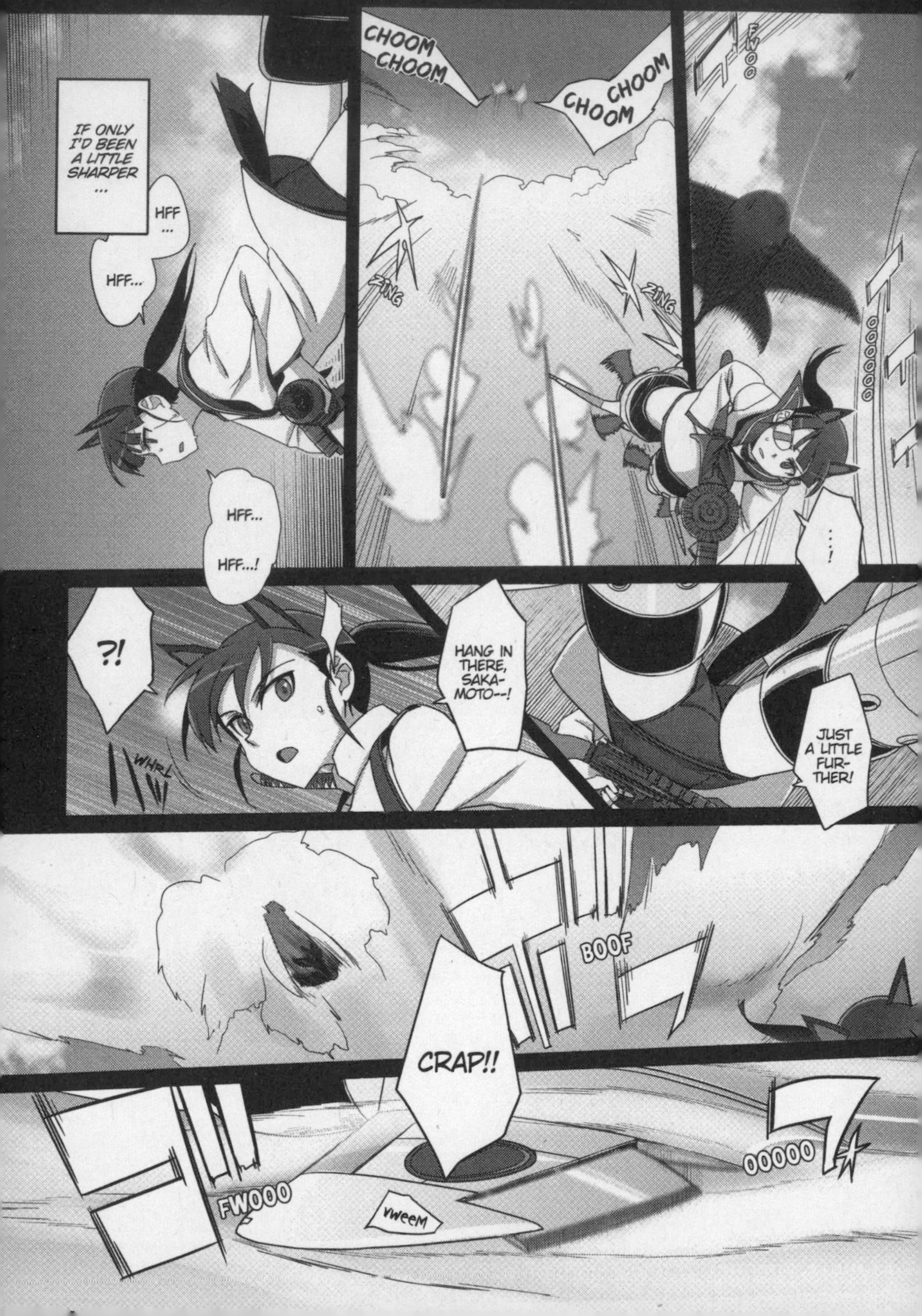
FWOO
OOOOOO
...!
CHOOM CHOOM
CHOOM CHOOM
ZING
ZING
IF ONLY I'D BEEN A LITTLE SHARPER ...
HFF ...
HFF...
HFF...
HFF...!
JUST A LITTLE FUR-THER!
HANG IN THERE, SAKA-MOTO--!
?!
WHRL
BOOF
CRAP!!
OOOOO
FWOOO
vweem

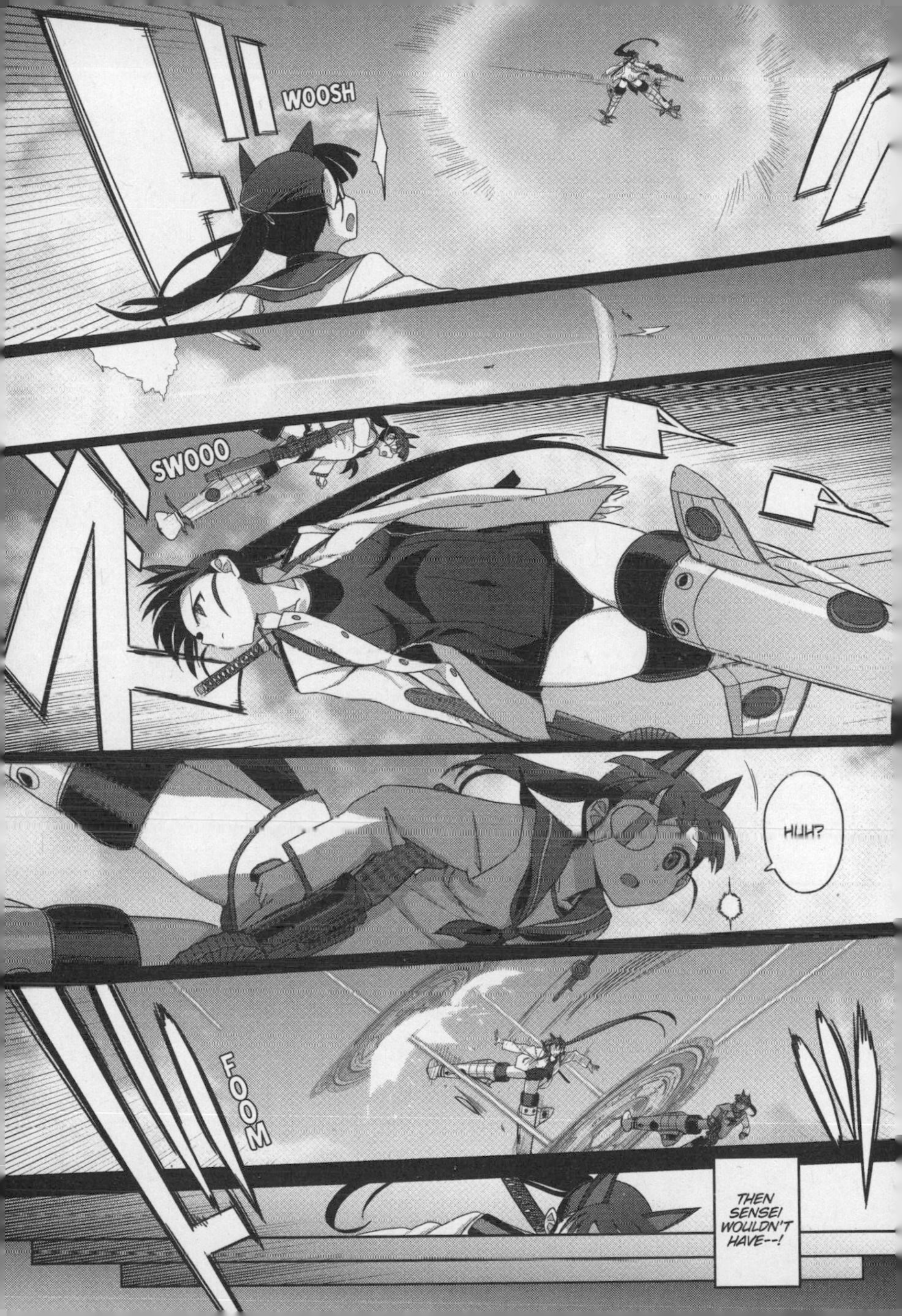
WOOSH
SWOOO
HUH?
FOOM
THEN SENSEI WOULDN'T HAVE--!

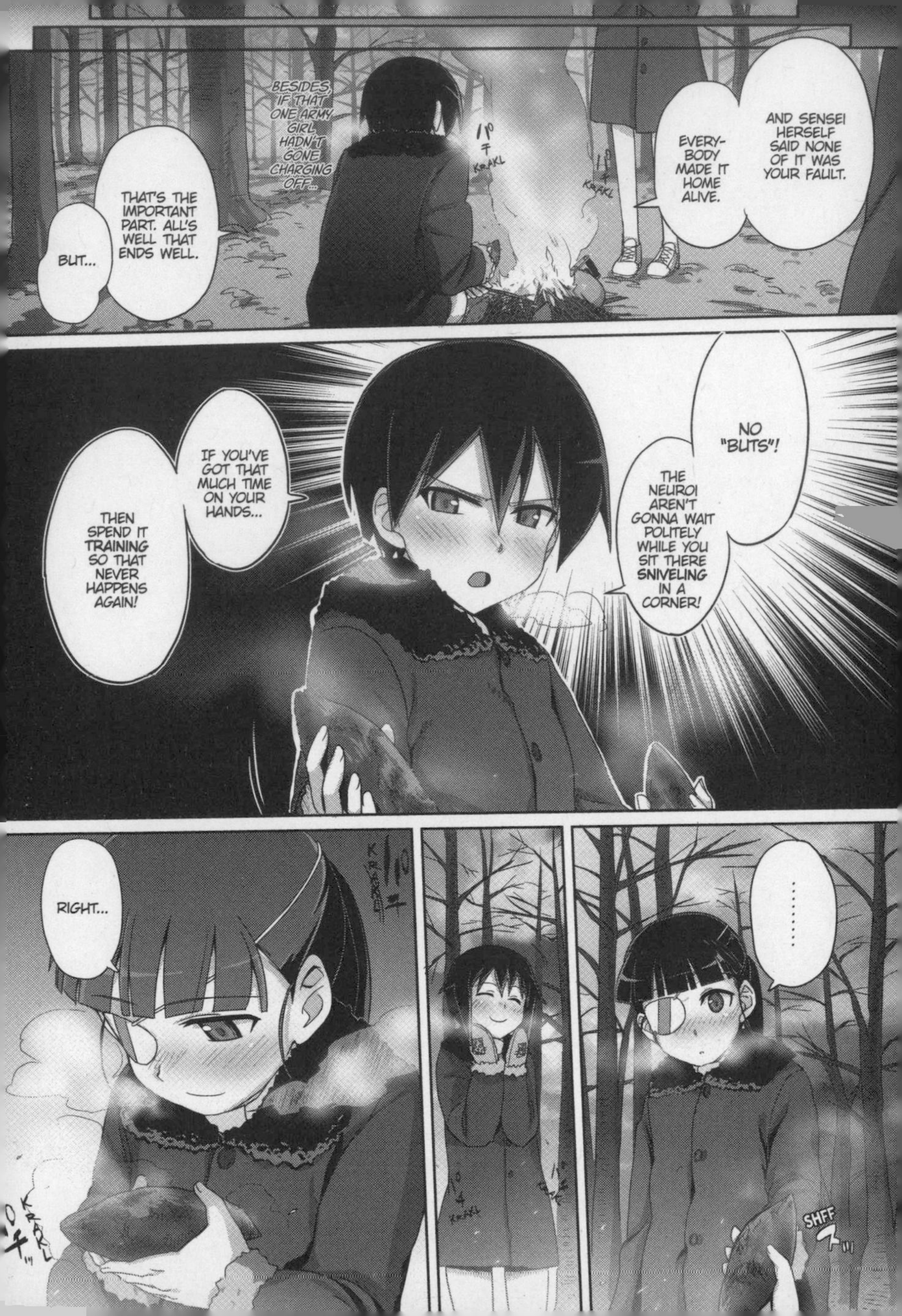
AND SENSEI HERSELF SAID NONE OF IT WAS YOUR FAULT.
EVERYBODY MADE IT HOME ALIVE.
KRAKL
KRAKL
BESIDES, IF THAT ONE ARMY GIRL HADN'T GONE CHARGING OFF...
THAT'S THE IMPORTANT PART. ALL'S WELL THAT ENDS WELL.
BUT...
NO "BUTS"!
THE NEUROI AREN'T GONNA WAIT POLITELY WHILE YOU SIT THERE SNIVELING IN A CORNER!
IF YOU'VE GOT THAT MUCH TIME ON YOUR HANDS...
THEN SPEND IT TRAINING SO THAT NEVER HAPPENS AGAIN!
......
SHFF
KRAKL
KRAKL
RIGHT...
KRAKL

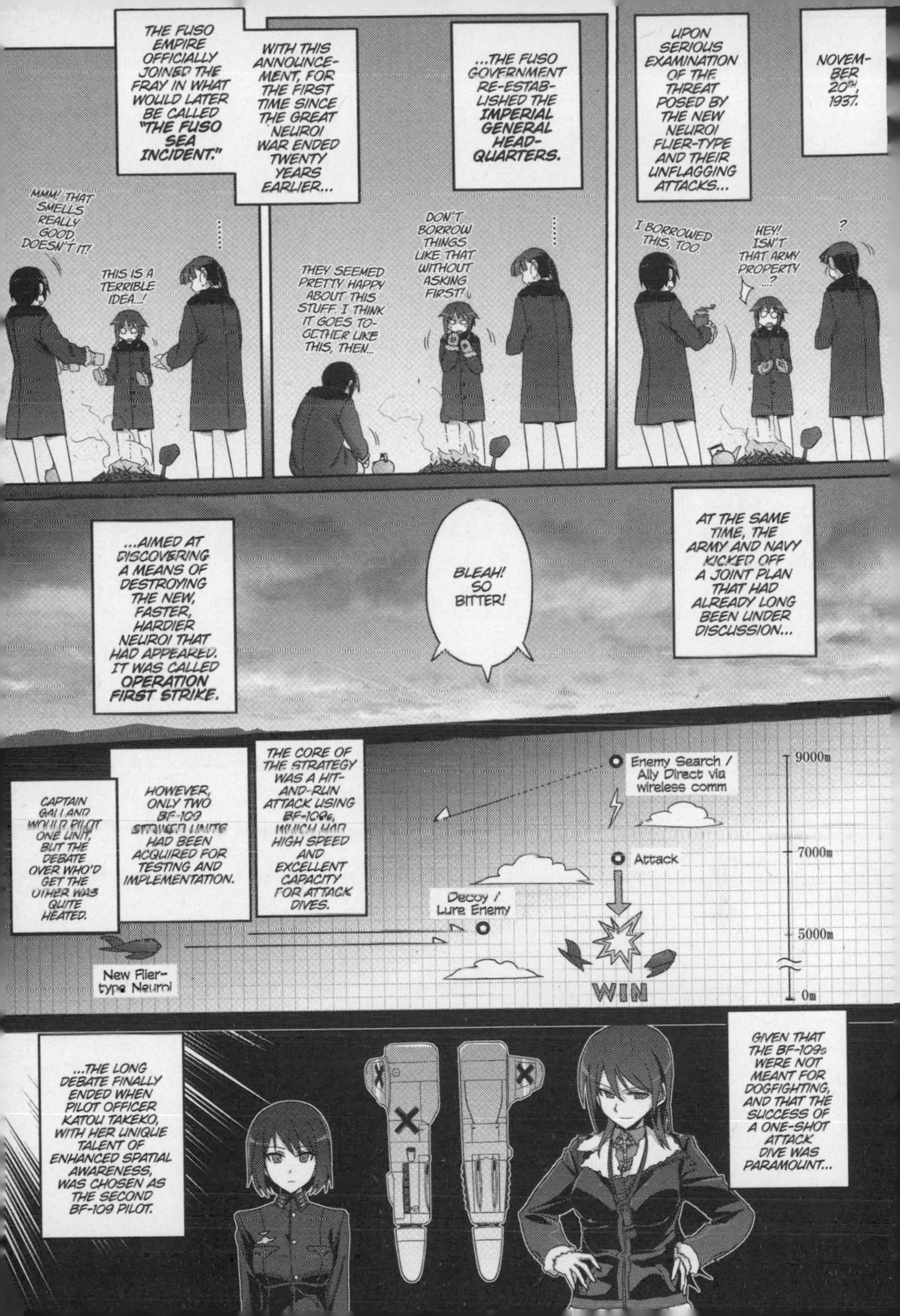
NOVEMBER 20TH, 1937.
UPON SERIOUS EXAMINATION OF THE THREAT POSED BY THE NEW NEUROI FLIER-TYPE AND THEIR UNFLAGGING ATTACKS...
?
HEY! ISN'T THAT ARMY PROPERTY...?
I BORROWED THIS, TOO
...THE FUSO GOVERNMENT RE-ESTABLISHED THE IMPERIAL GENERAL HEADQUARTERS.
.....
DON'T BORROW THINGS LIKE THAT WITHOUT ASKING FIRST!
THEY SEEMED PRETTY HAPPY ABOUT THIS STUFF. I THINK IT GOES TOGETHER LIKE THIS, THEN...
WITH THIS ANNOUNCEMENT, FOR THE FIRST TIME SINCE THE GREAT NEUROI WAR ENDED TWENTY YEARS EARLIER...
THE FUSO EMPIRE OFFICIALLY JOINED THE FRAY IN WHAT WOULD LATER BE CALLED "THE FUSO SEA INCIDENT."
.....
MMM! THAT SMELLS REALLY GOOD, DOESN'T IT!
THIS IS A TERRIBLE IDEA...!
AT THE SAME TIME, THE ARMY AND NAVY KICKED OFF A JOINT PLAN THAT HAD ALREADY LONG BEEN UNDER DISCUSSION...
BLEAH! SO BITTER!
...AIMED AT DISCOVERING A MEANS OF DESTROYING THE NEW, FASTER, HARDIER NEUROI THAT HAD APPEARED. IT WAS CALLED OPERATION FIRST STRIKE.
9000m
7000m
5000m
0m
Enemy Search / Ally Direct via wireless comm
Attack
Decoy / Lure Enemy
WIN
New Flier-type Neuroi
THE CORE OF THE STRATEGY WAS A HIT-AND-RUN ATTACK USING BF-109s, WHICH HAD HIGH SPEED AND EXCELLENT CAPACITY FOR ATTACK DIVES.
HOWEVER, ONLY TWO BF-109 STRIKER UNITS HAD BEEN ACQUIRED FOR TESTING AND IMPLEMENTATION.
CAPTAIN GALLAND WOULD PILOT ONE UNIT, BUT THE DEBATE OVER WHO'D GET THE OTHER WAS QUITE HEATED.
GIVEN THAT THE BF-109s WERE NOT MEANT FOR DOGFIGHTING, AND THAT THE SUCCESS OF A ONE-SHOT ATTACK DIVE WAS PARAMOUNT...
...THE LONG DEBATE FINALLY ENDED WHEN PILOT OFFICER KATOU TAKEKO, WITH HER UNIQUE TALENT OF ENHANCED SPATIAL AWARENESS, WAS CHOSEN AS THE SECOND BF-109 PILOT.

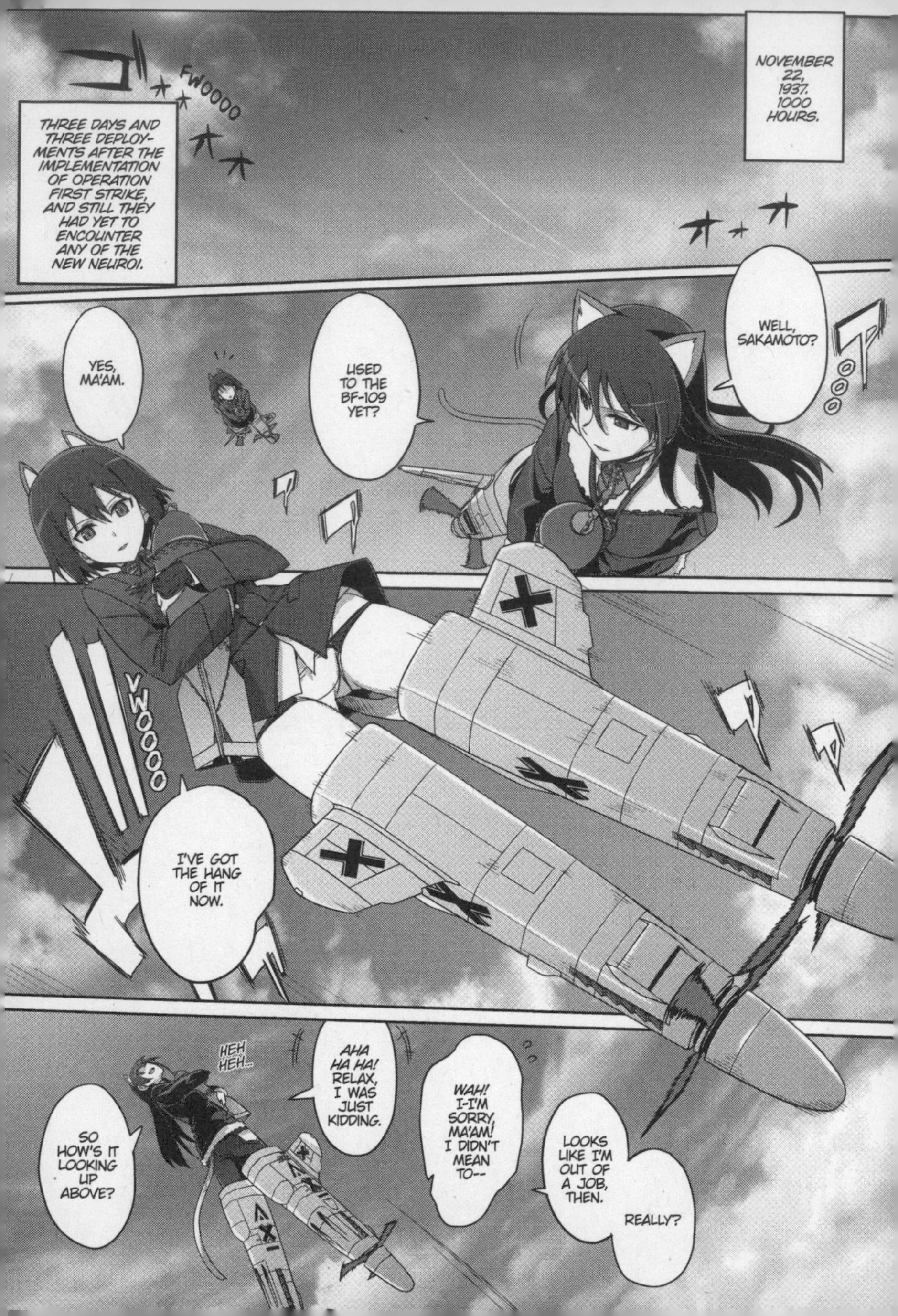
NOVEMBER 22, 1937. 1000 HOURS.
FWOOOO
THREE DAYS AND THREE DEPLOYMENTS AFTER THE IMPLEMENTATION OF OPERATION FIRST STRIKE, AND STILL THEY HAD YET TO ENCOUNTER ANY OF THE NEW NEUROI.
WELL, SAKAMOTO?
USED TO THE BF-109 YET?
YES, MA'AM.
VWOOOO
I'VE GOT THE HANG OF IT NOW.
REALLY?
LOOKS LIKE I'M OUT OF A JOB, THEN.
WAH! I-I'M SORRY, MA'AM! I DIDN'T MEAN TO--
AHA HA HA! RELAX, I WAS JUST KIDDING.
HEH HEH...
SO HOW'S IT LOOKING UP ABOVE?

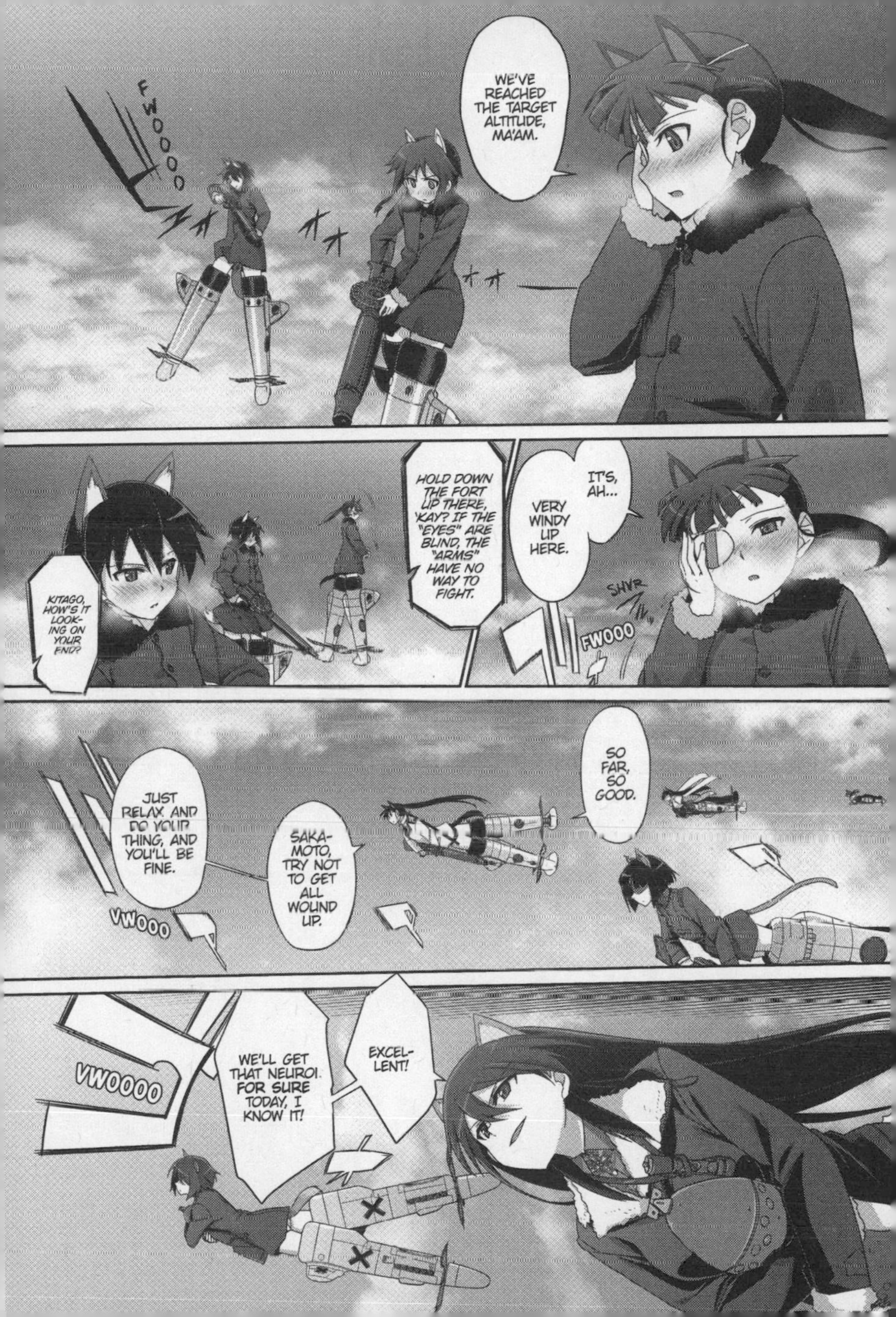
WE'VE REACHED THE TARGET ALTITUDE, MA'AM.
FWOOOO
IT'S, AH...
VERY WINDY UP HERE.
SHVR
FWOOO
HOLD DOWN THE FORT UP THERE, 'KAY? IF THE "EYES" ARE BLIND, THE "ARMS" HAVE NO WAY TO FIGHT.
KITAGO, HOW'S IT LOOKING ON YOUR END?
SO FAR, SO GOOD.
SAKAMOTO, TRY NOT TO GET ALL WOUND UP.
JUST RELAX AND DO YOUR THING, AND YOU'LL BE FINE.
VWOOO
EXCEL-LENT!
WE'LL GET THAT NEUROI FOR SURE TODAY, I KNOW IT!
VWOOOO

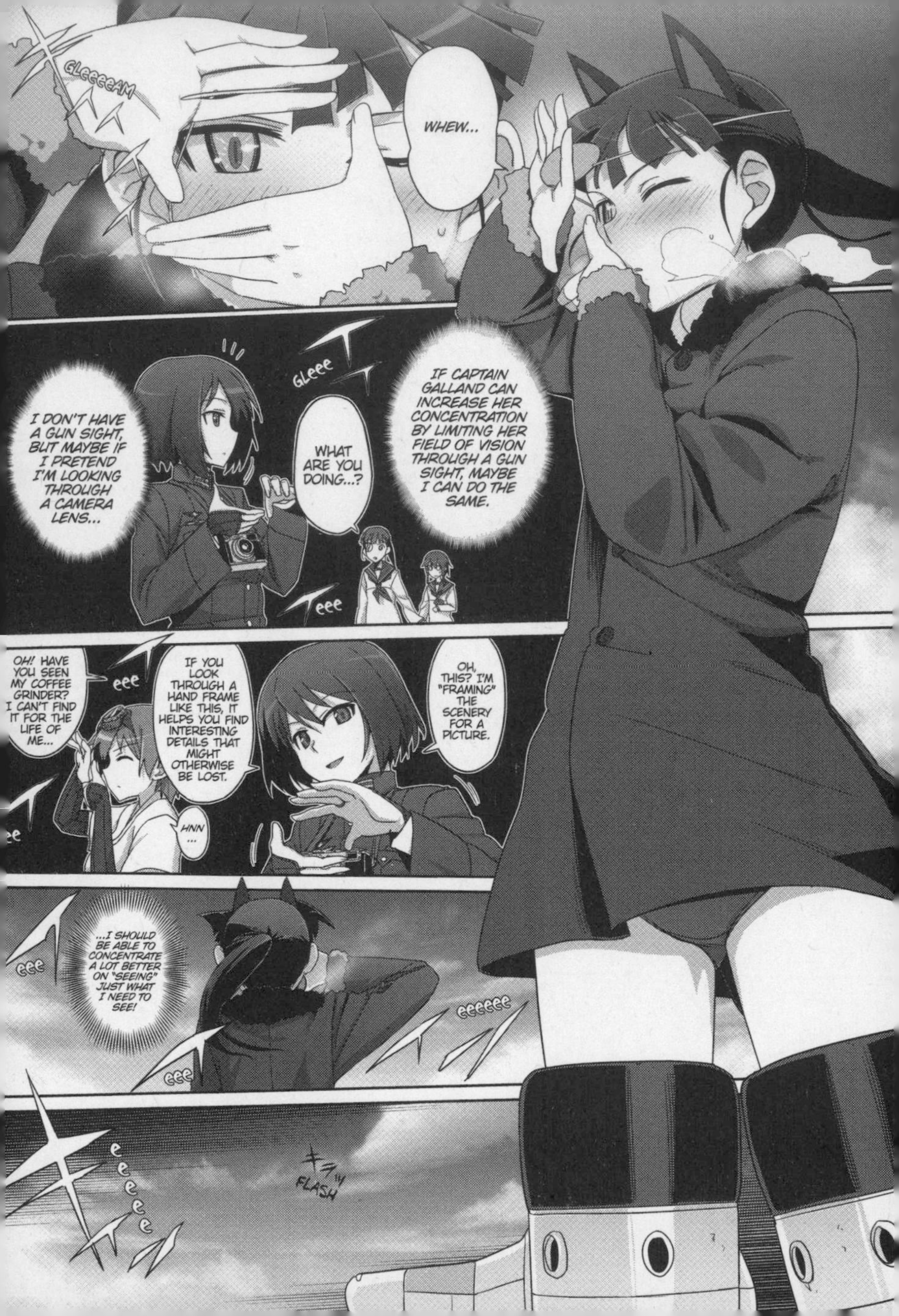
WHEW...
GLEEEEAM
IF CAPTAIN GALLAND CAN INCREASE HER CONCENTRATION BY LIMITING HER FIELD OF VISION THROUGH A GUN SIGHT, MAYBE I CAN DO THE SAME.
GLEEE
WHAT ARE YOU DOING...?
I DON'T HAVE A GUN SIGHT, BUT MAYBE IF I PRETEND I'M LOOKING THROUGH A CAMERA LENS...
Teee
OH, THIS? I'M "FRAMING" THE SCENERY FOR A PICTURE.
IF YOU LOOK THROUGH A HAND FRAME LIKE THIS, IT HELPS YOU FIND INTERESTING DETAILS THAT MIGHT OTHERWISE BE LOST.
HNN ...
OH! HAVE YOU SEEN MY COFFEE GRINDER? I CAN'T FIND IT FOR THE LIFE OF ME...
eee
...I SHOULD BE ABLE TO CONCENTRATE A LOT BETTER ON "SEEING" JUST WHAT I NEED TO SEE!
eeeeee
eee
FLASH
eeeee

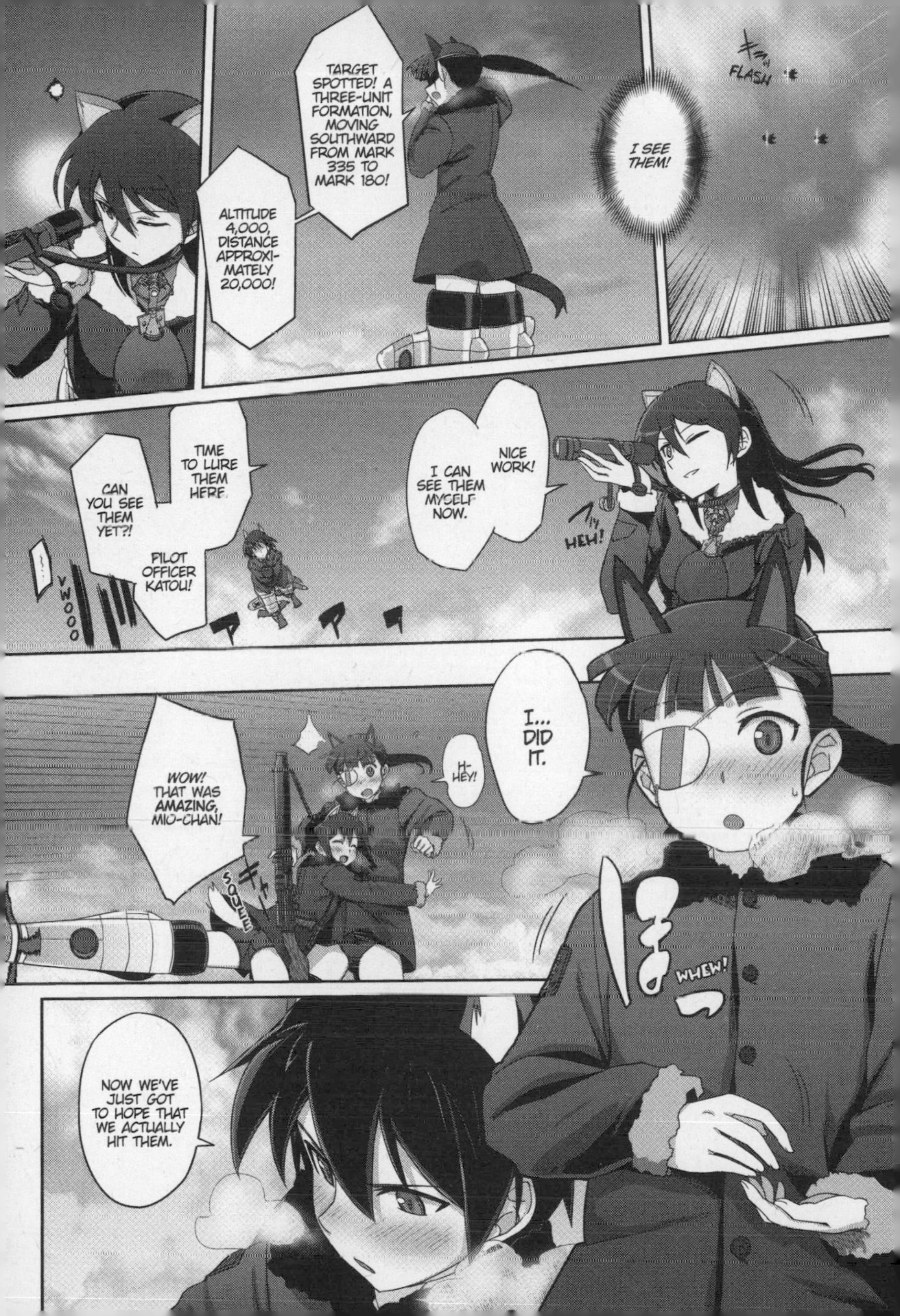
FLASH
I SEE THEM!
TARGET SPOTTED! A THREE-UNIT FORMATION, MOVING SOUTHWARD FROM MARK 335 TO MARK 180!
ALTITUDE 4,000, DISTANCE APPROXIMATELY 20,000!
NICE WORK! I CAN SEE THEM MYSELF NOW.
HEH!
TIME TO LURE THEM HERE.
CAN YOU SEE THEM YET?!
PILOT OFFICER KATOU!
VWOOOO
I... DID IT.
WHEW!
H-HEY!
WOW! THAT WAS AMAZING, MIO-CHAN!
SQUEE
NOW WE'VE JUST GOT TO HOPE THAT WE ACTUALLY HIT THEM.

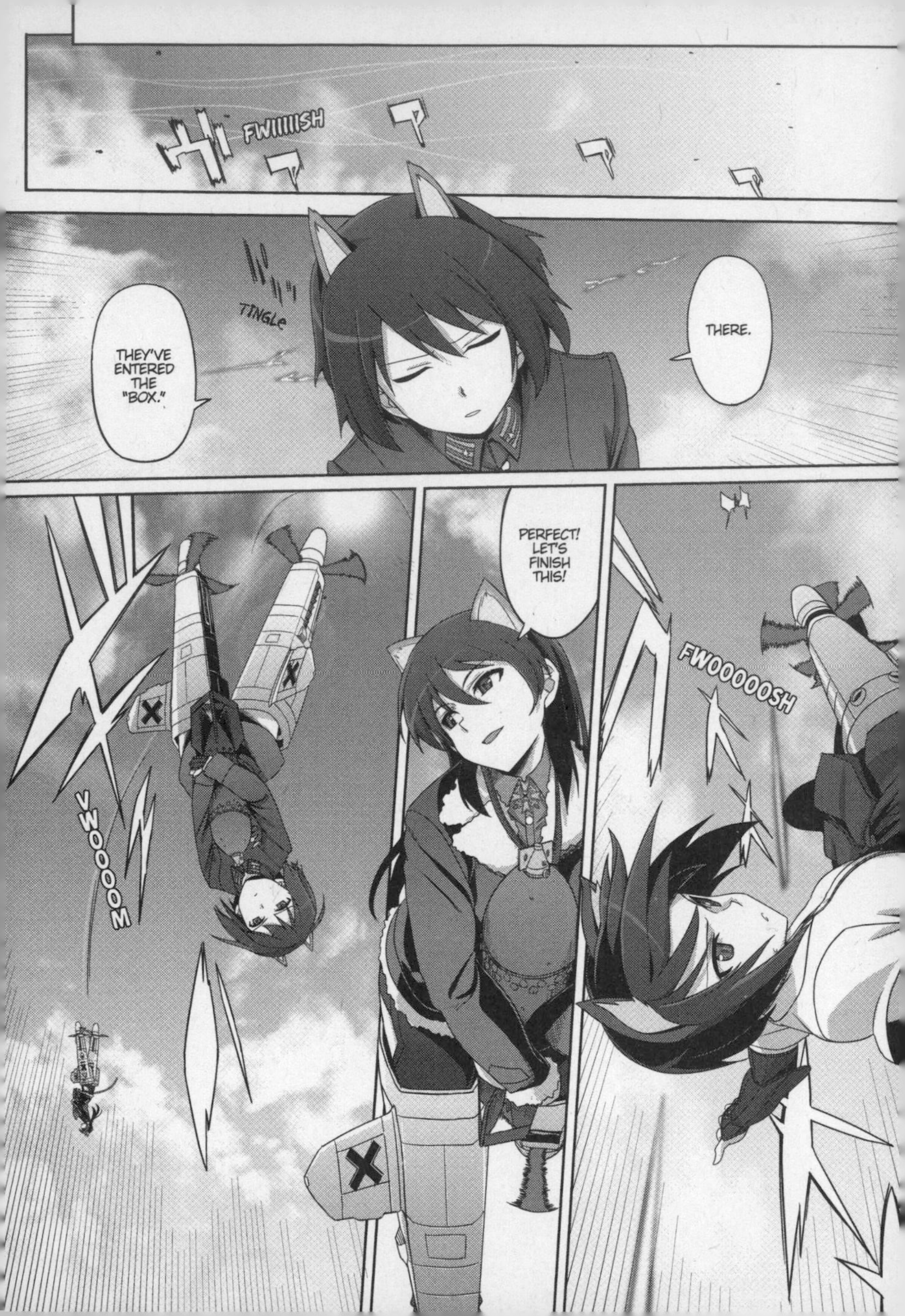
FWIIIIISH
THERE.
TINGLE
THEY'VE ENTERED THE "BOX."
FWOOOOOSH
PERFECT! LET'S FINISH THIS!
VWOOOOOM

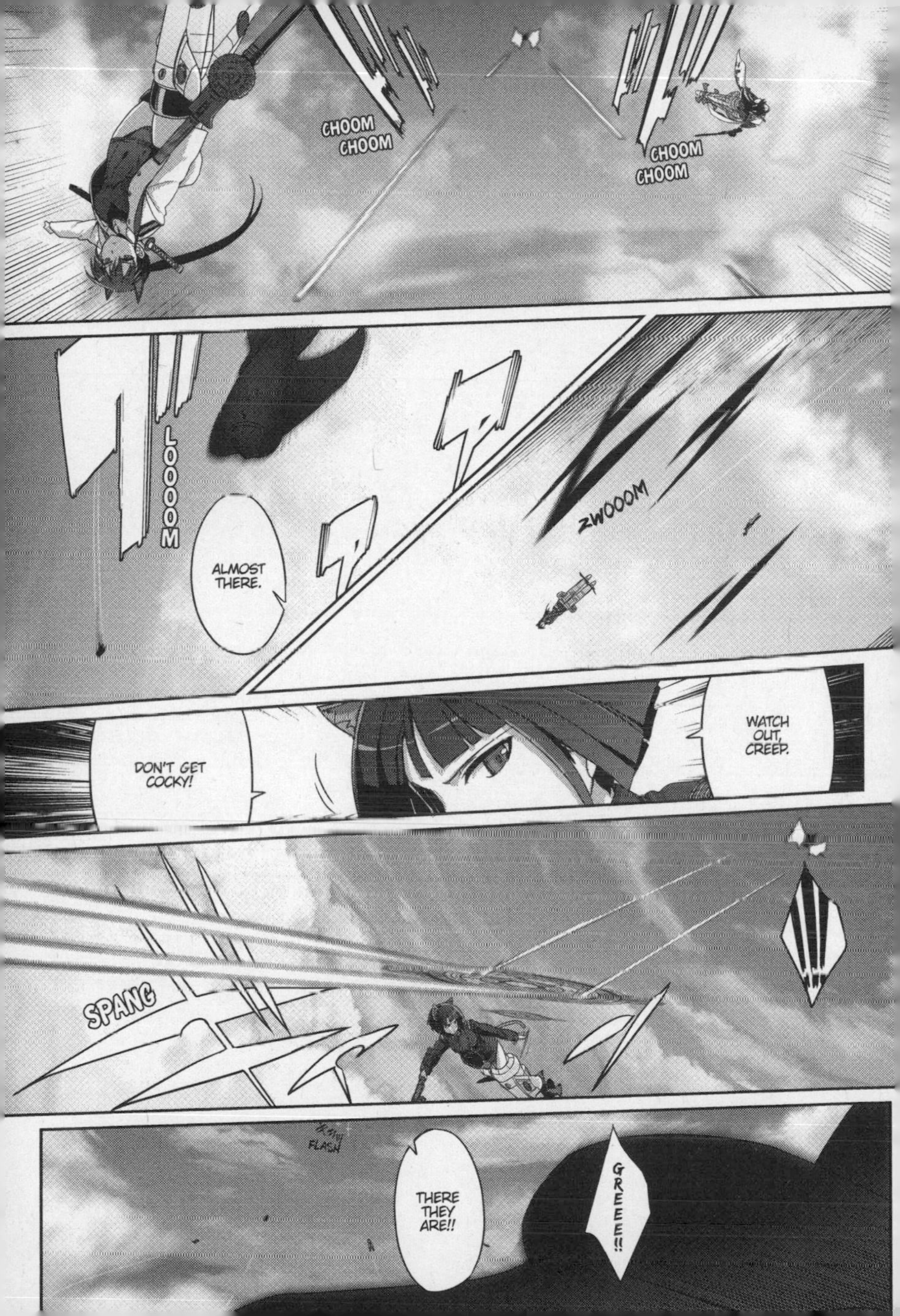
CHOOM
CHOOM
CHOOM
CHOOM
ZWOOOM
LOOOOOM
ALMOST THERE.
WATCH OUT, CREEP.
DON'T GET COCKY!
SPANG
GREEEE!!
FLASH
THERE THEY ARE!!

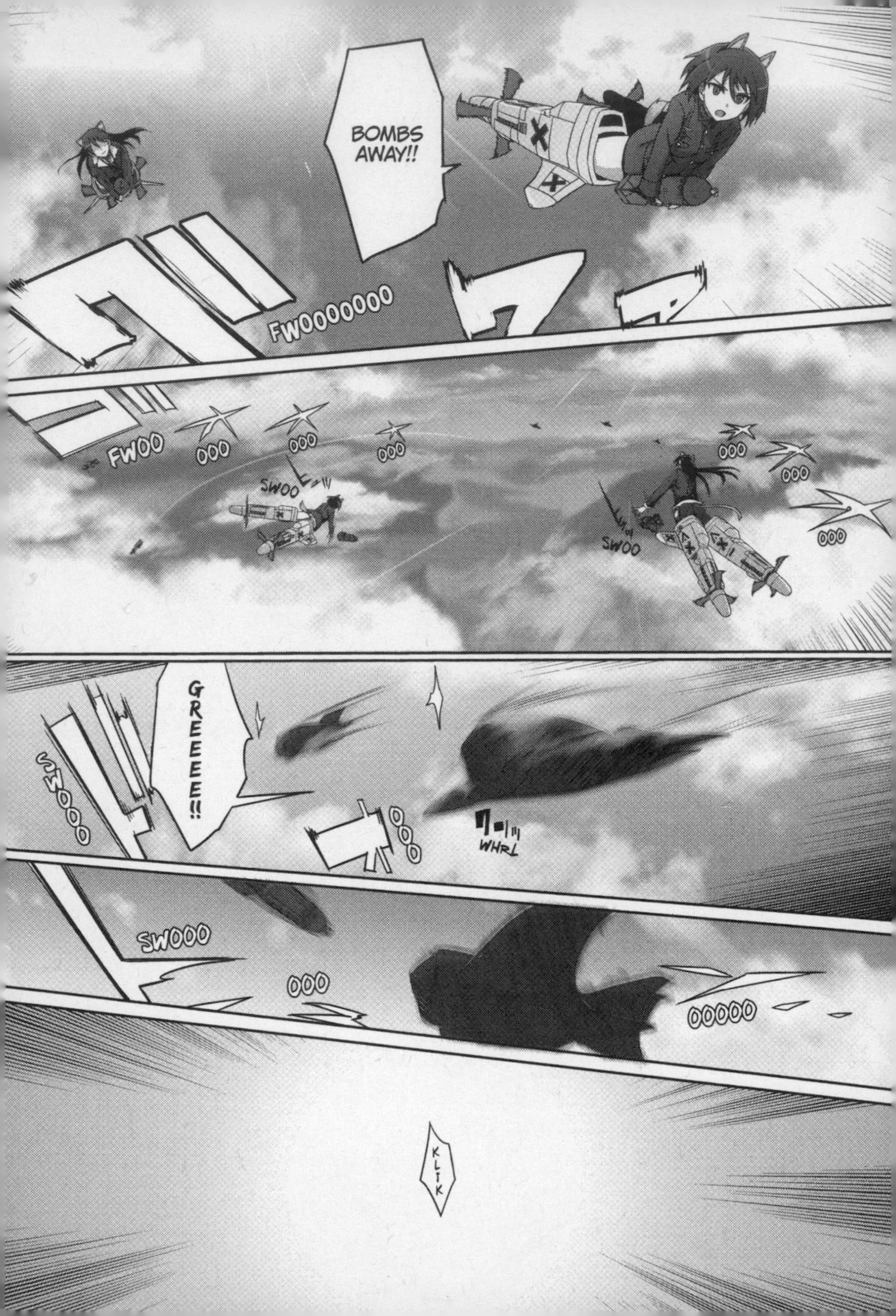
BOMBS AWAY!!
FWOOOOOOO
OOO
OOO
OOO
SWOO
FWOO
OOO
OOO
OOO
SWOO
GREEEEE!!
WHRL
OOO
SWOOOO
SWOOO
OOO
OOOOO
KLIK

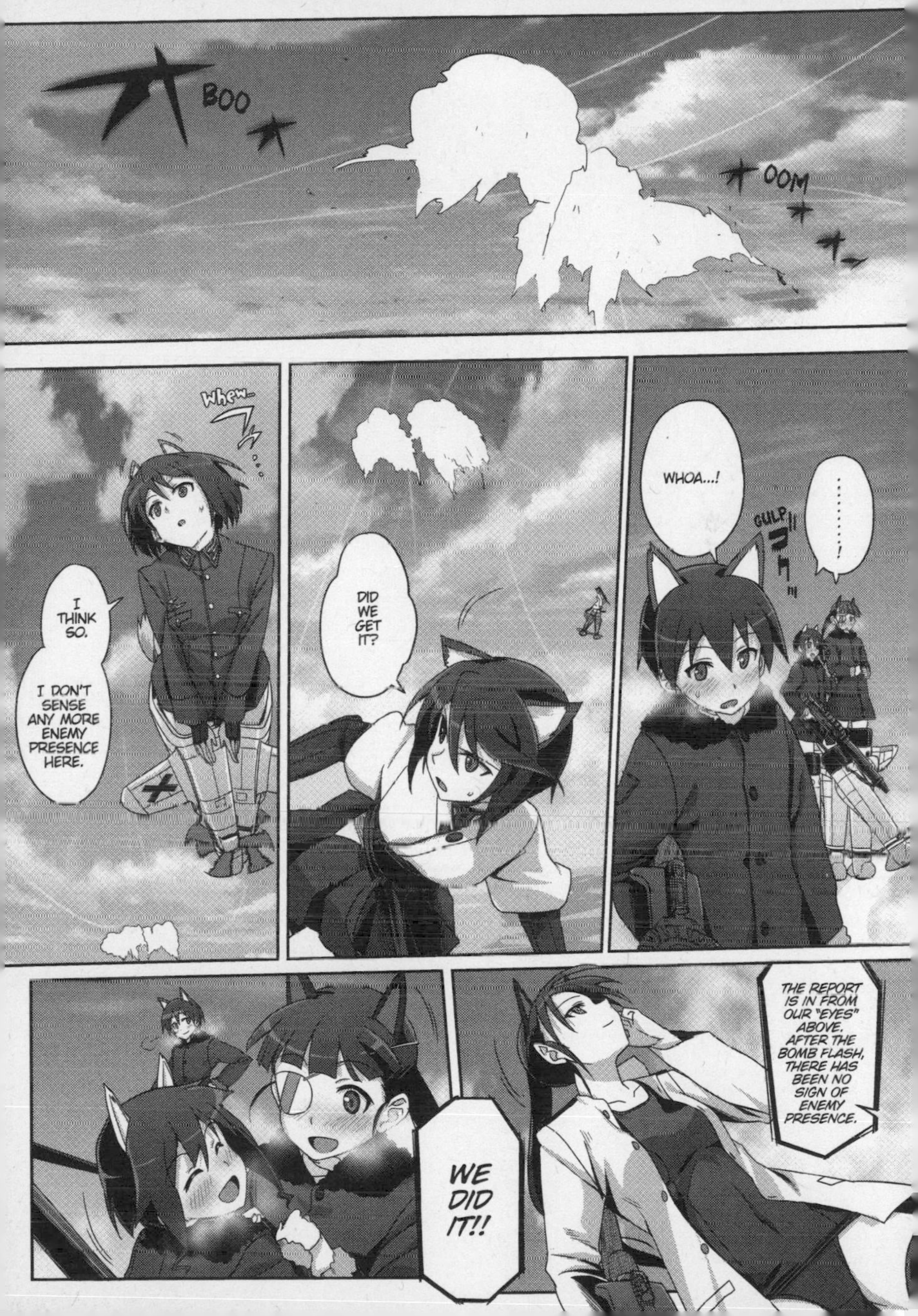
BOO
OOM
......!
GULP
WHOA...!
DID WE GET IT?
Whew...
I THINK SO.
I DON'T SENSE ANY MORE ENEMY PRESENCE HERE.
THE REPORT IS IN FROM OUR "EYES" ABOVE. AFTER THE BOMB FLASH, THERE HAS BEEN NO SIGN OF ENEMY PRESENCE.
WE DID IT!!

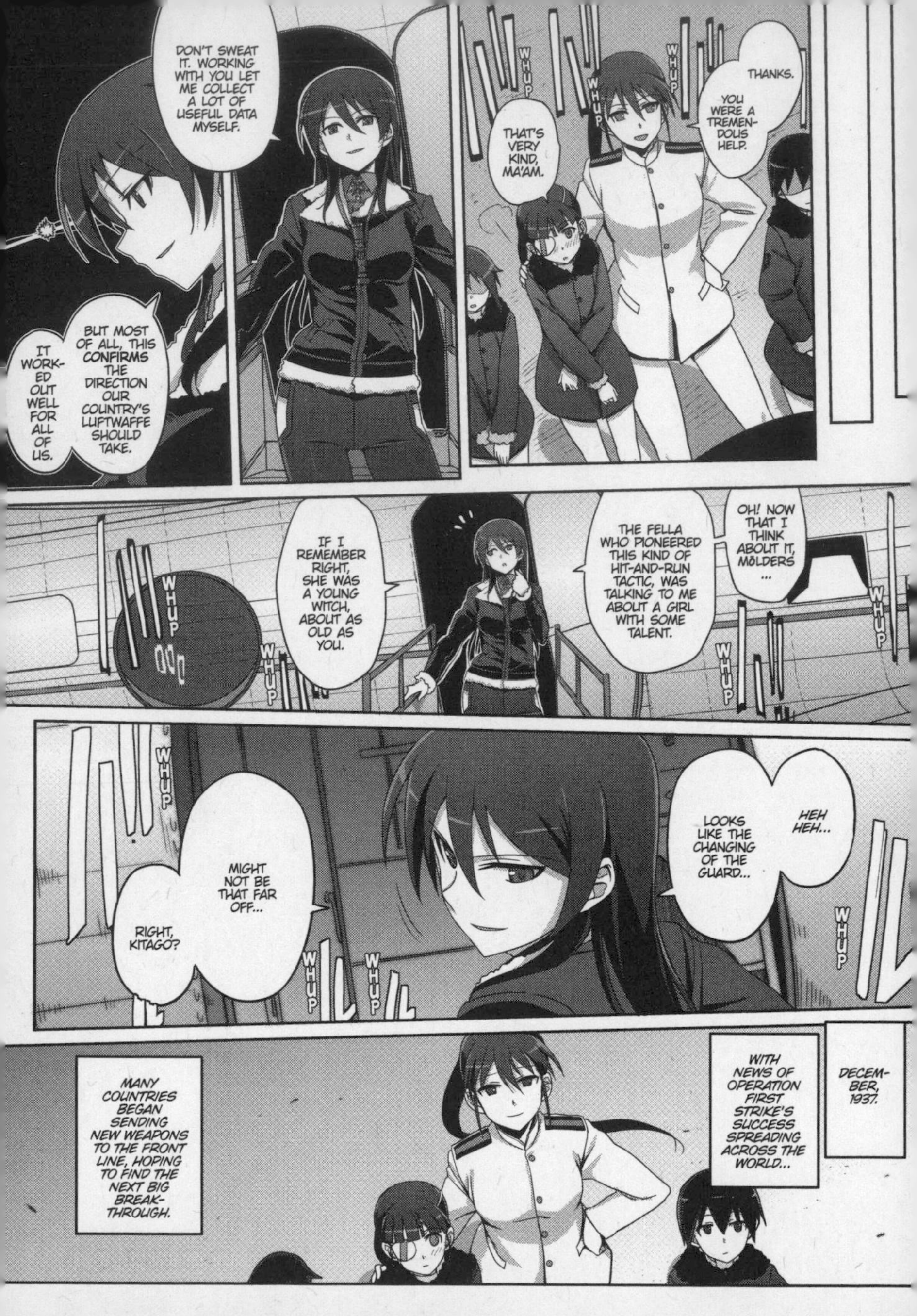
WHUP
WHUP
THANKS.
YOU WERE A TREMENDOUS HELP.
WHUP
THAT'S VERY KIND, MA'AM.
DON'T SWEAT IT. WORKING WITH YOU LET ME COLLECT A LOT OF USEFUL DATA MYSELF.
BUT MOST OF ALL, THIS CONFIRMS THE DIRECTION OUR COUNTRY'S LUFTWAFFE SHOULD TAKE.
IT WORKED OUT WELL FOR ALL OF US.
OH! NOW THAT I THINK ABOUT IT, MÖLDERS...
WHUP
THE FELLA WHO PIONEERED THIS KIND OF HIT-AND-RUN TACTIC, WAS TALKING TO ME ABOUT A GIRL WITH SOME TALENT.
WHUP
IF I REMEMBER RIGHT, SHE WAS A YOUNG WITCH, ABOUT AS OLD AS YOU.
WHUP
WHUP
WHUP
HEH HEH...
LOOKS LIKE THE CHANGING OF THE GUARD...
MIGHT NOT BE THAT FAR OFF...
RIGHT, KITAGO?
WHUP
WHUP
WHUP
DECEMBER, 1937.
WITH NEWS OF OPERATION FIRST STRIKE'S SUCCESS SPREADING ACROSS THE WORLD...
MANY COUNTRIES BEGAN SENDING NEW WEAPONS TO THE FRONT LINE, HOPING TO FIND THE NEXT BIG BREAKTHROUGH.

Chapter 4:
Operation First Strike
[Mission Complete]

CHAPTER 5:
A BRIEF HOLIDAY

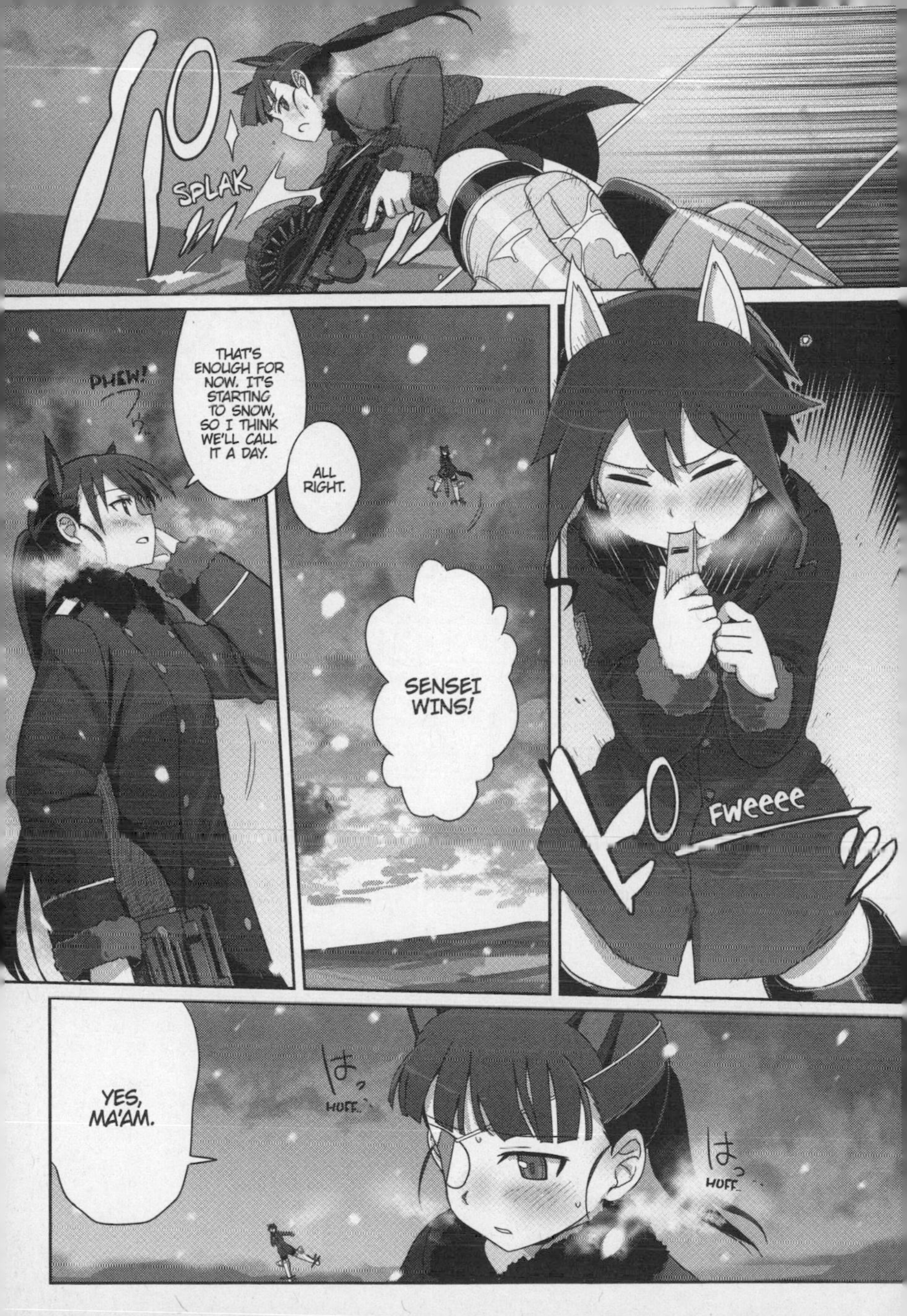
SPLAK
Fweeee
SENSEI WINS!
THAT'S ENOUGH FOR NOW. IT'S STARTING TO SNOW, SO I THINK WE'LL CALL IT A DAY.
ALL RIGHT.
PHEW!
HUFF...
HUFF...
YES, MA'AM.

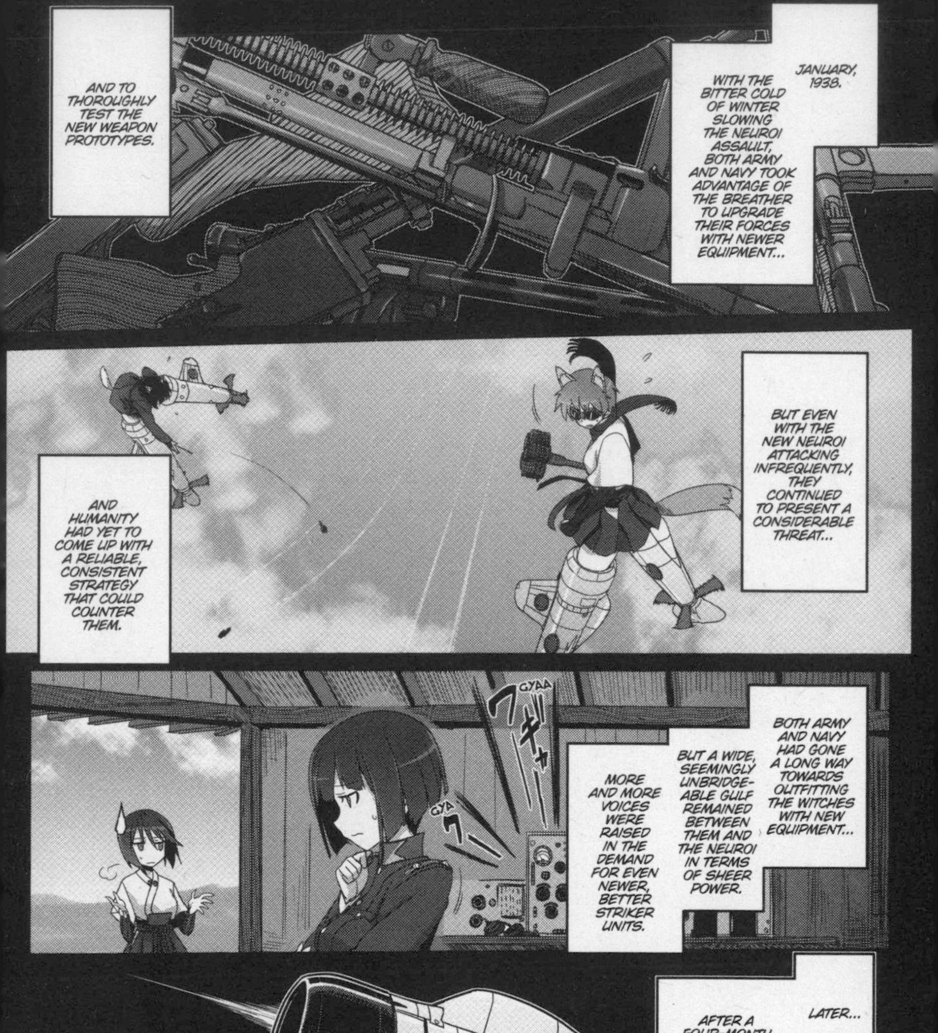
JANUARY, 1938.
WITH THE BITTER COLD OF WINTER SLOWING THE NEUROI ASSAULT, BOTH ARMY AND NAVY TOOK ADVANTAGE OF THE BREATHER TO UPGRADE THEIR FORCES WITH NEWER EQUIPMENT...
AND TO THOROUGHLY TEST THE NEW WEAPON PROTOTYPES.
BUT EVEN WITH THE NEW NEUROI ATTACKING INFREQUENTLY, THEY CONTINUED TO PRESENT A CONSIDERABLE THREAT...
AND HUMANITY HAD YET TO COME UP WITH A RELIABLE, CONSISTENT STRATEGY THAT COULD COUNTER THEM.
GYAA
BOTH ARMY AND NAVY HAD GONE A LONG WAY TOWARDS OUTFITTING THE WITCHES WITH NEW EQUIPMENT...
BUT A WIDE, SEEMINGLY UNBRIDGE-ABLE GULF REMAINED BETWEEN THEM AND THE NEUROI IN TERMS OF SHEER POWER.
MORE AND MORE VOICES WERE RAISED IN THE DEMAND FOR EVEN NEWER, BETTER STRIKER UNITS.
GYA
LATER...
AFTER A FOUR-MONTH DELAY, THE ORDER WAS FINALLY GIVEN TO BEGIN WORK ON A STRIKER UNIT THAT I WOULD EVENTUALLY MAKE MUCH USE OF--THE MIYAHISHI A6M "ZERO."
AS FOR THE ARMY, THEY BEGAN WORKING ON BOTH THE NAGASHIMA KI-43 "HAYABUSA" AND THE NAGASHIMA KI-44 "SHOKI" UNITS.

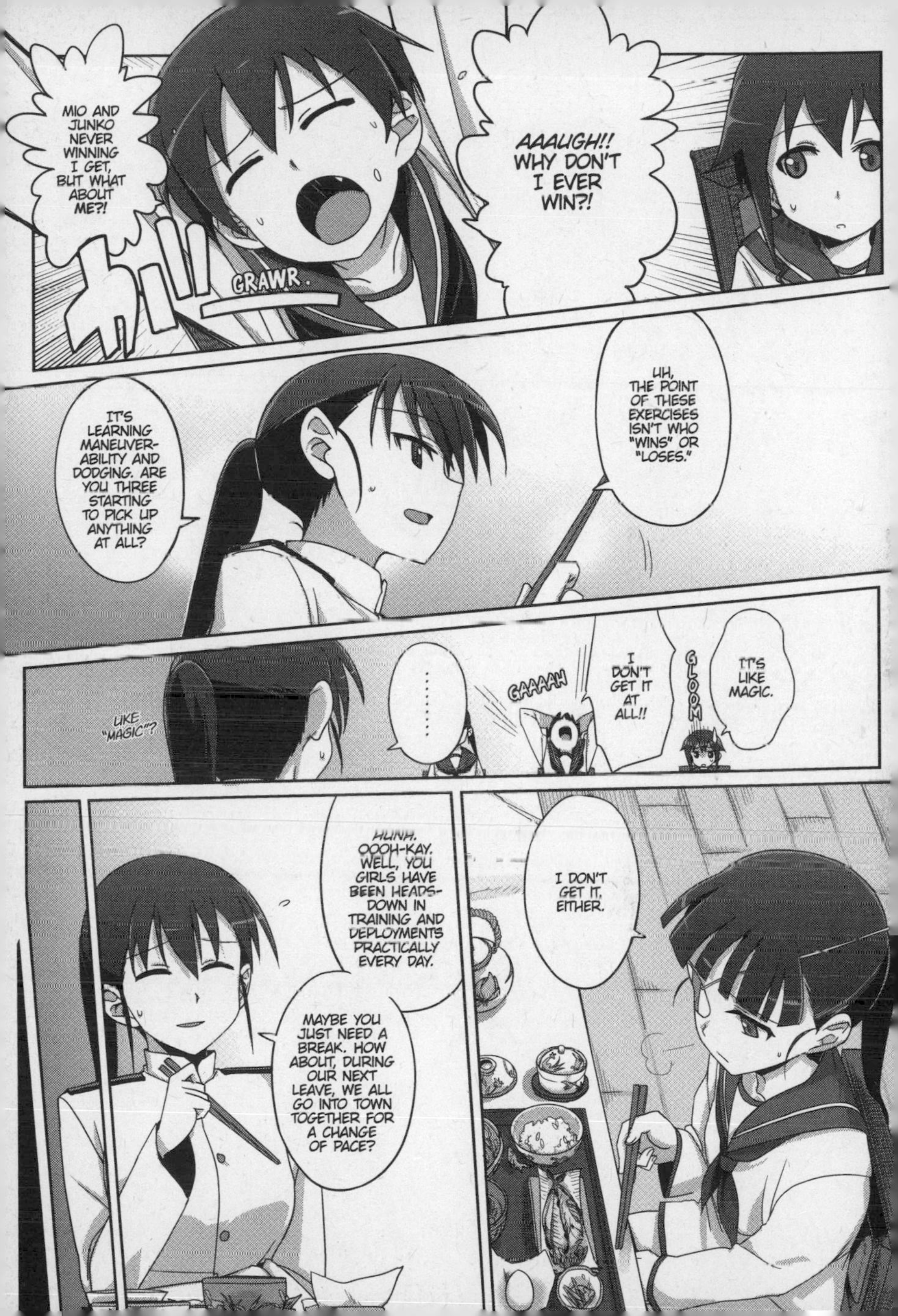
AAAUGH!! WHY DON'T I EVER WIN?!
MIO AND JUNKO NEVER WINNING I GET, BUT WHAT ABOUT ME?!
GRAWR.
UH, THE POINT OF THESE EXERCISES ISN'T WHO "WINS" OR "LOSES."
IT'S LEARNING MANEUVER-ABILITY AND DODGING. ARE YOU THREE STARTING TO PICK UP ANYTHING AT ALL?
IT'S LIKE MAGIC.
GLOOM
I DON'T GET IT AT ALL!!
GAAAAH
......
LIKE "MAGIC"?
I DON'T GET IT, EITHER.
HUNH. OOOH-KAY. WELL, YOU GIRLS HAVE BEEN HEADS-DOWN IN TRAINING AND DEPLOYMENTS PRACTICALLY EVERY DAY.
MAYBE YOU JUST NEED A BREAK. HOW ABOUT, DURING OUR NEXT LEAVE, WE ALL GO INTO TOWN TOGETHER FOR A CHANGE OF PACE?

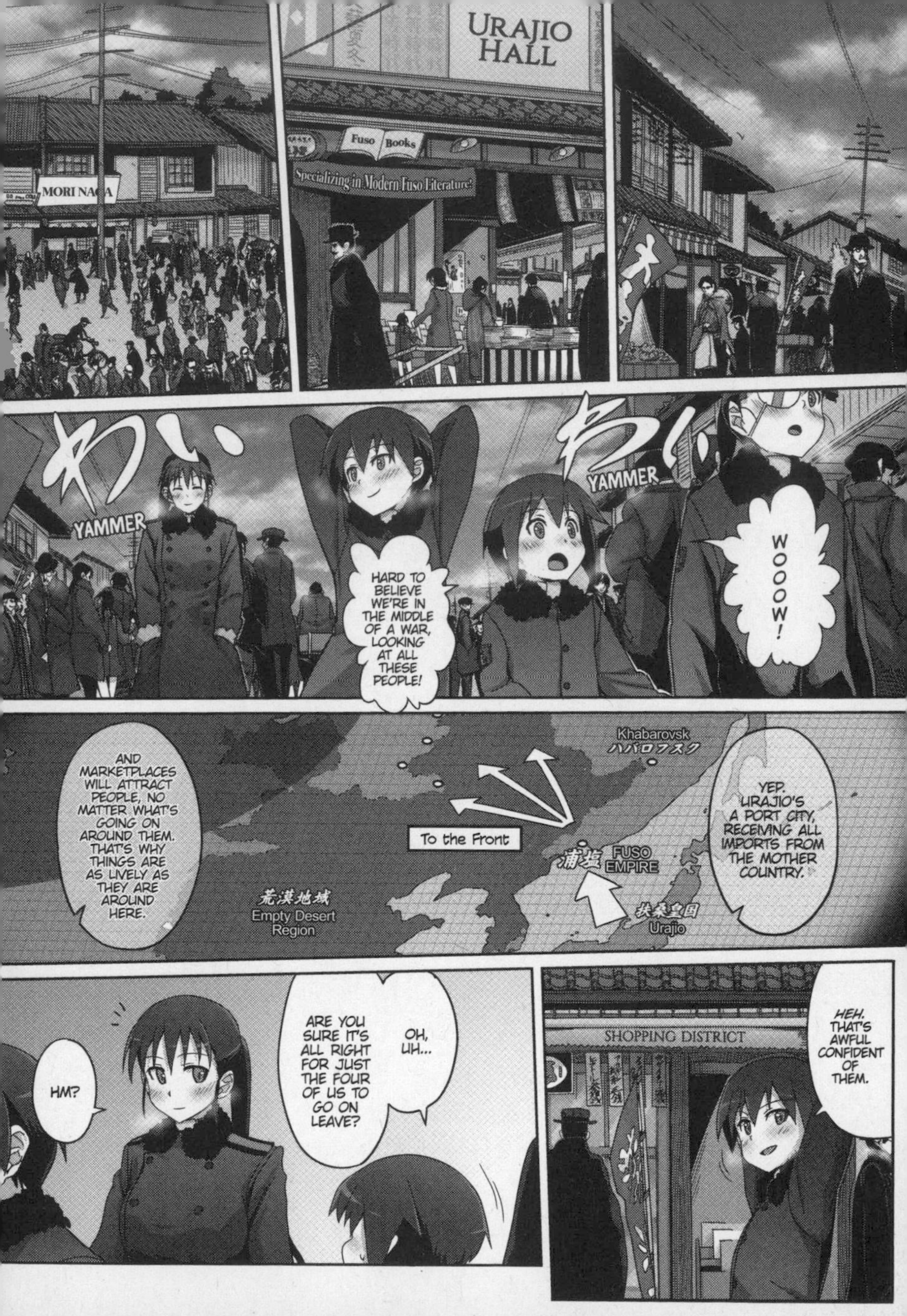
URAJIO HALL
Fuso Books
Specializing in Modern Fuso Literature!
MORI NAGA
わい
YAMMER
WOOOW!
HARD TO BELIEVE WE'RE IN THE MIDDLE OF A WAR, LOOKING AT ALL THESE PEOPLE!
わい
YAMMER
YEP. URAJIO'S A PORT CITY, RECEIVING ALL IMPORTS FROM THE MOTHER COUNTRY.
Khabarovsk
ハバロフスク
To the Front
浦塩
FUSO EMPIRE
扶桑皇国
Urajio
荒漠地域
Empty Desert Region
AND MARKETPLACES WILL ATTRACT PEOPLE, NO MATTER WHAT'S GOING ON AROUND THEM. THAT'S WHY THINGS ARE AS LIVELY AS THEY ARE AROUND HERE.
SHOPPING DISTRICT
HEH. THAT'S AWFUL CONFIDENT OF THEM.
OH, UH...
ARE YOU SURE IT'S ALL RIGHT FOR JUST THE FOUR OF US TO GO ON LEAVE?
HM?

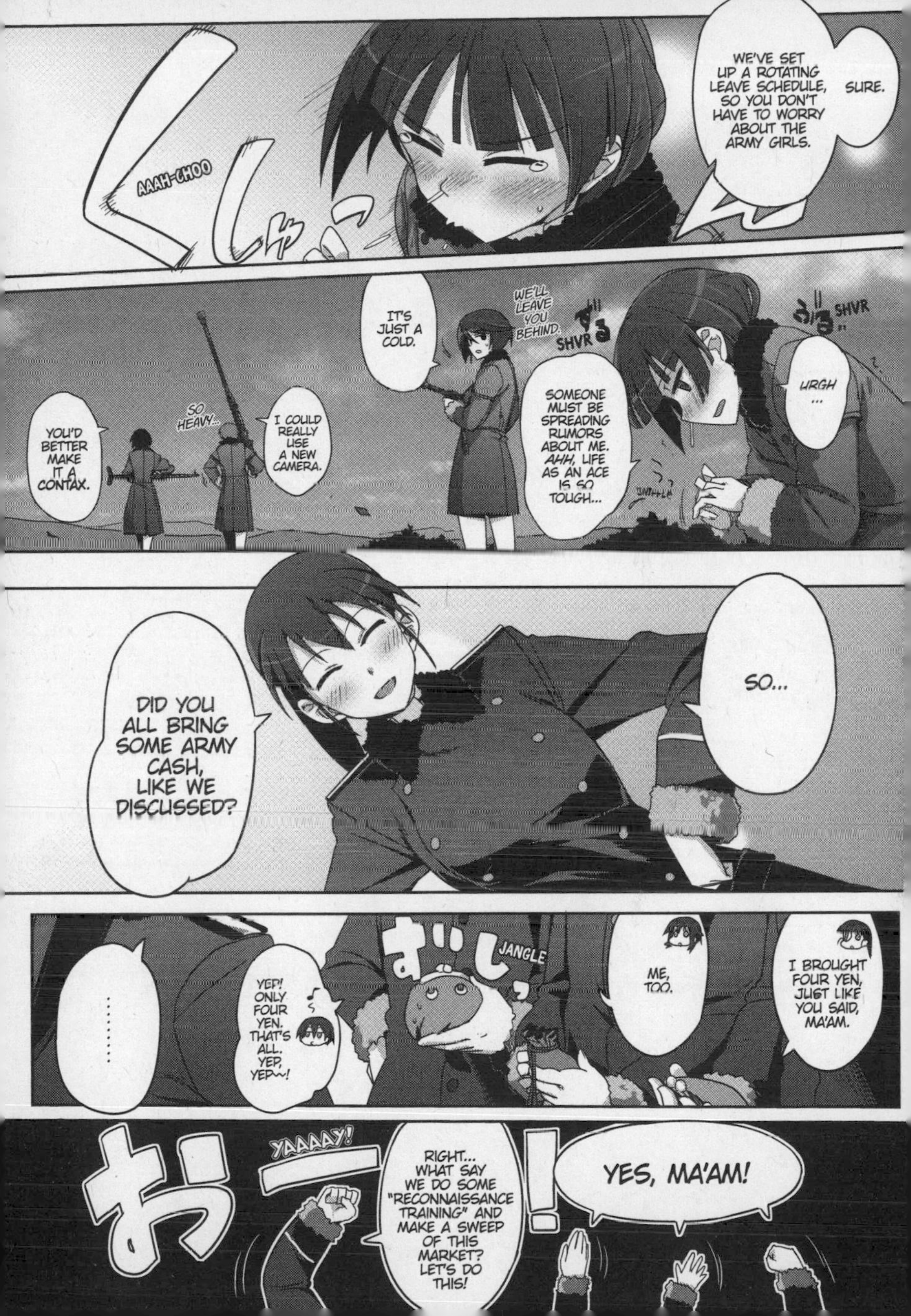
WE'VE SET UP A ROTATING LEAVE SCHEDULE, SO YOU DON'T HAVE TO WORRY ABOUT THE ARMY GIRLS. SURE.
AAAH-CHOO
SHVR
URGH...
SHVR
SOMEONE MUST BE SPREADING RUMORS ABOUT ME. AHH, LIFE AS AN ACE IS SO TOUGH...
WE'LL LEAVE YOU BEHIND.
IT'S JUST A COLD.
I COULD REALLY USE A NEW CAMERA.
SO HEAVY...
YOU'D BETTER MAKE IT A CONTAX.
SO...
DID YOU ALL BRING SOME ARMY CASH, LIKE WE DISCUSSED?
I BROUGHT FOUR YEN, JUST LIKE YOU SAID, MA'AM.
ME, TOO.
JANGLE
YEP! ONLY FOUR YEN. THAT'S ALL. YEP, YEP~!
......
YES, MA'AM!
RIGHT... WHAT SAY WE DO SOME "RECONNAISSANCE TRAINING" AND MAKE A SWEEP OF THIS MARKET? LET'S DO THIS!
YAAAAY!

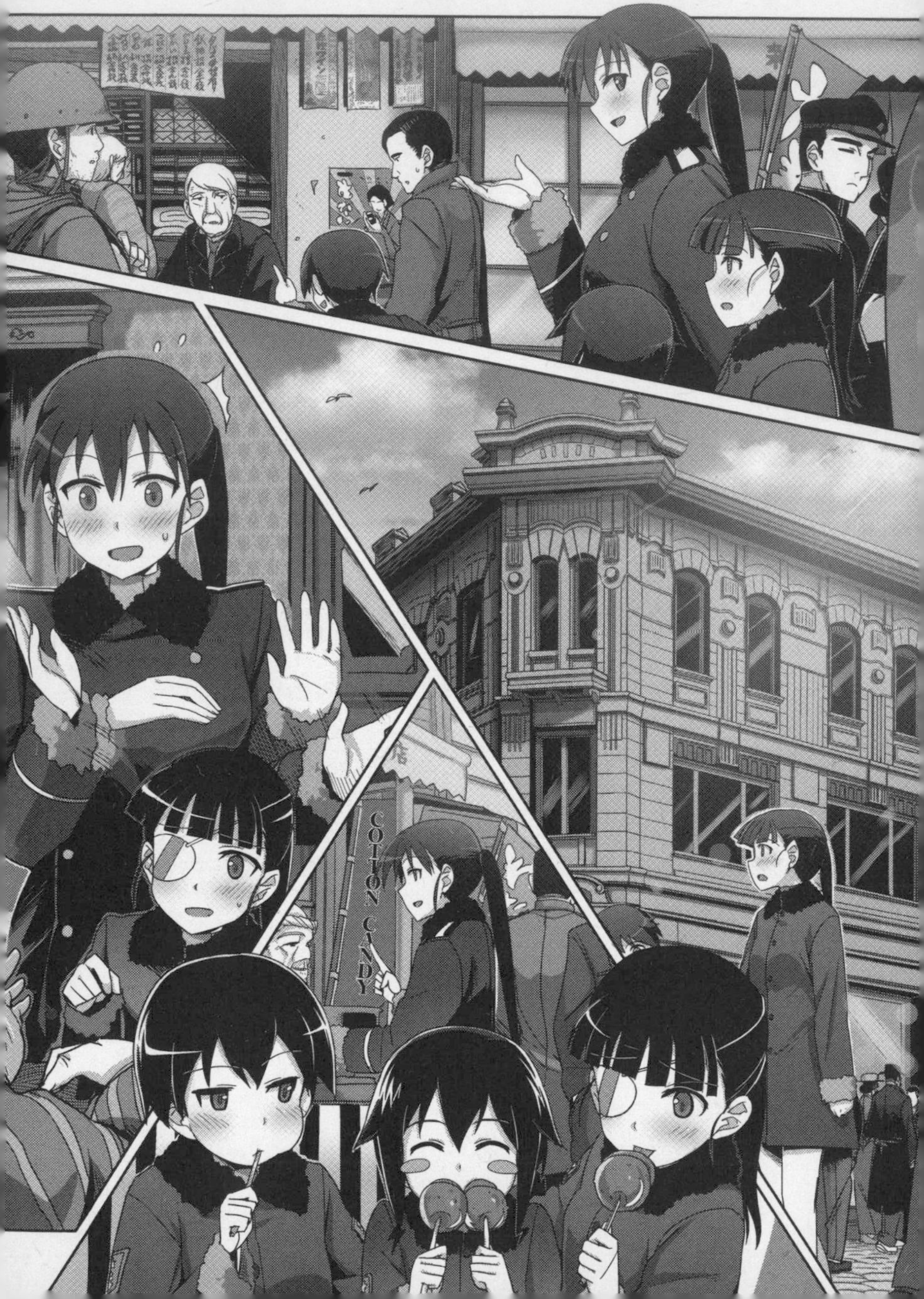
COTTON CANDY

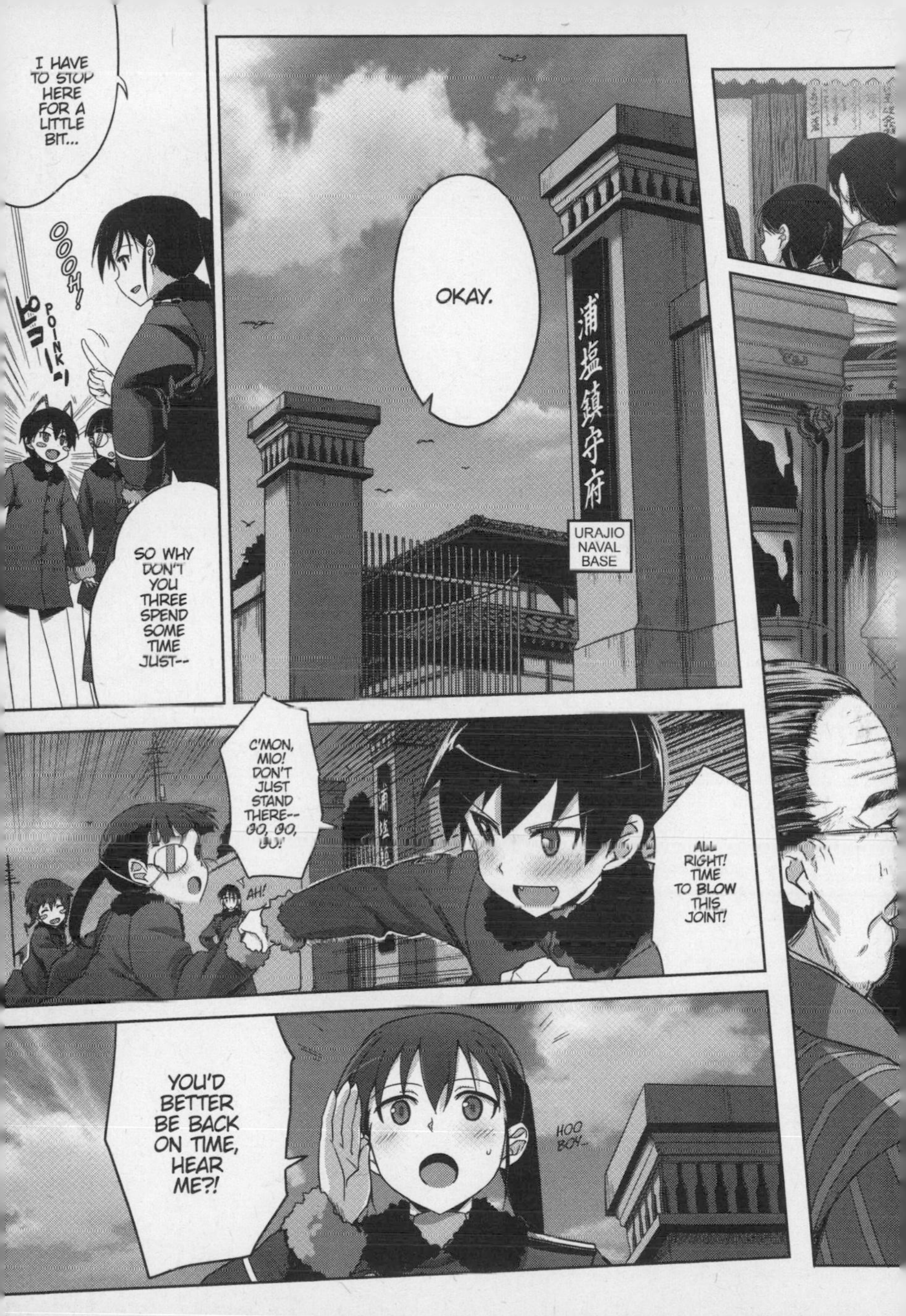
OKAY.
浦塩鎮守府
URAJIO NAVAL BASE
I HAVE TO STOP HERE FOR A LITTLE BIT...
OOOH!
POINK
SO WHY DON'T YOU THREE SPEND SOME TIME JUST--
ALL RIGHT! TIME TO BLOW THIS JOINT!
C'MON, MIO! DON'T JUST STAND THERE-- GO, GO, GO!
AH!
HOO BOY...
YOU'D BETTER BE BACK ON TIME, HEAR ME?!

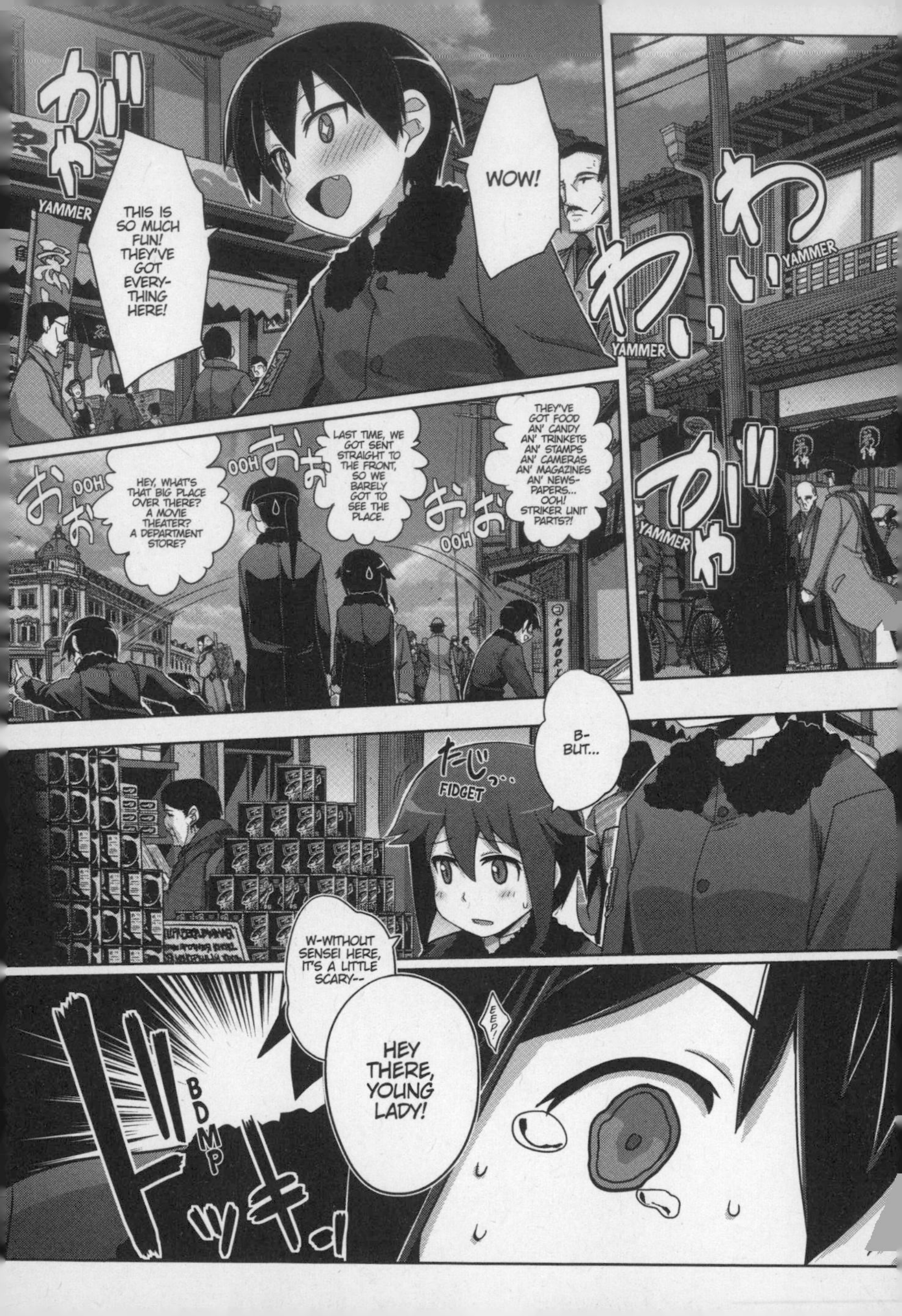

YAMMER
YAMMER
YAMMER
YAMMER
WOW!
THIS IS SO MUCH FUN! THEY'VE GOT EVERYTHING HERE!
YAMMER
THEY'VE GOT FOOD AN' CANDY AN' TRINKETS AN' STAMPS AN' CAMERAS AN' MAGAZINES AN' NEWSPAPERS... OOH! STRIKER UNIT PARTS?!
OOH
LAST TIME, WE GOT SENT STRAIGHT TO THE FRONT, SO WE BARELY GOT TO SEE THE PLACE.
OOH
HEY, WHAT'S THAT BIG PLACE OVER THERE? A MOVIE THEATER? A DEPARTMENT STORE?
OOH
KOMORY
B-BUT...
FIDGET
W-WITHOUT SENSEI HERE, IT'S A LITTLE SCARY--
EEP!
HEY THERE, YOUNG LADY!
BDMP

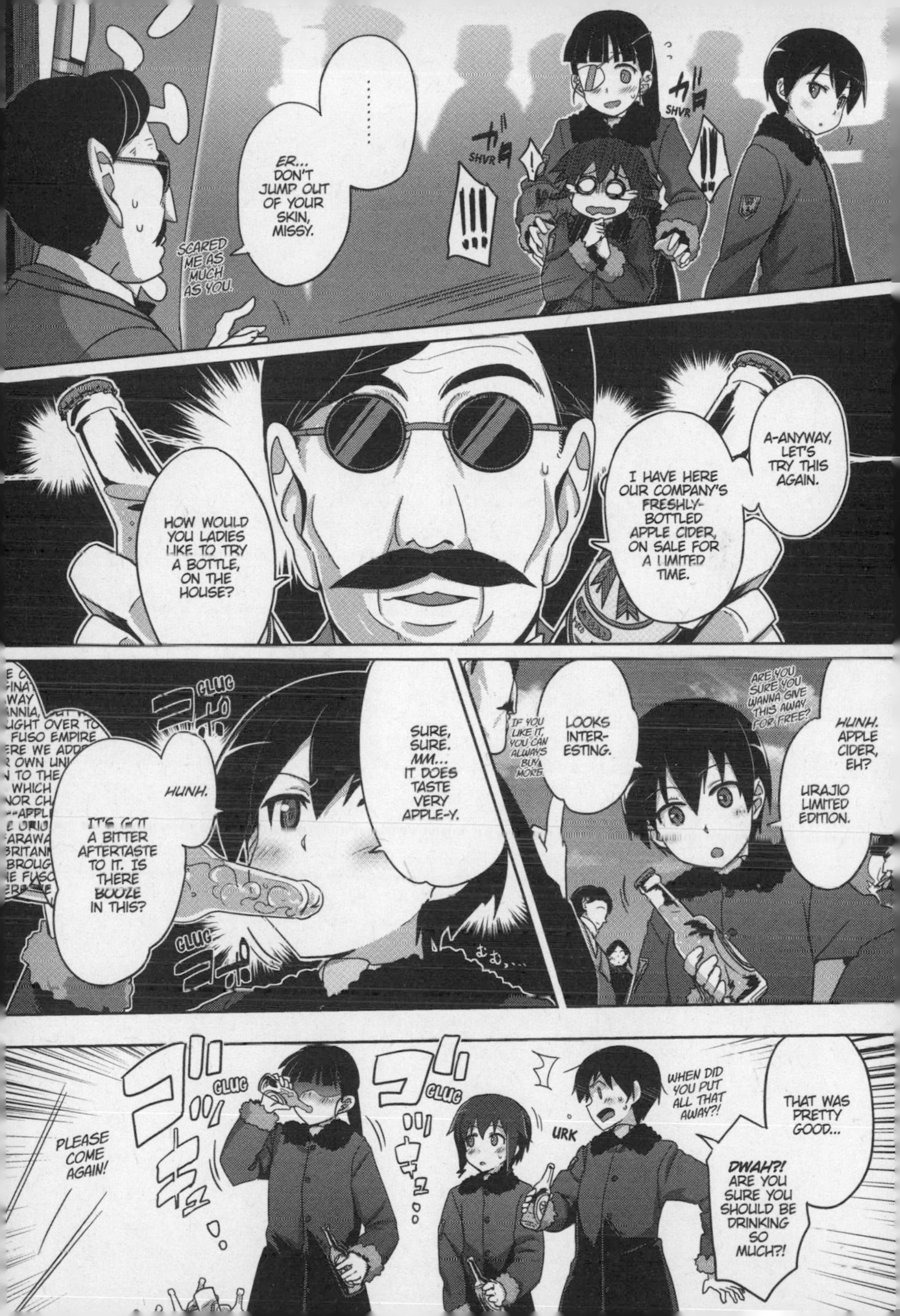
SHVR
SHVR
......
ER... DON'T JUMP OUT OF YOUR SKIN, MISSY.
SCARED ME AS MUCH AS YOU.
A-ANYWAY, LET'S TRY THIS AGAIN.
I HAVE HERE OUR COMPANY'S FRESHLY-BOTTLED APPLE CIDER, ON SALE FOR A LIMITED TIME.
HOW WOULD YOU LADIES LIKE TO TRY A BOTTLE, ON THE HOUSE?
HUNH. APPLE CIDER, EH?
URAJIO LIMITED EDITION.
ARE YOU SURE YOU WANNA GIVE THIS AWAY FOR FREE?
LOOKS INTER-ESTING.
IF YOU LIKE IT, YOU CAN ALWAYS BUY MORE.
SURE, SURE. MM... IT DOES TASTE VERY APPLE-Y.
GLUG
HUNH.
IT'S GOT A BITTER AFTERTASTE TO IT. IS THERE BOOZE IN THIS?
GLUG
むむ、、、
THAT WAS PRETTY GOOD...
DWAH?! ARE YOU SURE YOU SHOULD BE DRINKING SO MUCH?!
WHEN DID YOU PUT ALL THAT AWAY?!
URK
GLUG
GLUG
PLEASE COME AGAIN!

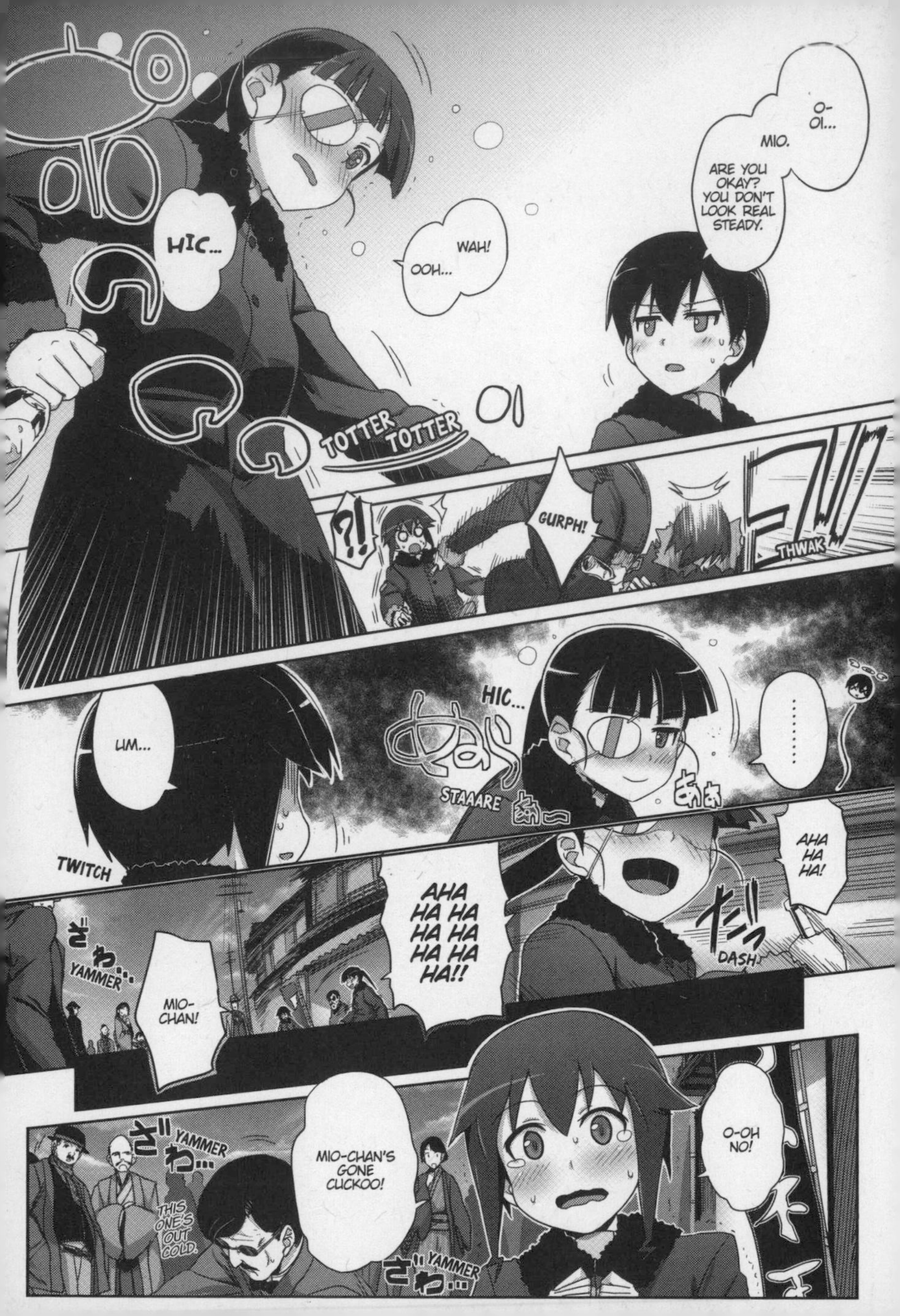
O-OI...
MIO.
ARE YOU OKAY? YOU DON'T LOOK REAL STEADY.
WAH! OOH...
HIC...
OI
TOTTER TOTTER
THWAK
GURPH!
?!
......
HIC...
STAAARE
UM...
TWITCH
AHA HA HA!
DASH
AHA HA HA HA HA HA HA HA HA!!
MIO-CHAN!
YAMMER
O-OH NO!
MIO-CHAN'S GONE CUCKOO!
YAMMER
THIS ONE'S OUT COLD.
YAMMER

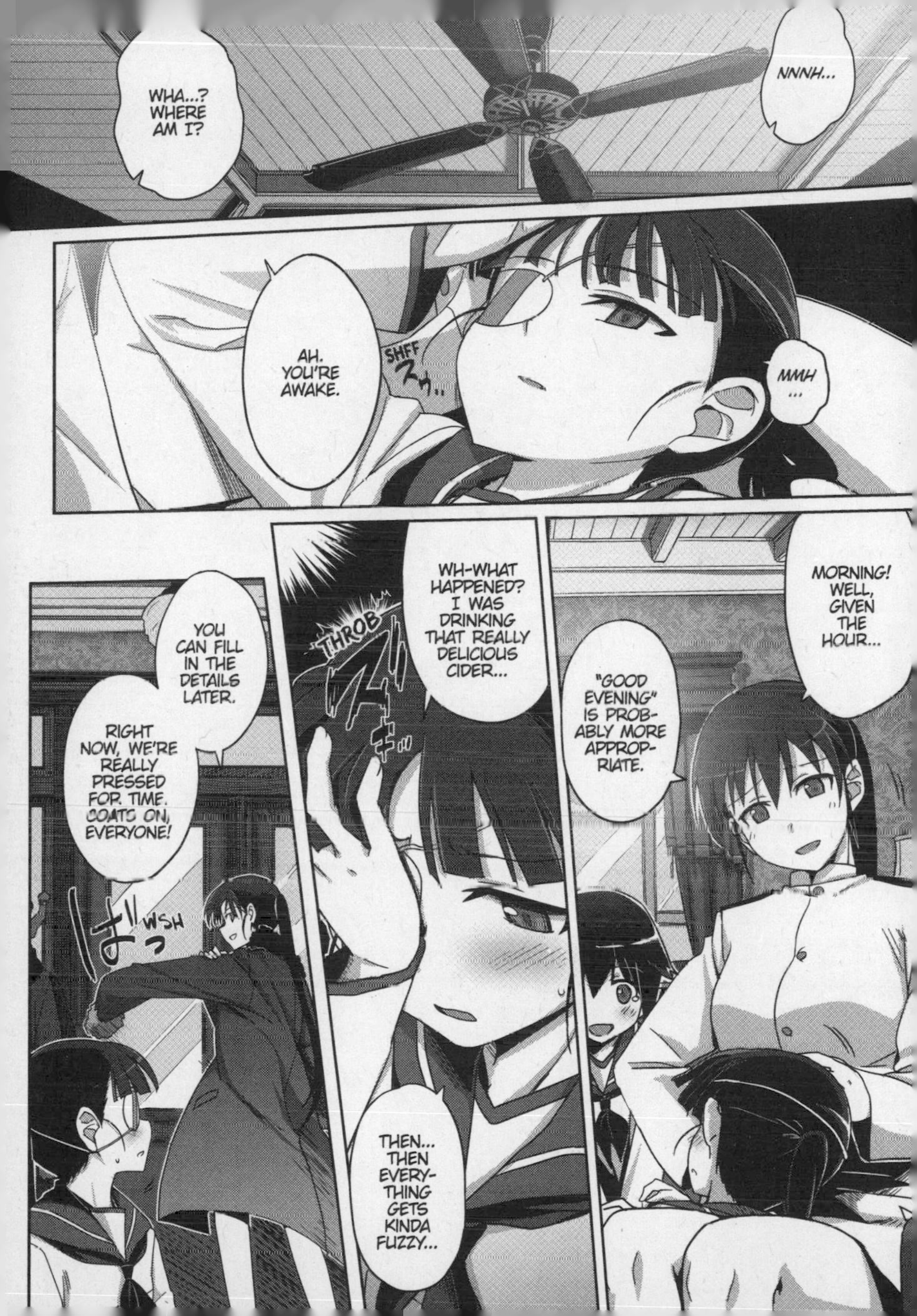
NNNH...
WHA...? WHERE AM I?
MMH ...
SHFF
AH. YOU'RE AWAKE.
MORNING! WELL, GIVEN THE HOUR...
"GOOD EVENING" IS PROBABLY MORE APPROPRIATE.
WH-WHAT HAPPENED? I WAS DRINKING THAT REALLY DELICIOUS CIDER...
THROB
THEN... THEN EVERYTHING GETS KINDA FUZZY...
YOU CAN FILL IN THE DETAILS LATER.
RIGHT NOW, WE'RE REALLY PRESSED FOR TIME. COATS ON, EVERYONE!
WSH

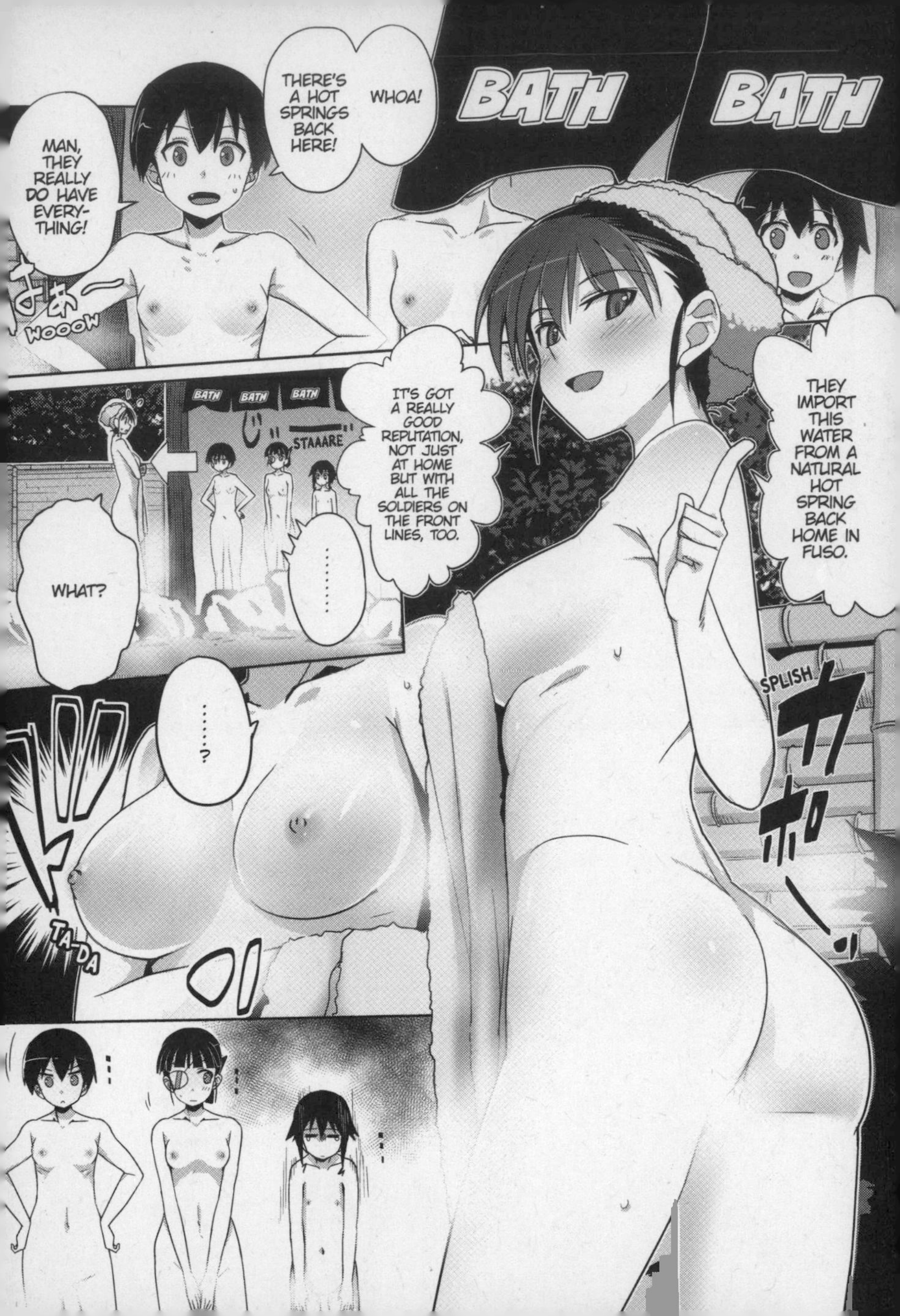
BATH
BATH
THEY IMPORT THIS WATER FROM A NATURAL HOT SPRING BACK HOME IN FUSO.
IT'S GOT A REALLY GOOD REPUTATION, NOT JUST AT HOME BUT WITH ALL THE SOLDIERS ON THE FRONT LINES, TOO.
SPLISH
WHOA!
THERE'S A HOT SPRINGS BACK HERE!
MAN, THEY REALLY DO HAVE EVERYTHING!
WOOOW
BATH
BATH
BATH
STAARE
......
WHAT?
......?
TA-DA

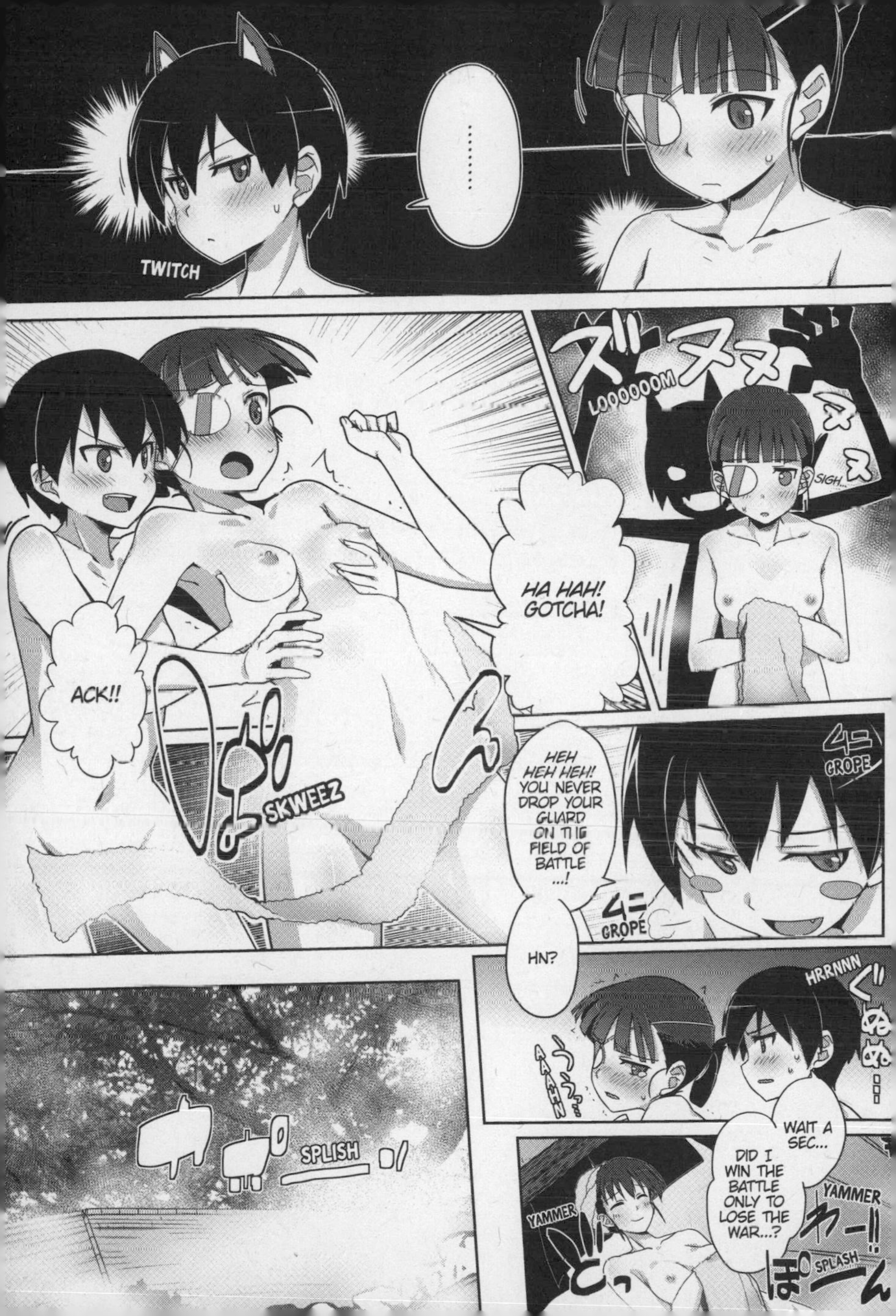
......
TWITCH
LOOOOOOM
SIGH...
GROPE
HEH HEH HEH! YOU NEVER DROP YOUR GUARD ON THE FIELD OF BATTLE ...!
GROPE
HN?
HA HAH! GOTCHA!
ACK!!
SKWEEZ
HRRNNN
AAAAHN
WAIT A SEC...
DID I WIN THE BATTLE ONLY TO LOSE THE WAR...?
YAMMER
YAMMER
SPLASH
SPLISH

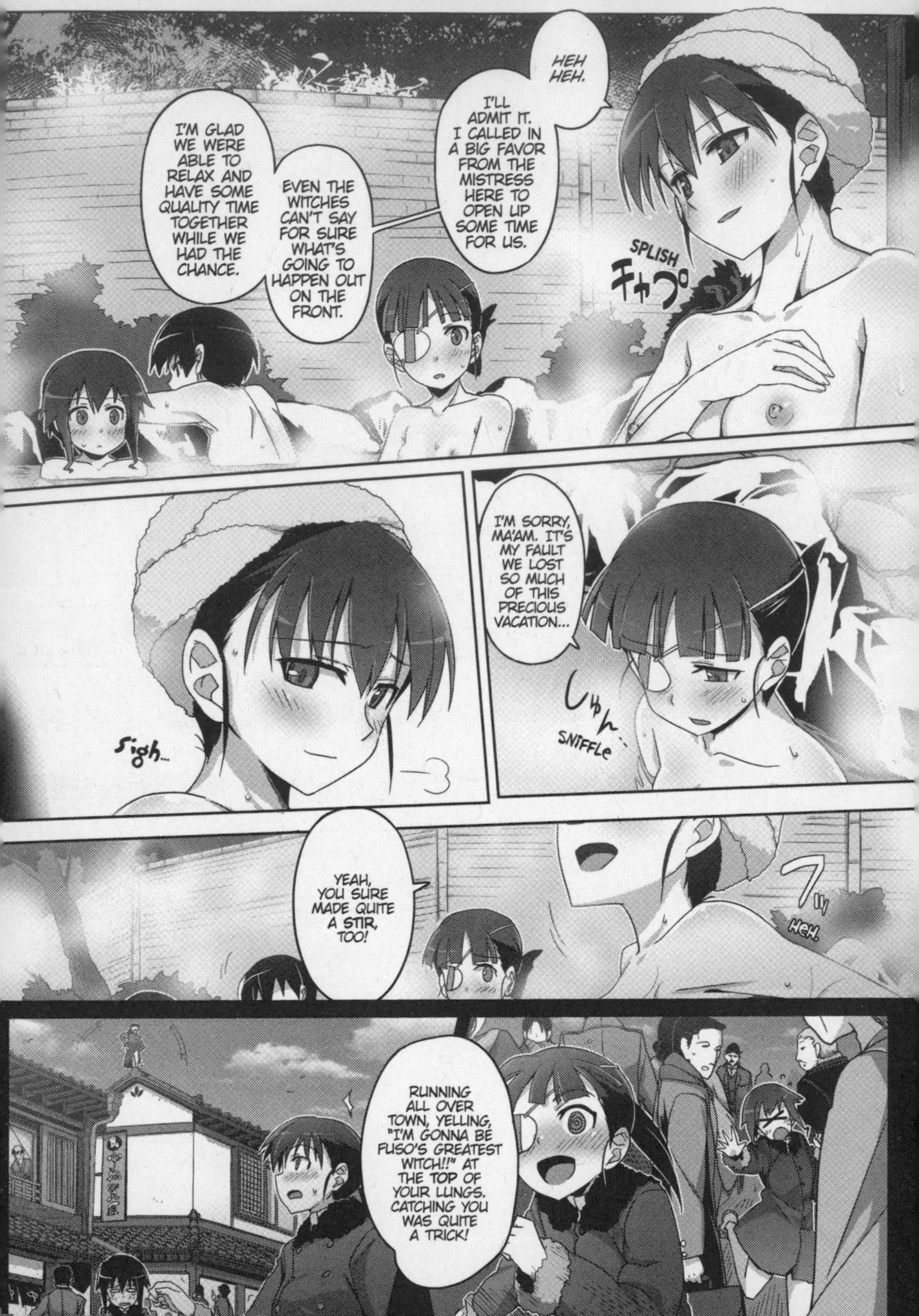
HEH HEH.
I'LL ADMIT IT. I CALLED IN A BIG FAVOR FROM THE MISTRESS HERE TO OPEN UP SOME TIME FOR US.
SPLISH チャプ
EVEN THE WITCHES CAN'T SAY FOR SURE WHAT'S GOING TO HAPPEN OUT ON THE FRONT.
I'M GLAD WE WERE ABLE TO RELAX AND HAVE SOME QUALITY TIME TOGETHER WHILE WE HAD THE CHANCE.
I'M SORRY, MA'AM. IT'S MY FAULT WE LOST SO MUCH OF THIS PRECIOUS VACATION...
しゅん SNIFFLE
sigh...
フッ HEH.
YEAH, YOU SURE MADE QUITE A STIR, TOO!
RUNNING ALL OVER TOWN, YELLING, "I'M GONNA BE FUSO'S GREATEST WITCH!!" AT THE TOP OF YOUR LUNGS. CATCHING YOU WAS QUITE A TRICK!

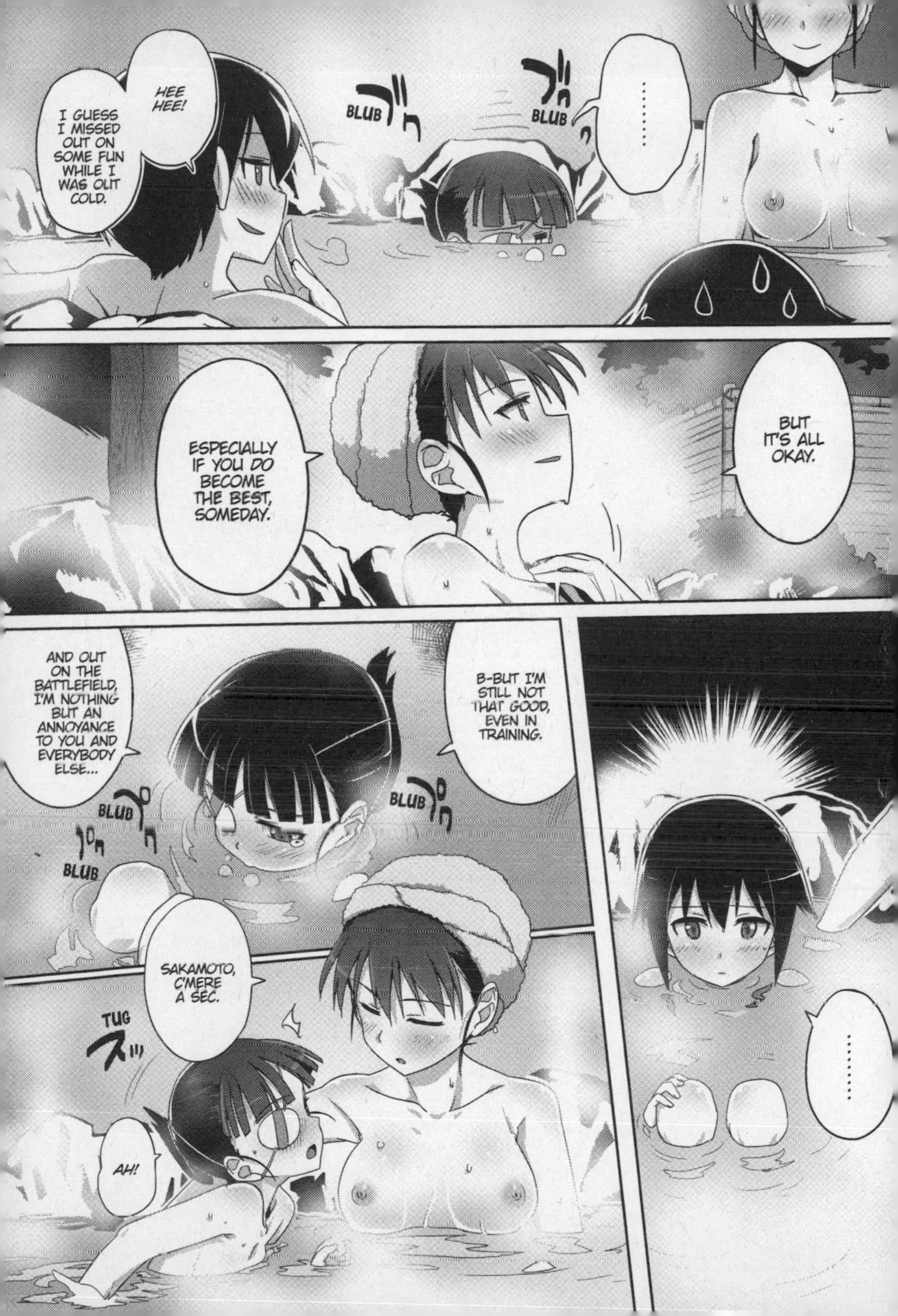
......
BLUB
BLUB
HEE HEE!
I GUESS I MISSED OUT ON SOME FUN WHILE I WAS OUT COLD.
BUT IT'S ALL OKAY.
ESPECIALLY IF YOU DO BECOME THE BEST, SOMEDAY.
......
B-BUT I'M STILL NOT THAT GOOD, EVEN IN TRAINING.
AND OUT ON THE BATTLEFIELD, I'M NOTHING BUT AN ANNOYANCE TO YOU AND EVERYBODY ELSE...
BLUB
BLUB
BLUB
SAKAMOTO, C'MERE A SEC.
TUG
AH!

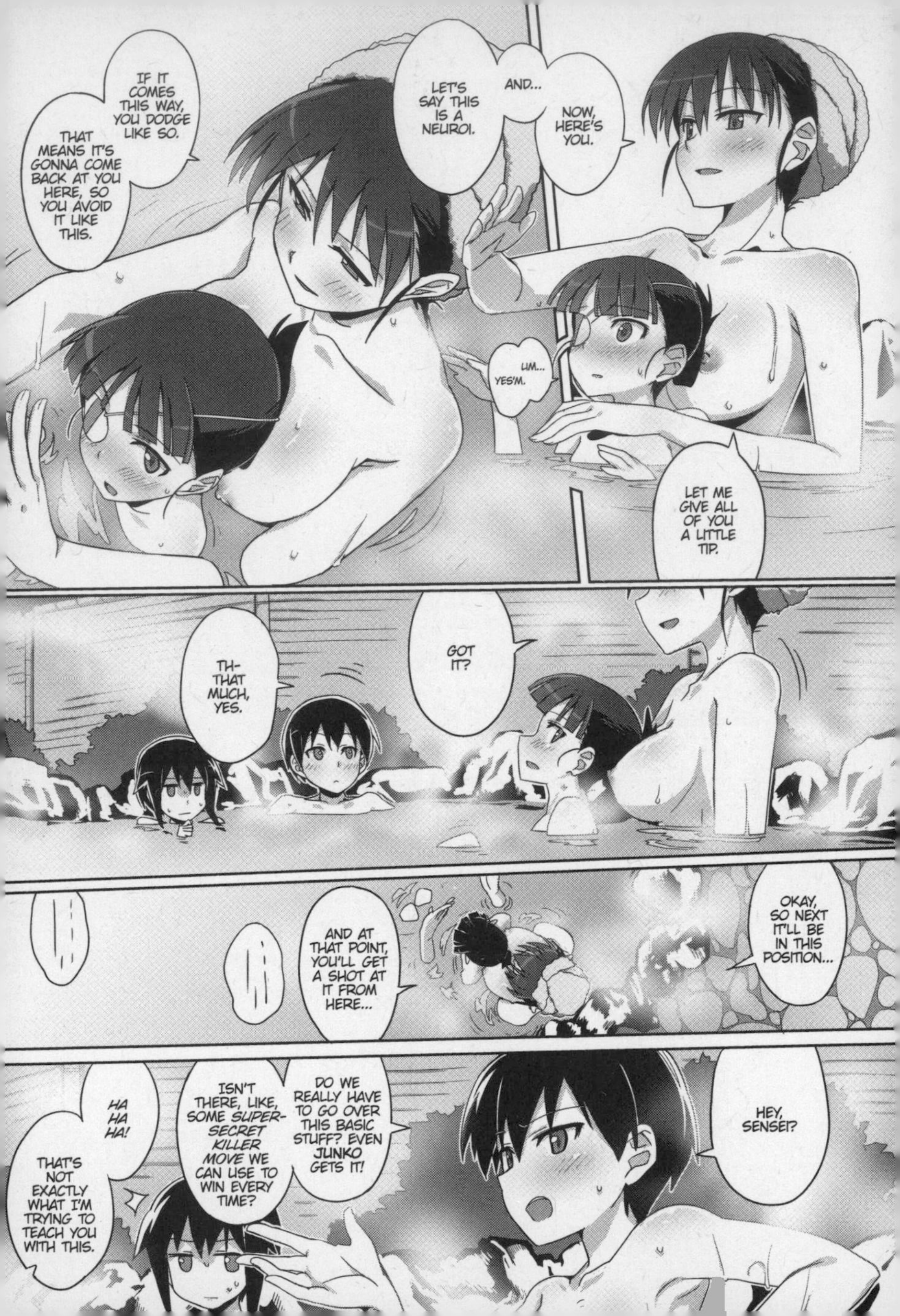
LET'S SAY THIS IS A NEUROI.
AND...
NOW, HERE'S YOU.
UM... YES'M.
LET ME GIVE ALL OF YOU A LITTLE TIP.
IF IT COMES THIS WAY, YOU DODGE LIKE SO.
THAT MEANS IT'S GONNA COME BACK AT YOU HERE, SO YOU AVOID IT LIKE THIS.
GOT IT?
TH-THAT MUCH, YES.
OKAY, SO NEXT IT'LL BE IN THIS POSITION...
AND AT THAT POINT, YOU'LL GET A SHOT AT IT FROM HERE...
HEY, SENSEI?
DO WE REALLY HAVE TO GO OVER THIS BASIC STUFF? EVEN JUNKO GETS IT!
ISN'T THERE, LIKE, SOME *SUPER-SECRET KILLER MOVE* WE CAN USE TO WIN EVERY TIME?
HA HA HA!
THAT'S NOT EXACTLY WHAT I'M TRYING TO TEACH YOU WITH THIS.

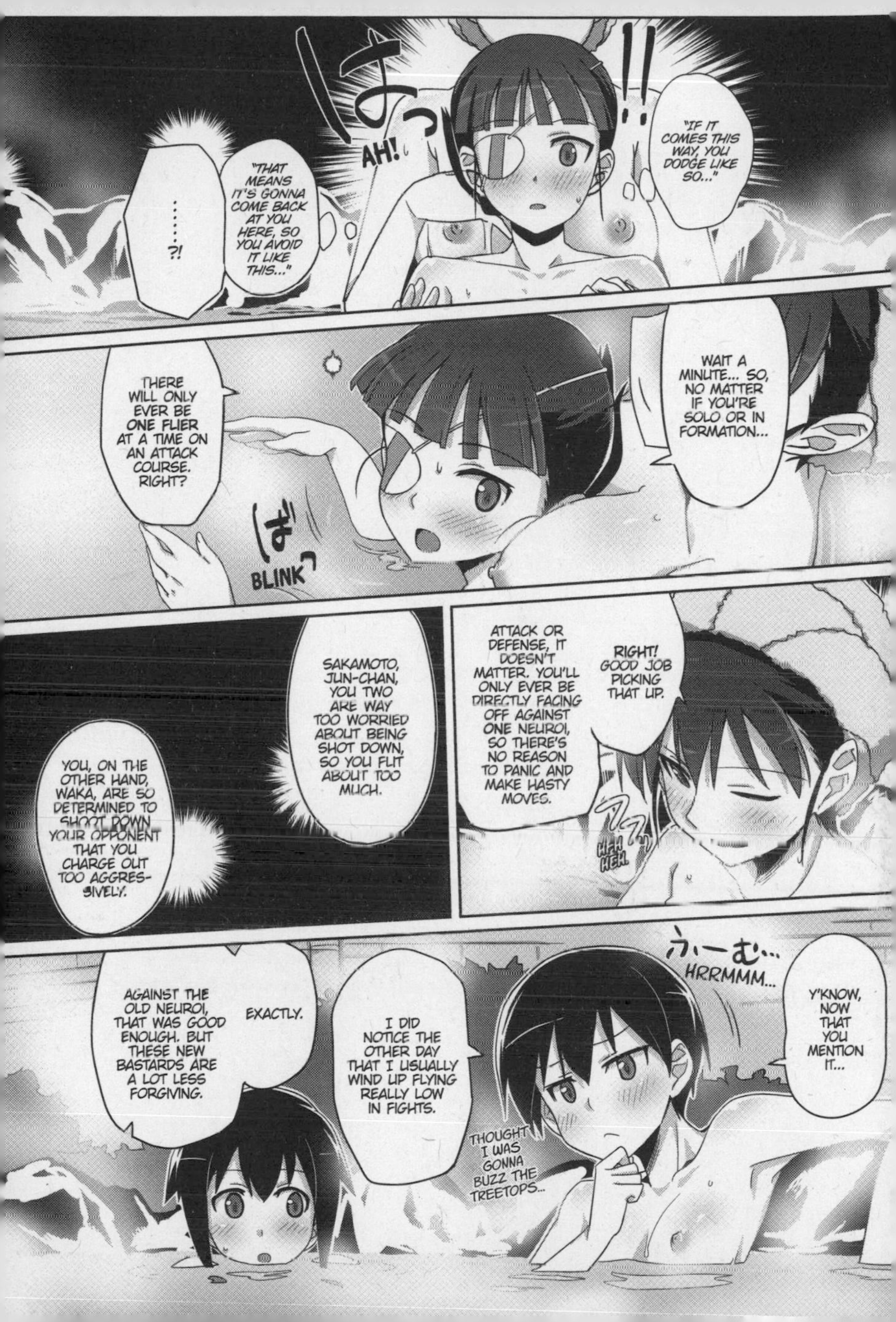
"IF IT COMES THIS WAY, YOU DODGE LIKE SO..."
はっ
AH!
!!
"THAT MEANS IT'S GONNA COME BACK AT YOU HERE, SO YOU AVOID IT LIKE THIS..."
......?!
WAIT A MINUTE... SO, NO MATTER IF YOU'RE SOLO OR IN FORMATION...
THERE WILL ONLY EVER BE ONE FLIER AT A TIME ON AN ATTACK COURSE. RIGHT?
ぱっ
BLINK
RIGHT! GOOD JOB PICKING THAT UP.
ATTACK OR DEFENSE, IT DOESN'T MATTER. YOU'LL ONLY EVER BE DIRECTLY FACING OFF AGAINST ONE NEUROI, SO THERE'S NO REASON TO PANIC AND MAKE HASTY MOVES.
HEH HEH.
SAKAMOTO, JUN-CHAN, YOU TWO ARE WAY TOO WORRIED ABOUT BEING SHOT DOWN, SO YOU FLIT ABOUT TOO MUCH.
YOU, ON THE OTHER HAND, WAKA, ARE SO DETERMINED TO SHOOT DOWN YOUR OPPONENT THAT YOU CHARGE OUT TOO AGGRES-SIVELY.
ふーむ...
HRRMMM...
Y'KNOW, NOW THAT YOU MENTION IT...
THOUGHT I WAS GONNA BUZZ THE TREETOPS...
I DID NOTICE THE OTHER DAY THAT I USUALLY WIND UP FLYING REALLY LOW IN FIGHTS.
EXACTLY.
AGAINST THE OLD NEUROI, THAT WAS GOOD ENOUGH. BUT THESE NEW BASTARDS ARE A LOT LESS FORGIVING.

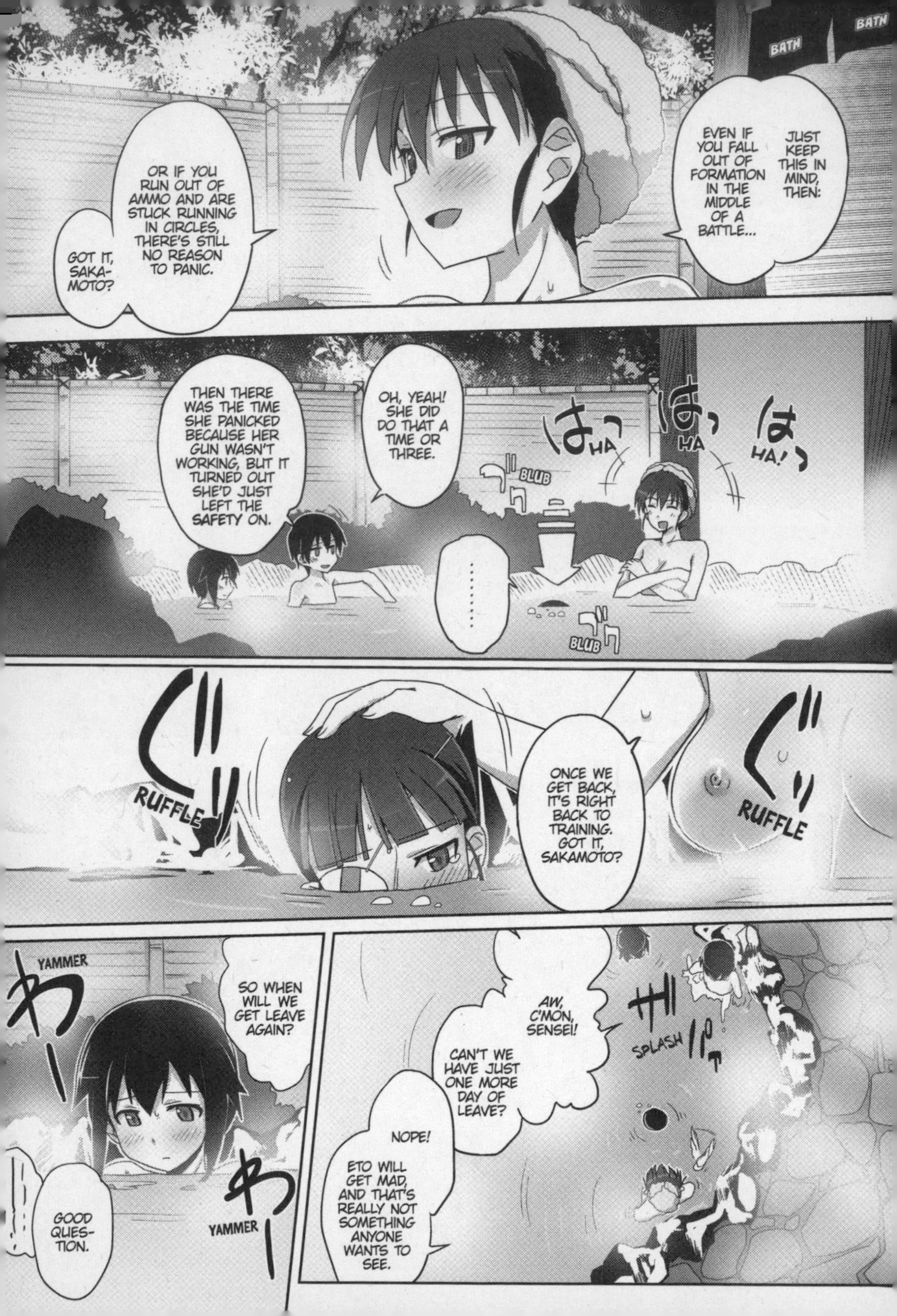
BATH
BATH
JUST KEEP THIS IN MIND, THEN:
EVEN IF YOU FALL OUT OF FORMATION IN THE MIDDLE OF A BATTLE...
OR IF YOU RUN OUT OF AMMO AND ARE STUCK RUNNING IN CIRCLES, THERE'S STILL NO REASON TO PANIC.
GOT IT, SAKAMOTO?
HA!
HA
HA
OH, YEAH! SHE DID DO THAT A TIME OR THREE.
THEN THERE WAS THE TIME SHE PANICKED BECAUSE HER GUN WASN'T WORKING, BUT IT TURNED OUT SHE'D JUST LEFT THE SAFETY ON.
BLUB
......
BLUB
RUFFLE
ONCE WE GET BACK, IT'S RIGHT BACK TO TRAINING. GOT IT, SAKAMOTO?
RUFFLE
SPLASH
AW, C'MON, SENSEI!
CAN'T WE HAVE JUST ONE MORE DAY OF LEAVE?
NOPE!
ETO WILL GET MAD, AND THAT'S REALLY NOT SOMETHING ANYONE WANTS TO SEE.
YAMMER
SO WHEN WILL WE GET LEAVE AGAIN?
GOOD QUESTION.
YAMMER

Chapter 5:
A Brief Holiday
[Mission Complete]

CHAPTER 6:
WHAT MAKES AN ACE

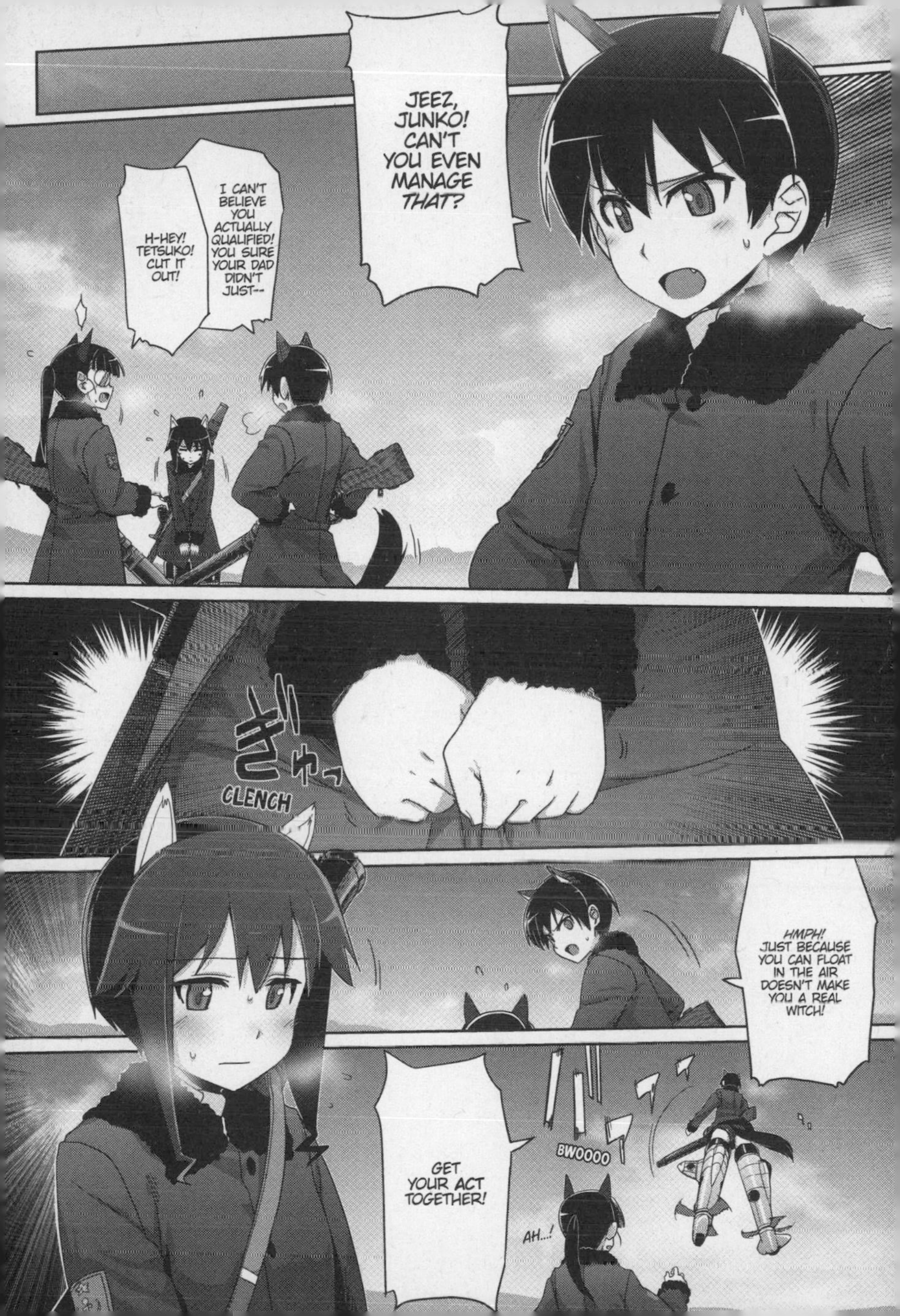
JEEZ, JUNKO! CAN'T YOU EVEN MANAGE *THAT?*
I CAN'T BELIEVE YOU ACTUALLY QUALIFIED! YOU SURE YOUR DAD DIDN'T JUST--
H-HEY! TETSUKO! CUT IT OUT!
きゅっ
CLENCH
HMPH! JUST BECAUSE YOU CAN FLOAT IN THE AIR DOESN'T MAKE YOU A REAL WITCH!
GET YOUR ACT TOGETHER!
BWOOOO
AH...!

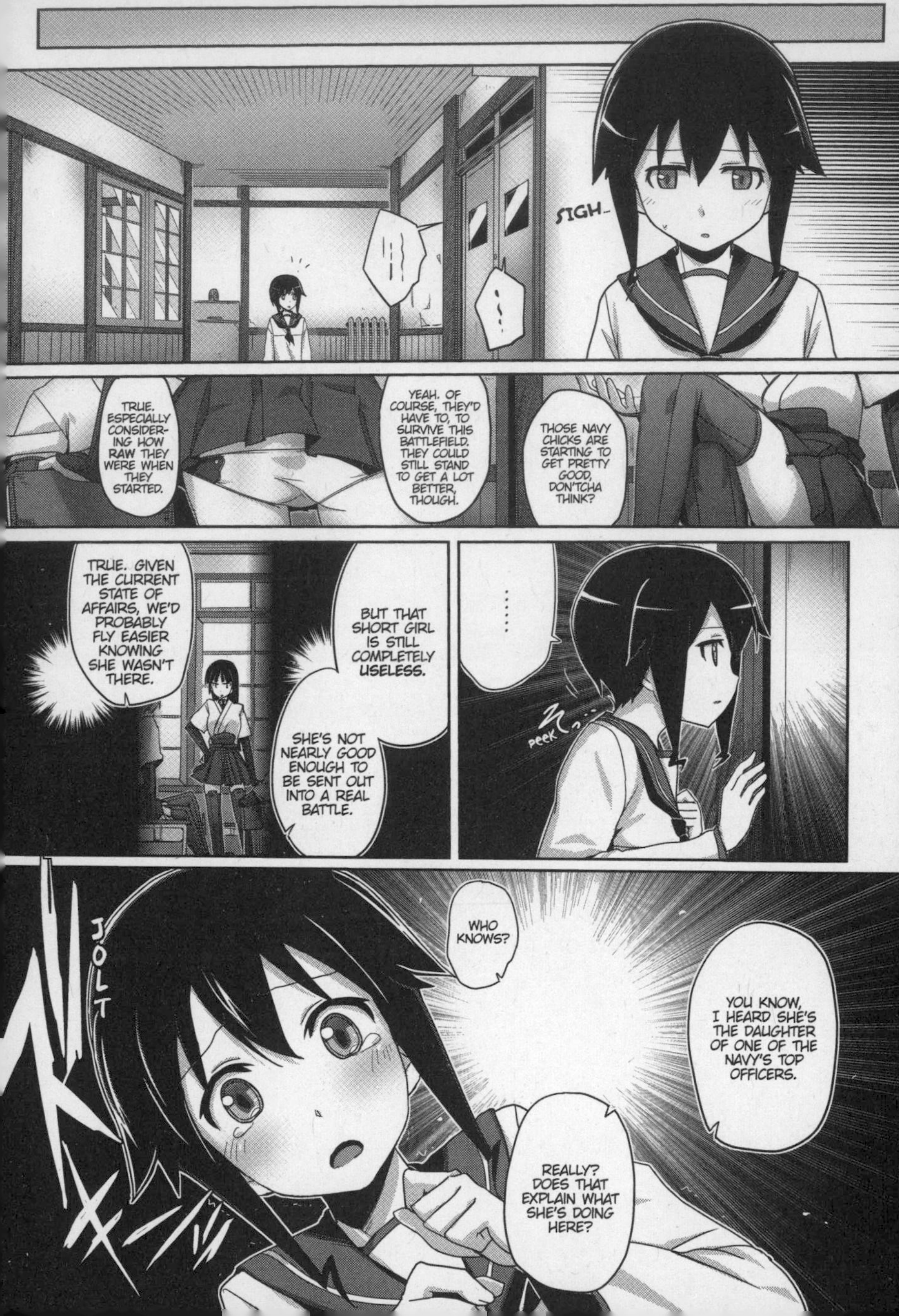
SIGH...
!!
...
THOSE NAVY CHICKS ARE STARTING TO GET PRETTY GOOD, DON'TCHA THINK?
YEAH. OF COURSE, THEY'D HAVE TO, TO SURVIVE THIS BATTLEFIELD. THEY COULD STILL STAND TO GET A LOT BETTER, THOUGH.
TRUE. ESPECIALLY CONSIDERING HOW RAW THEY WERE WHEN THEY STARTED.
......
PEEK
BUT THAT SHORT GIRL IS STILL COMPLETELY USELESS.
SHE'S NOT NEARLY GOOD ENOUGH TO BE SENT OUT INTO A REAL BATTLE.
TRUE. GIVEN THE CURRENT STATE OF AFFAIRS, WE'D PROBABLY FLY EASIER KNOWING SHE WASN'T THERE.
JOLT
YOU KNOW, I HEARD SHE'S THE DAUGHTER OF ONE OF THE NAVY'S TOP OFFICERS.
REALLY? DOES THAT EXPLAIN WHAT SHE'S DOING HERE?
WHO KNOWS?

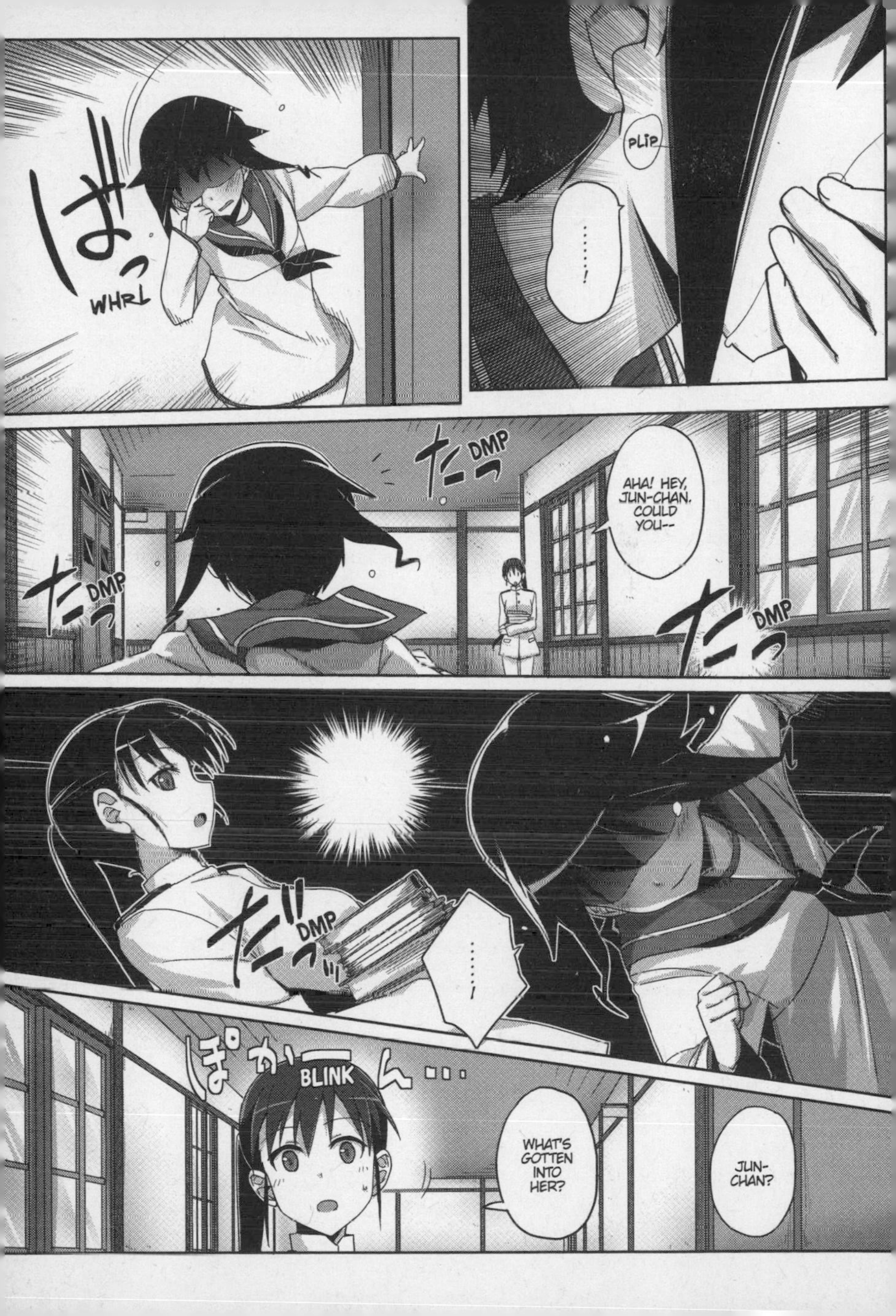
PLIP
......!
ぱっ
WHRL
たっ
DMP
AHA! HEY, JUN-CHAN, COULD YOU--
たーっ
DMP
たっ
DMP
たたっ
DMP
......!
JUN-CHAN?
WHAT'S GOTTEN INTO HER?
ぽかーん...
BLINK

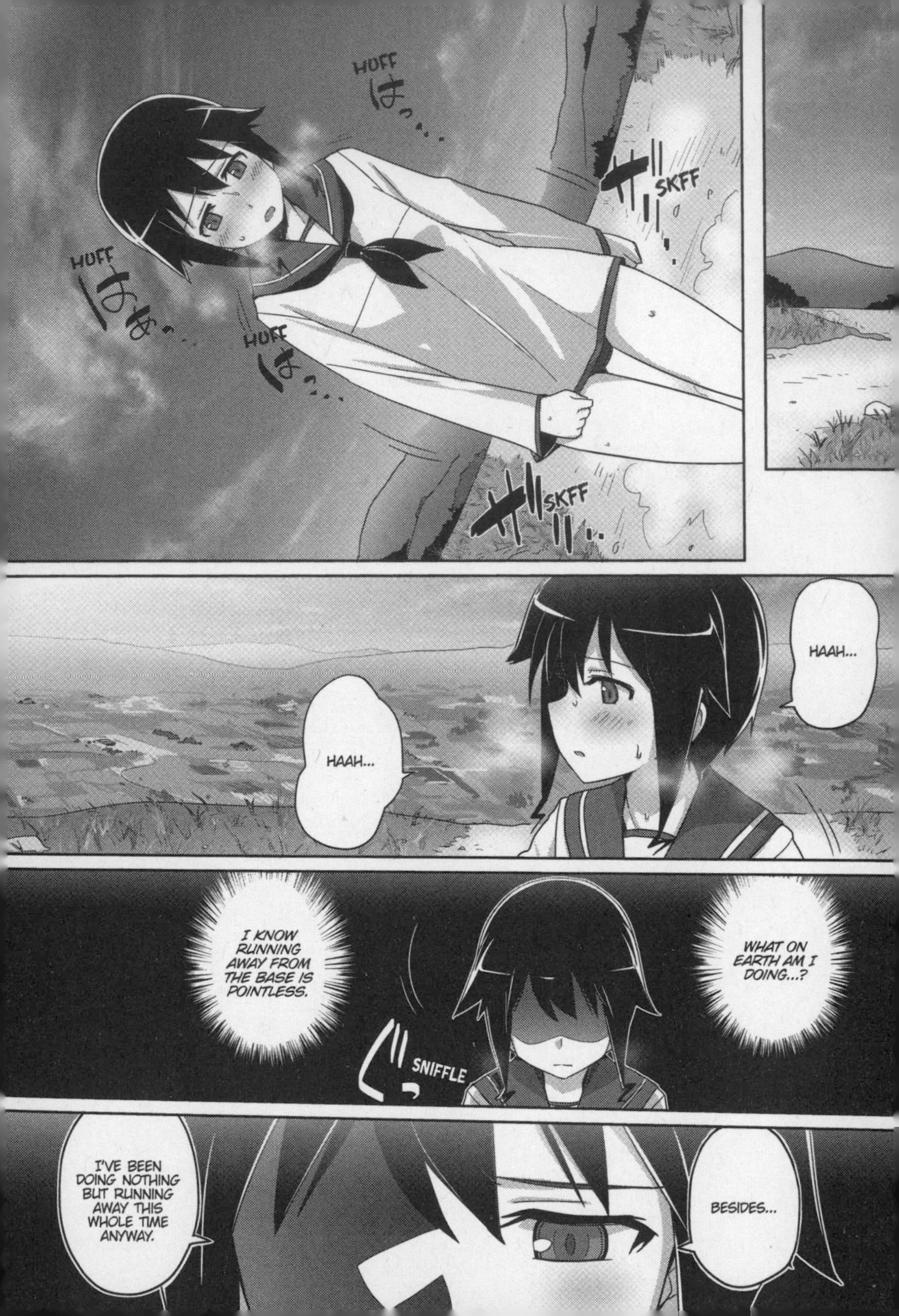
HUFF
はっ…
SKFF
HUFF
はぁ…
HUFF
はっ…
SKFF
HAAH...
HAAH...
WHAT ON EARTH AM I DOING...?
I KNOW RUNNING AWAY FROM THE BASE IS POINTLESS.
SNIFFLE
BESIDES...
I'VE BEEN DOING NOTHING BUT RUNNING AWAY THIS WHOLE TIME ANYWAY.

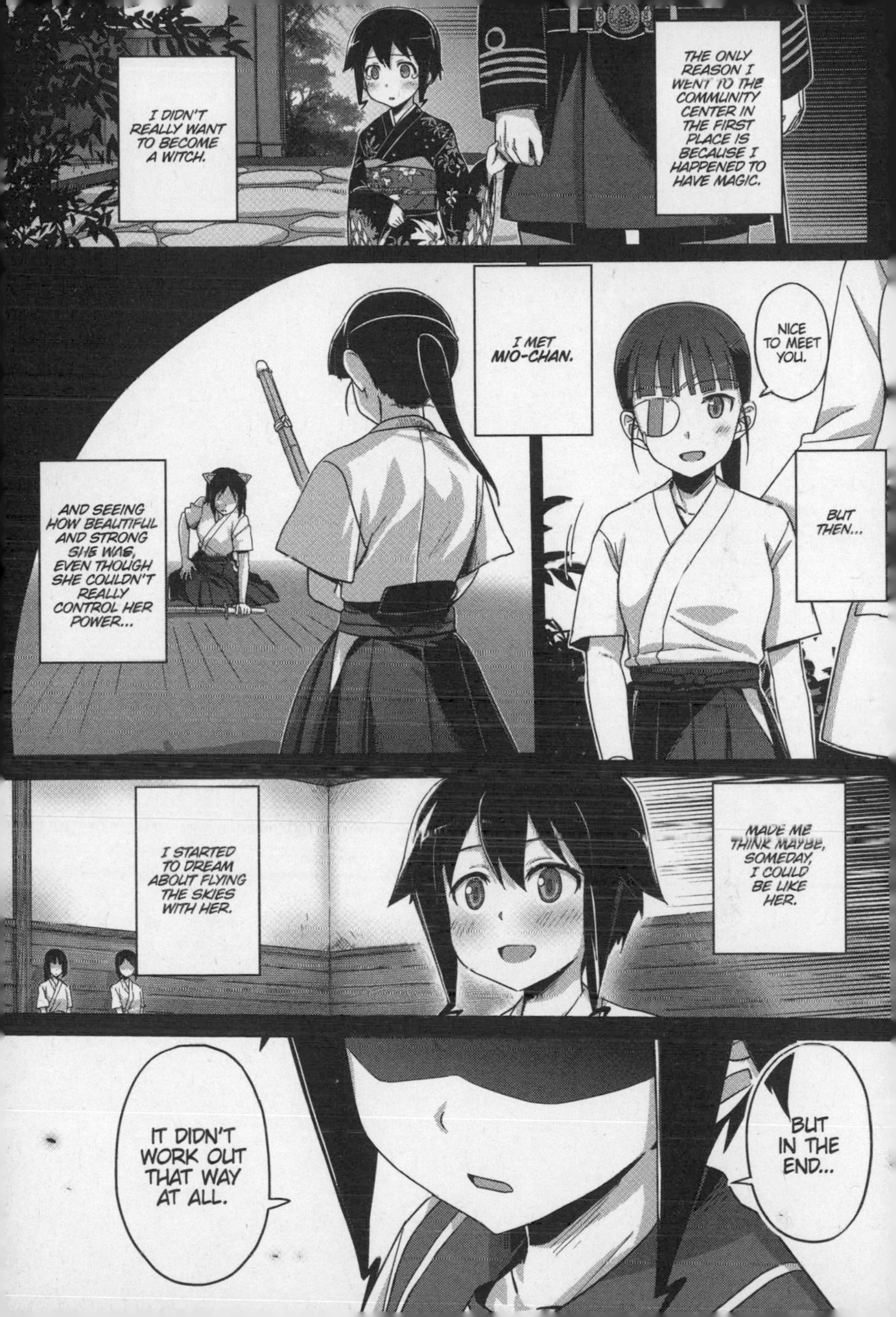
THE ONLY REASON I WENT TO THE COMMUNITY CENTER IN THE FIRST PLACE IS BECAUSE I HAPPENED TO HAVE MAGIC.
I DIDN'T REALLY WANT TO BECOME A WITCH.
NICE TO MEET YOU.
I MET MIO-CHAN.
BUT THEN...
AND SEEING HOW BEAUTIFUL AND STRONG SHE WAS, EVEN THOUGH SHE COULDN'T REALLY CONTROL HER POWER...
MADE ME THINK MAYBE, SOMEDAY, I COULD BE LIKE HER.
I STARTED TO DREAM ABOUT FLYING THE SKIES WITH HER.
BUT IN THE END...
IT DIDN'T WORK OUT THAT WAY AT ALL.

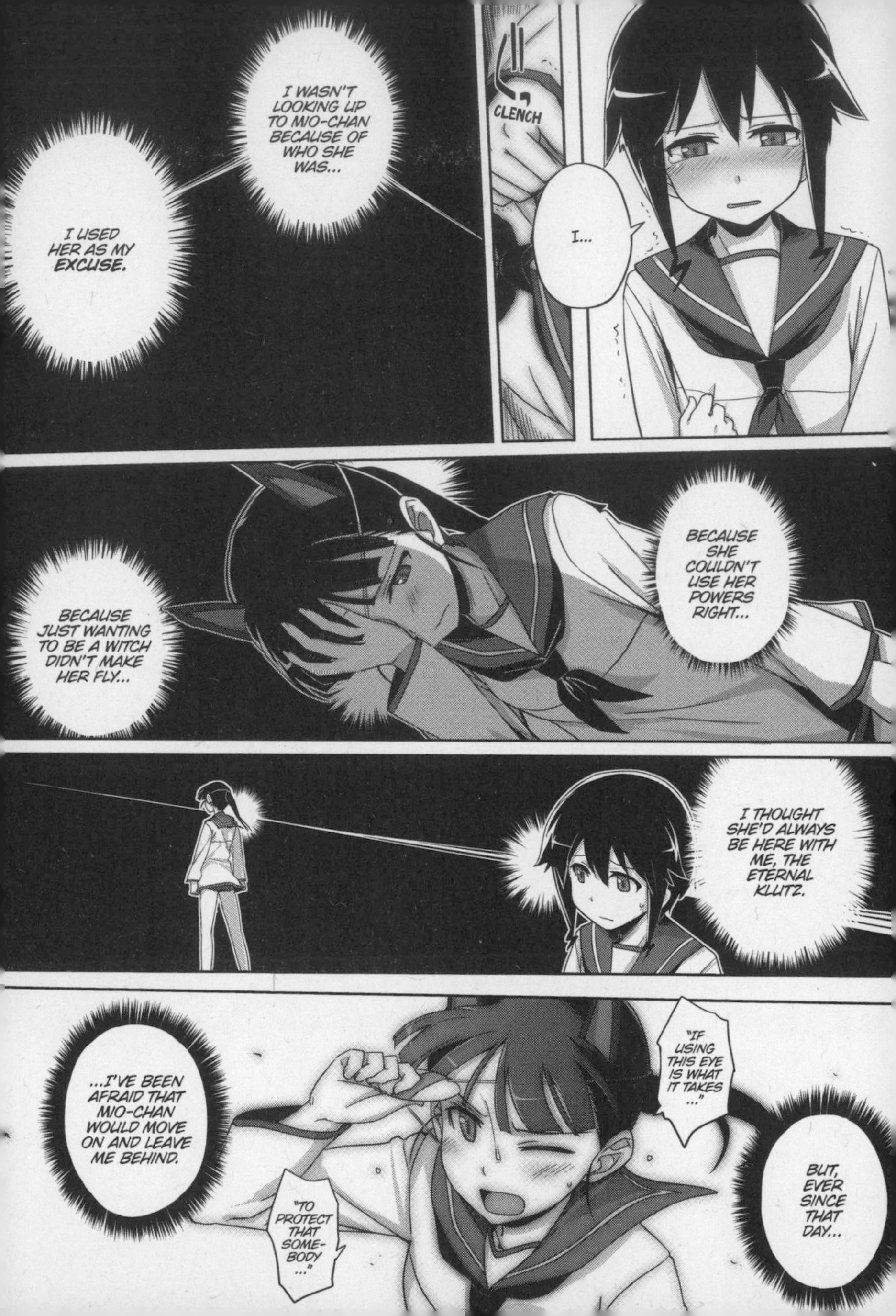
I...
CLENCH
I WASN'T LOOKING UP TO MIO-CHAN BECAUSE OF WHO SHE WAS...
I USED HER AS MY EXCUSE.
BECAUSE SHE COULDN'T USE HER POWERS RIGHT...
BECAUSE JUST WANTING TO BE A WITCH DIDN'T MAKE HER FLY...
I THOUGHT SHE'D ALWAYS BE HERE WITH ME, THE ETERNAL KLUTZ.
BUT, EVER SINCE THAT DAY...
"IF USING THIS EYE IS WHAT IT TAKES..."
"TO PROTECT THAT SOME-BODY..."
...I'VE BEEN AFRAID THAT MIO-CHAN WOULD MOVE ON AND LEAVE ME BEHIND.

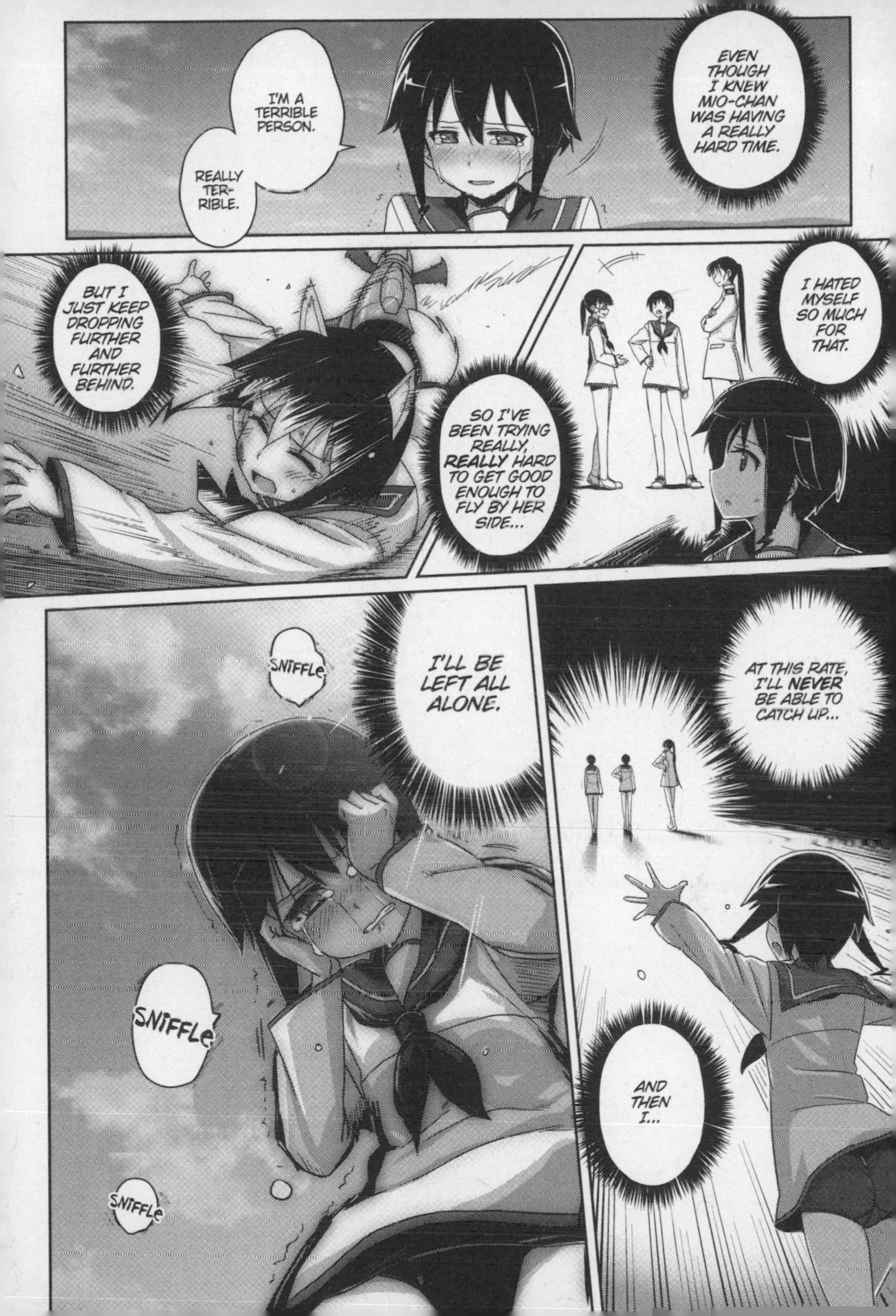
EVEN THOUGH I KNEW MIO-CHAN WAS HAVING A REALLY HARD TIME.
I'M A TERRIBLE PERSON.
REALLY TERRIBLE.
I HATED MYSELF SO MUCH FOR THAT.
SO I'VE BEEN TRYING REALLY, REALLY HARD TO GET GOOD ENOUGH TO FLY BY HER SIDE...
BUT I JUST KEEP DROPPING FURTHER AND FURTHER BEHIND.
AT THIS RATE, I'LL NEVER BE ABLE TO CATCH UP...
AND THEN I...
I'LL BE LEFT ALL ALONE.
SNIFFLE
SNIFFLE
SNIFFLE

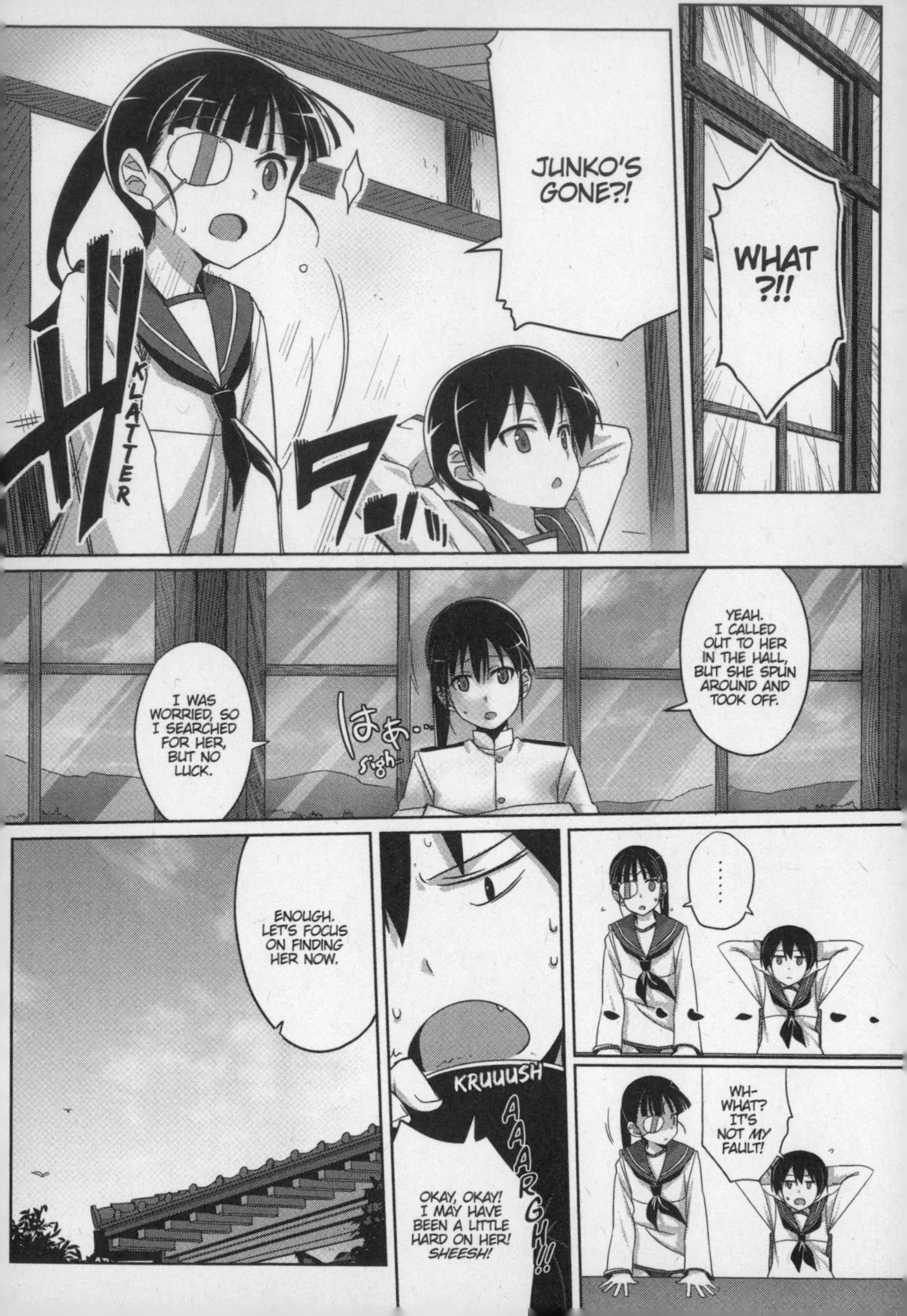
WHAT?!!
JUNKO'S GONE?!
KLATTER
YEAH. I CALLED OUT TO HER IN THE HALL, BUT SHE SPUN AROUND AND TOOK OFF.
はぁ…
sigh
I WAS WORRIED, SO I SEARCHED FOR HER, BUT NO LUCK.
......
WH-WHAT? IT'S NOT MY FAULT!
KRUUUSH
AAAARGH!!
OKAY, OKAY! I MAY HAVE BEEN A LITTLE HARD ON HER! SHEESH!
ENOUGH. LET'S FOCUS ON FINDING HER NOW.

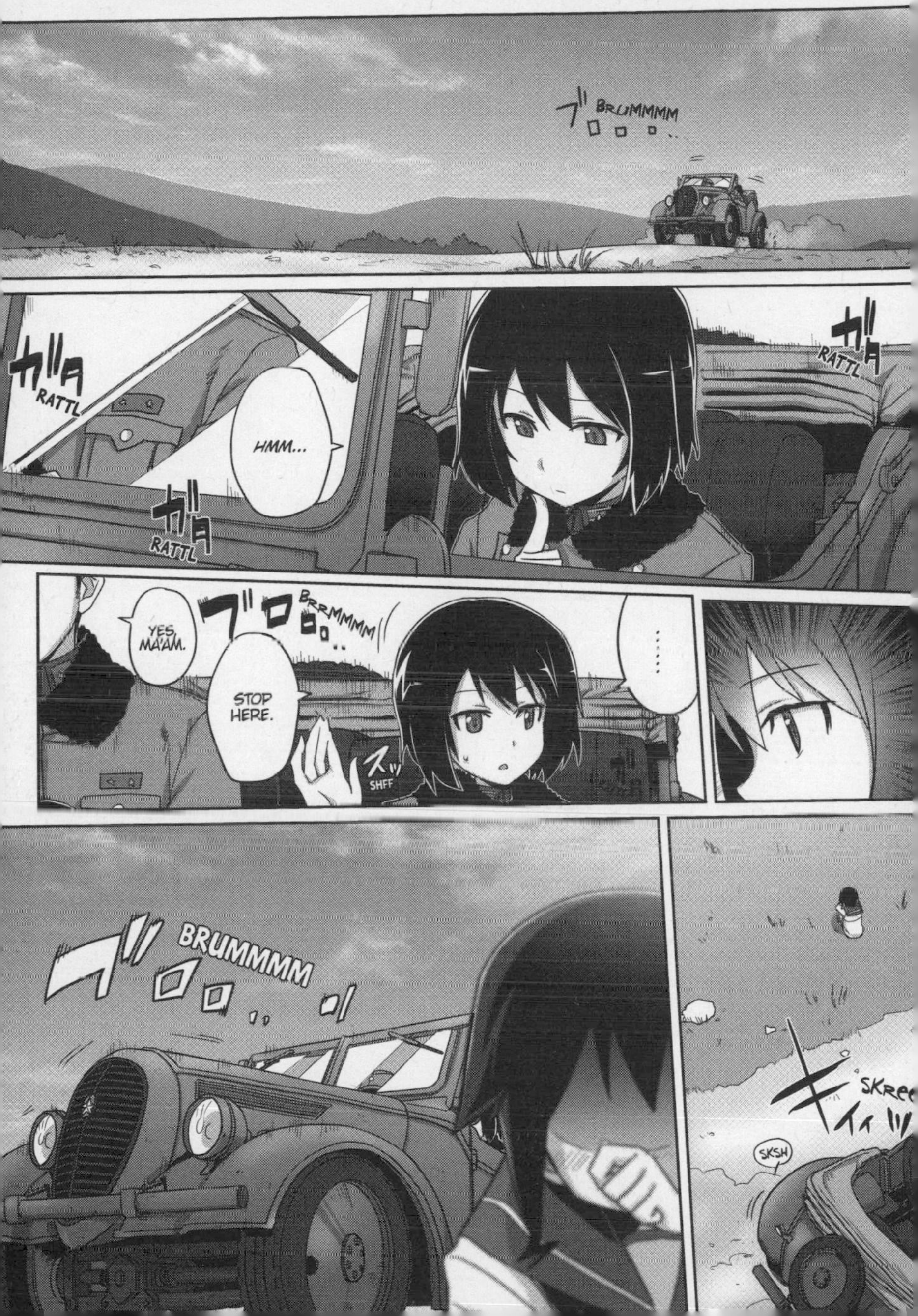
BRUMMMM
RATTL
HMM...
RATTL
RATTL
......
BRRMMMM
STOP HERE.
YES MA'AM.
SHFF
SKREE
SKSH
BRUMMMM

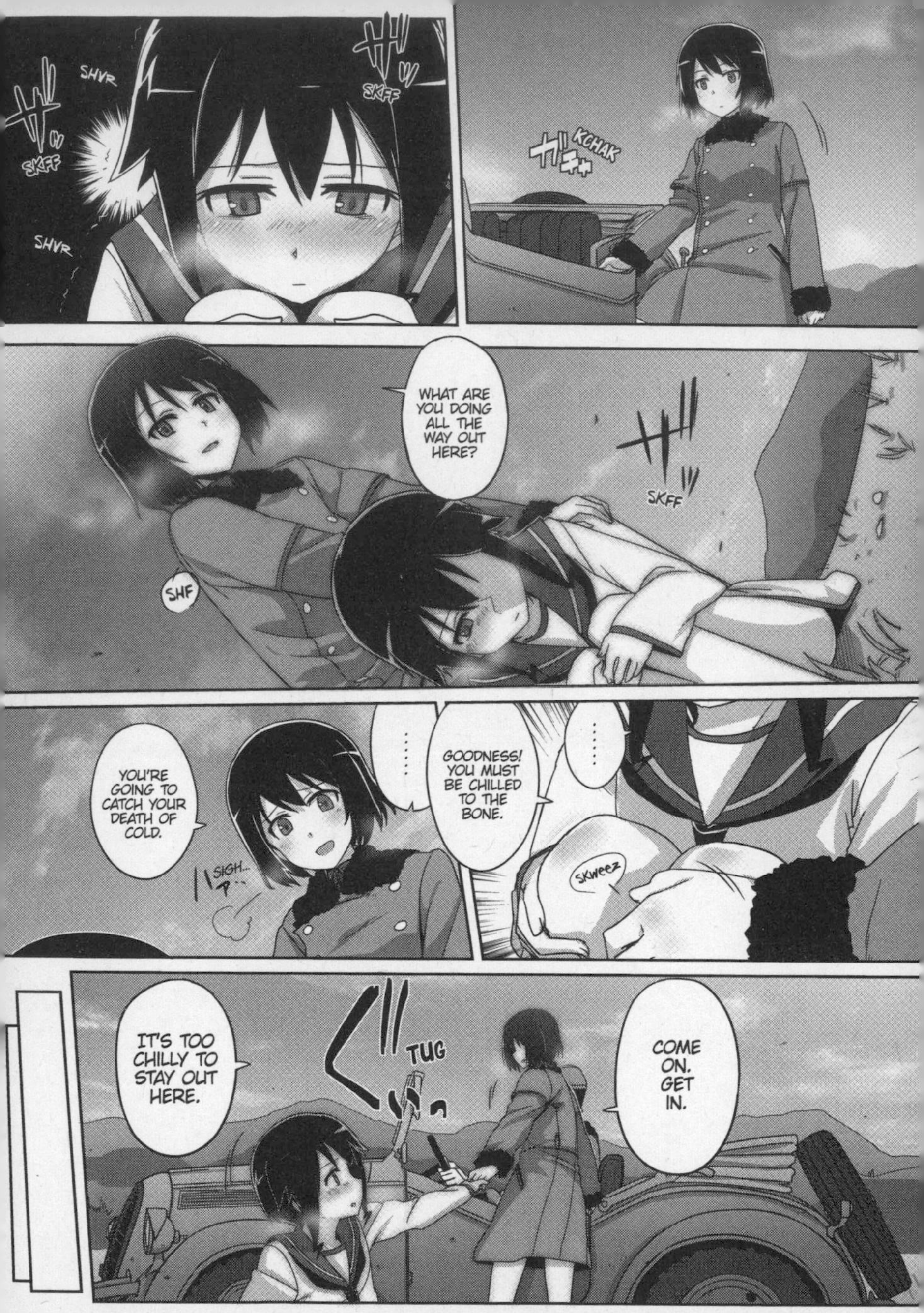
KCHAK
SHVR
SKFF
SHVR
SKFF
WHAT ARE YOU DOING ALL THE WAY OUT HERE?
SKFF
SHF
......
SKWEEZ
GOODNESS! YOU MUST BE CHILLED TO THE BONE.
......
YOU'RE GOING TO CATCH YOUR DEATH OF COLD.
SIGH...
COME ON. GET IN.
TUG
IT'S TOO CHILLY TO STAY OUT HERE.

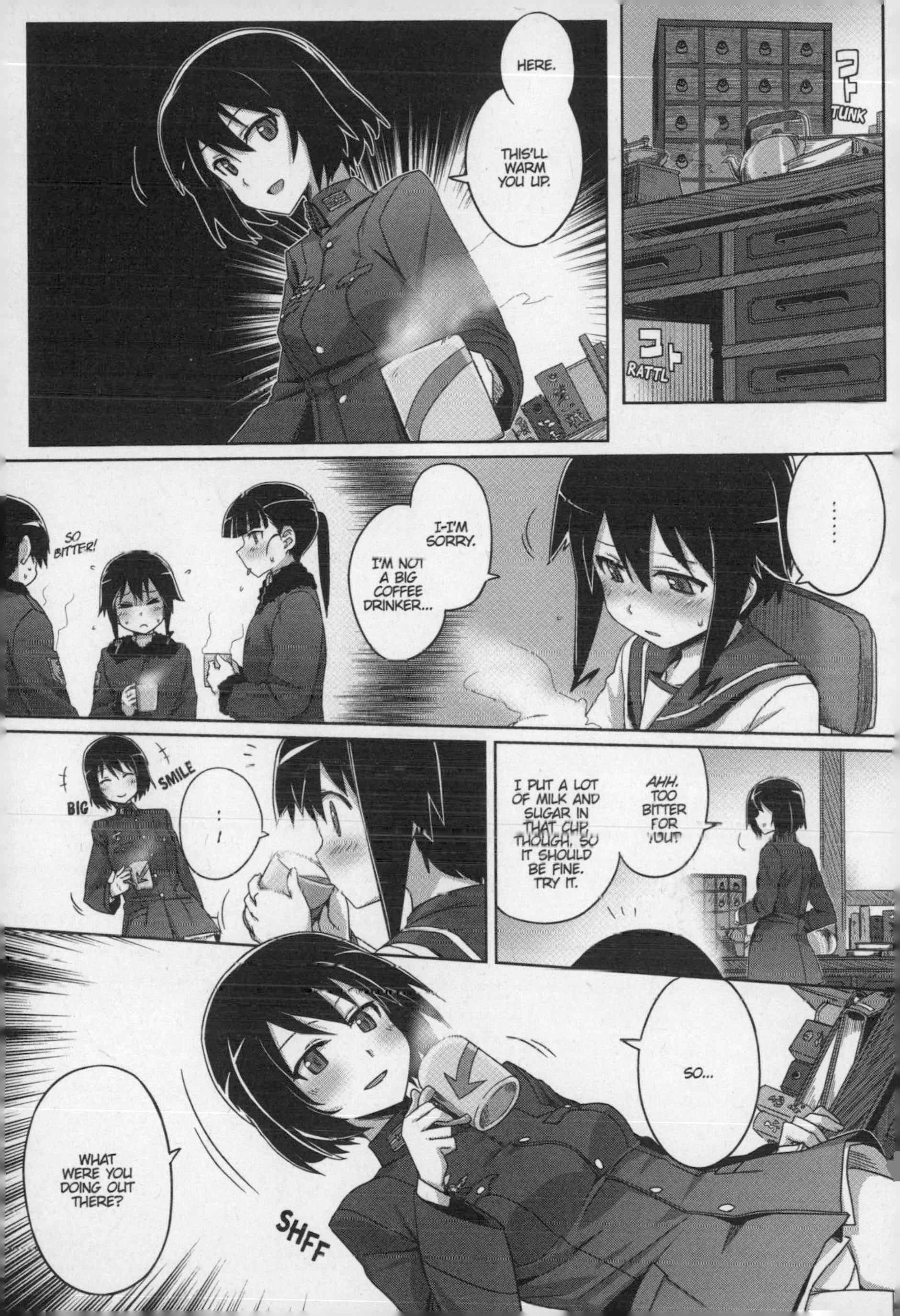

コト
TUNK
コト
RATTL
HERE.
THIS'LL WARM YOU UP.
......
I-I'M SORRY.
I'M NOT A BIG COFFEE DRINKER...
SO BITTER!
AHH. TOO BITTER FOR YOU?
I PUT A LOT OF MILK AND SUGAR IN THAT CUP, THOUGH, SO IT SHOULD BE FINE. TRY IT.
...!
BIG SMILE
SO...
WHAT WERE YOU DOING OUT THERE?
SHFF

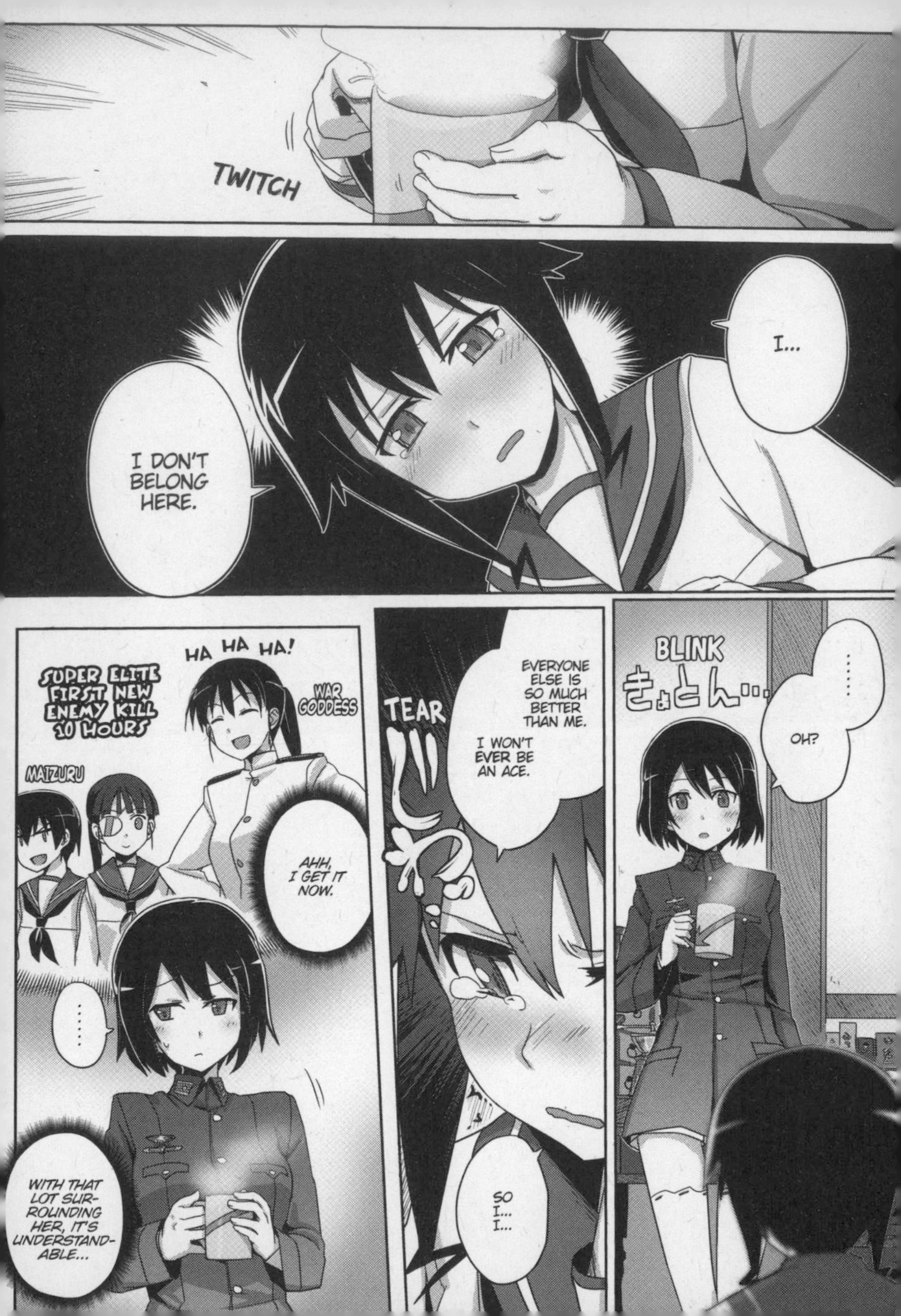
TWITCH
I...
I DON'T BELONG HERE.
BLINK
きょとん…
……
OH?
TEAR
EVERYONE ELSE IS SO MUCH BETTER THAN ME.
I WON'T EVER BE AN ACE.
SO I... I...
HA HA HA!
WAR GODDESS
SUPER ELITE FIRST NEW ENEMY KILL 10 HOURS
MAIZURU
AHH, I GET IT NOW.
……
WITH THAT LOT SUR-ROUNDING HER, IT'S UNDERSTAND-ABLE...

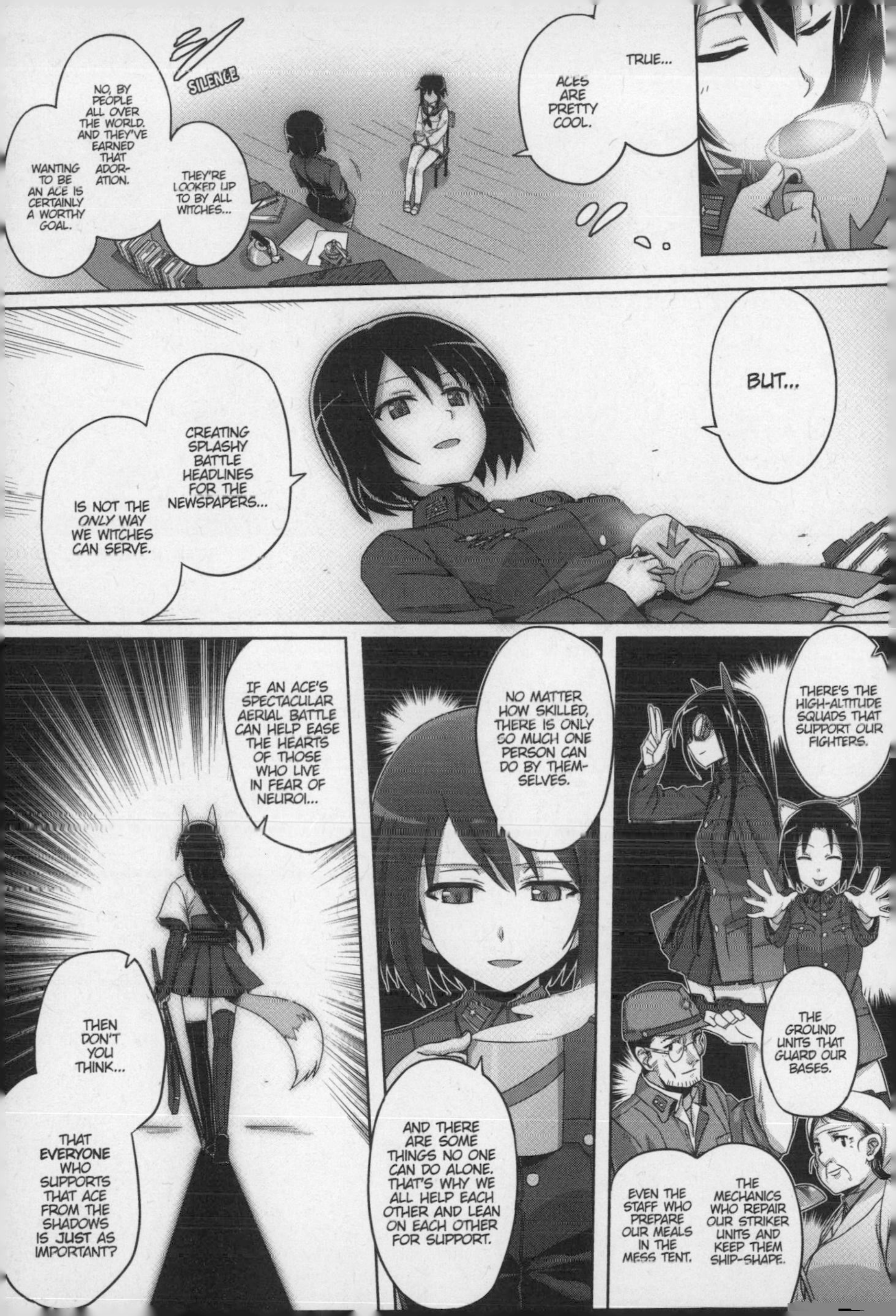
TRUE...
ACES ARE PRETTY COOL.
SILENCE
THEY'RE LOOKED UP TO BY ALL WITCHES...
NO, BY PEOPLE ALL OVER THE WORLD. AND THEY'VE EARNED THAT ADORATION.
WANTING TO BE AN ACE IS CERTAINLY A WORTHY GOAL.
BUT...
CREATING SPLASHY BATTLE HEADLINES FOR THE NEWSPAPERS...
IS NOT THE *ONLY* WAY WE WITCHES CAN SERVE.
THERE'S THE HIGH-ALTITUDE SQUADS THAT SUPPORT OUR FIGHTERS.
THE GROUND UNITS THAT GUARD OUR BASES.
THE MECHANICS WHO REPAIR OUR STRIKER UNITS AND KEEP THEM SHIP-SHAPE.
EVEN THE STAFF WHO PREPARE OUR MEALS IN THE MESS TENT.
NO MATTER HOW SKILLED, THERE IS ONLY SO MUCH ONE PERSON CAN DO BY THEM-SELVES.
AND THERE ARE SOME THINGS NO ONE CAN DO ALONE. THAT'S WHY WE ALL HELP EACH OTHER AND LEAN ON EACH OTHER FOR SUPPORT.
IF AN ACE'S SPECTACULAR AERIAL BATTLE CAN HELP EASE THE HEARTS OF THOSE WHO LIVE IN FEAR OF NEUROI...
THEN DON'T YOU THINK...
THAT **EVERYONE** WHO SUPPORTS THAT ACE FROM THE SHADOWS IS JUST AS IMPORTANT?

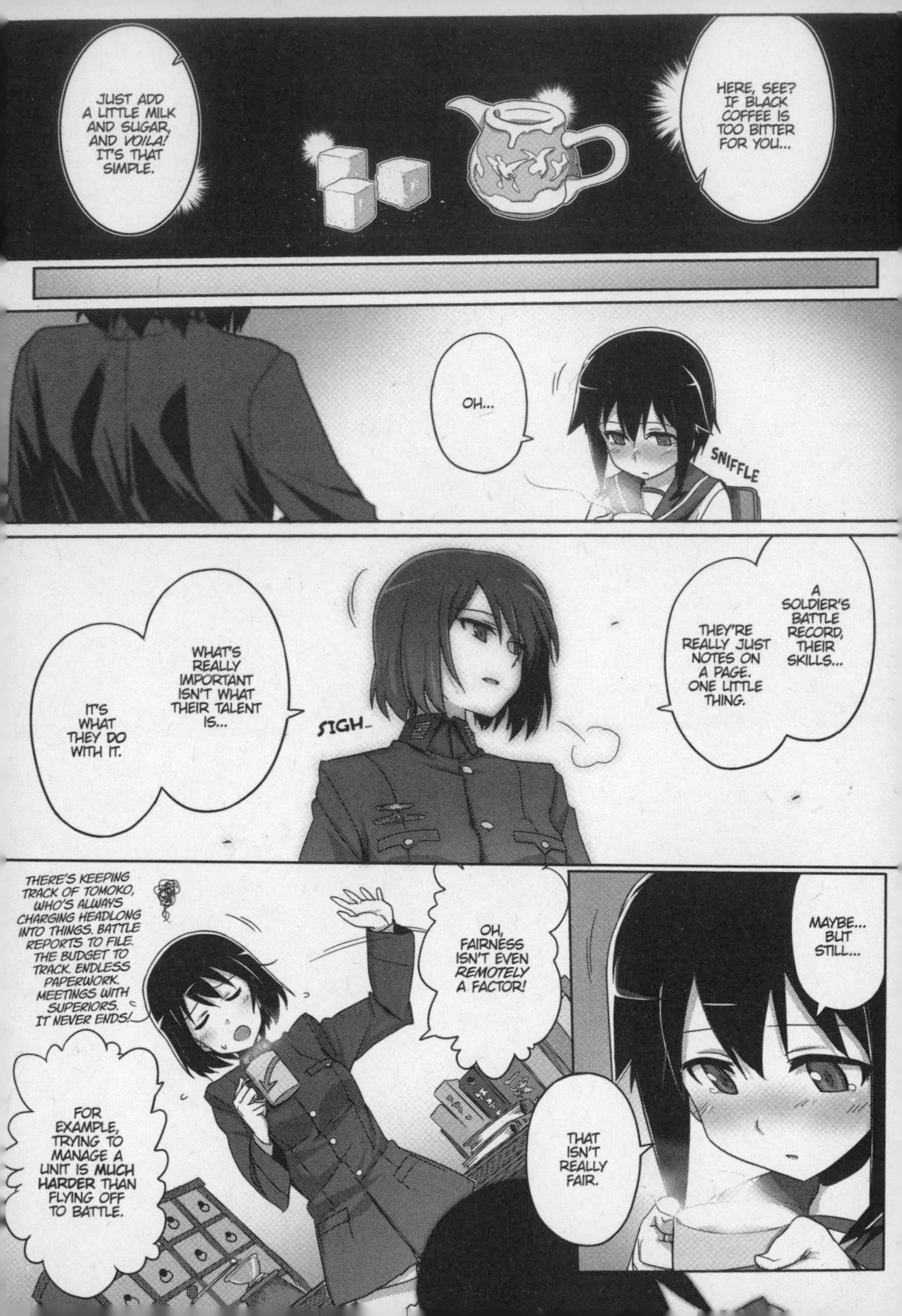
HERE, SEE? IF BLACK COFFEE IS TOO BITTER FOR YOU...
JUST ADD A LITTLE MILK AND SUGAR, AND *VOILA!* IT'S THAT SIMPLE.
OH...
SNIFFLE
A SOLDIER'S BATTLE RECORD, THEIR SKILLS...
THEY'RE REALLY JUST NOTES ON A PAGE. ONE LITTLE THING.
SIGH...
WHAT'S REALLY IMPORTANT ISN'T WHAT THEIR TALENT IS...
IT'S WHAT THEY DO WITH IT.
MAYBE... BUT STILL...
THAT ISN'T REALLY FAIR.
OH, FAIRNESS ISN'T EVEN *REMOTELY* A FACTOR!
THERE'S KEEPING TRACK OF TOMOKO, WHO'S ALWAYS CHARGING HEADLONG INTO THINGS. BATTLE REPORTS TO FILE. THE BUDGET TO TRACK. ENDLESS PAPERWORK. MEETINGS WITH SUPERIORS. IT NEVER ENDS!
FOR EXAMPLE, TRYING TO MANAGE A UNIT IS **MUCH HARDER** THAN FLYING OFF TO BATTLE.

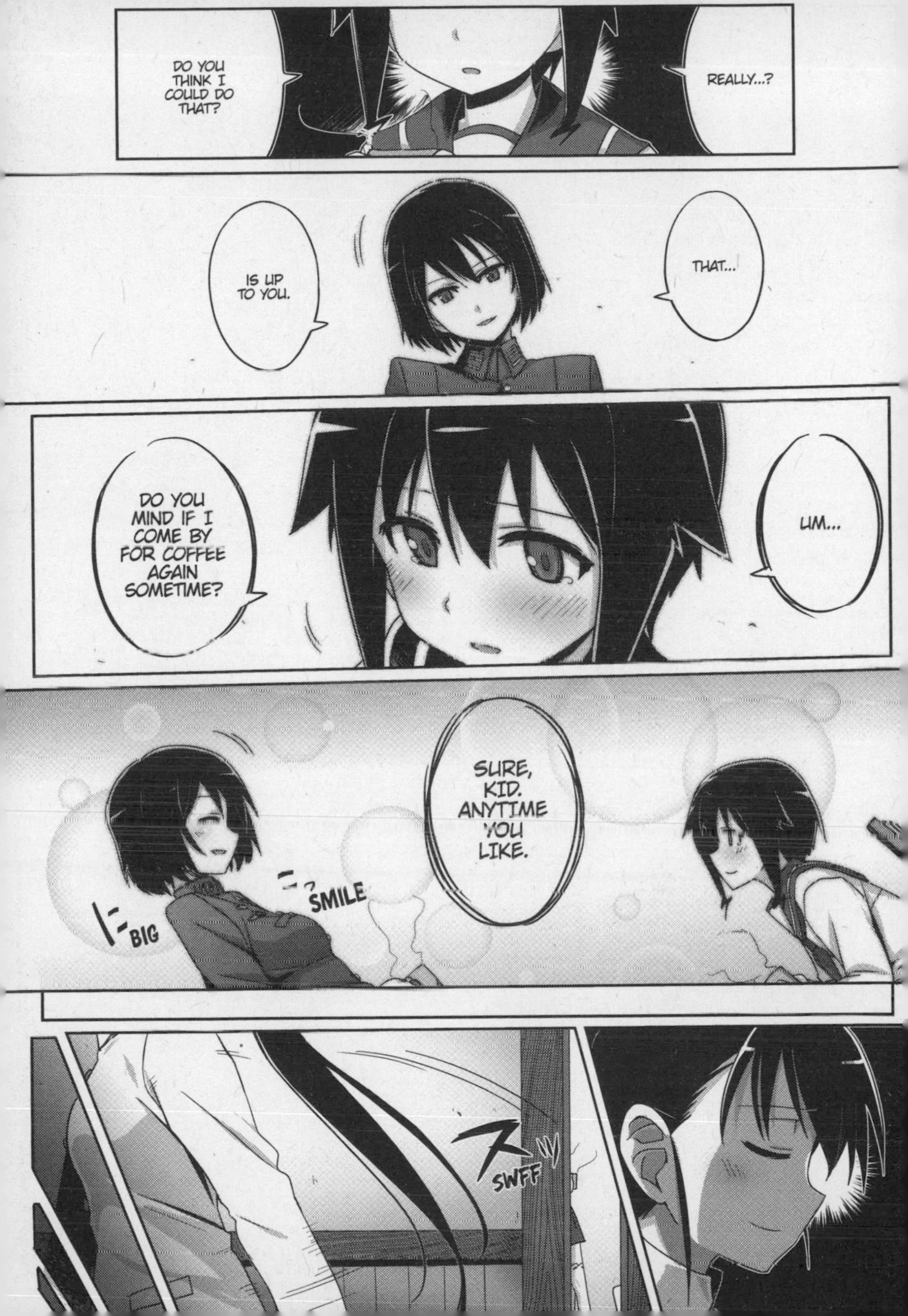
REALLY...?
DO YOU THINK I COULD DO THAT?
THAT...
IS UP TO YOU.
UM...
DO YOU MIND IF I COME BY FOR COFFEE AGAIN SOMETIME?
SURE, KID. ANYTIME YOU LIKE.
SMILE
BIG
SWFF

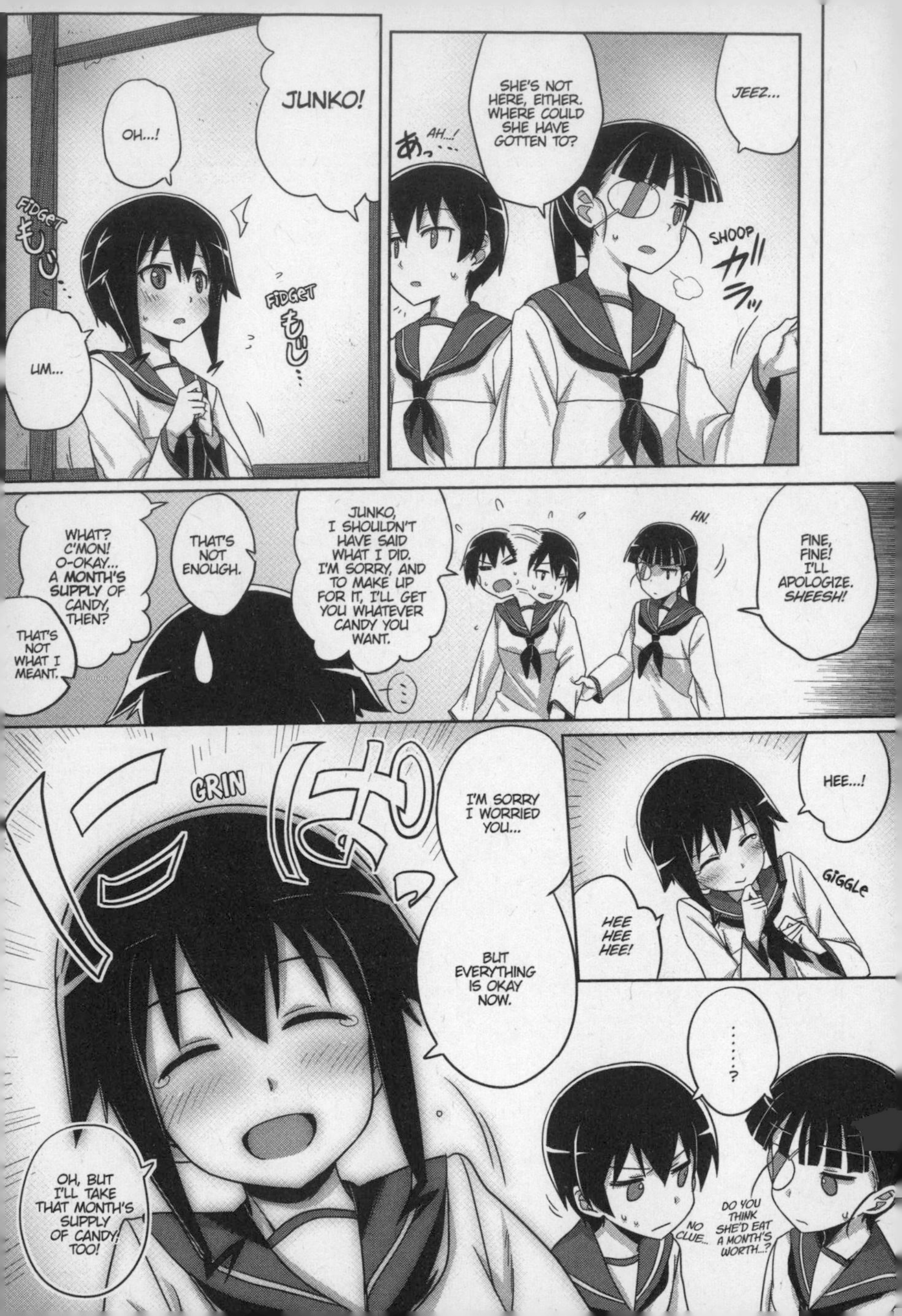
JEEZ...
SHOOP
ガラッ
SHE'S NOT HERE, EITHER. WHERE COULD SHE HAVE GOTTEN TO?
あっ…
AH...!
JUNKO!
OH...!
FIDGET
もじ
FIDGET
もじ…
UM...
FINE, FINE! I'LL APOLOGIZE. SHEESH!
HN.
JUNKO, I SHOULDN'T HAVE SAID WHAT I DID. I'M SORRY, AND TO MAKE UP FOR IT, I'LL GET YOU WHATEVER CANDY YOU WANT.
THAT'S NOT ENOUGH.
WHAT? C'MON! O-OKAY... A MONTH'S SUPPLY OF CANDY, THEN?
THAT'S NOT WHAT I MEANT.
…
HEE...!
GIGGLE
HEE HEE HEE!
......?
DO YOU THINK SHE'D EAT A MONTH'S WORTH...?
NO CLUE...
I'M SORRY I WORRIED YOU...
BUT EVERYTHING IS OKAY NOW.
GRIN
にぱっ
OH, BUT I'LL TAKE THAT MONTH'S SUPPLY OF CANDY, TOO!

Chapter 6:
What Makes an Ace
[Mission Complete]

CHAPTER 00:
FLASH IN THE FUSO SEA

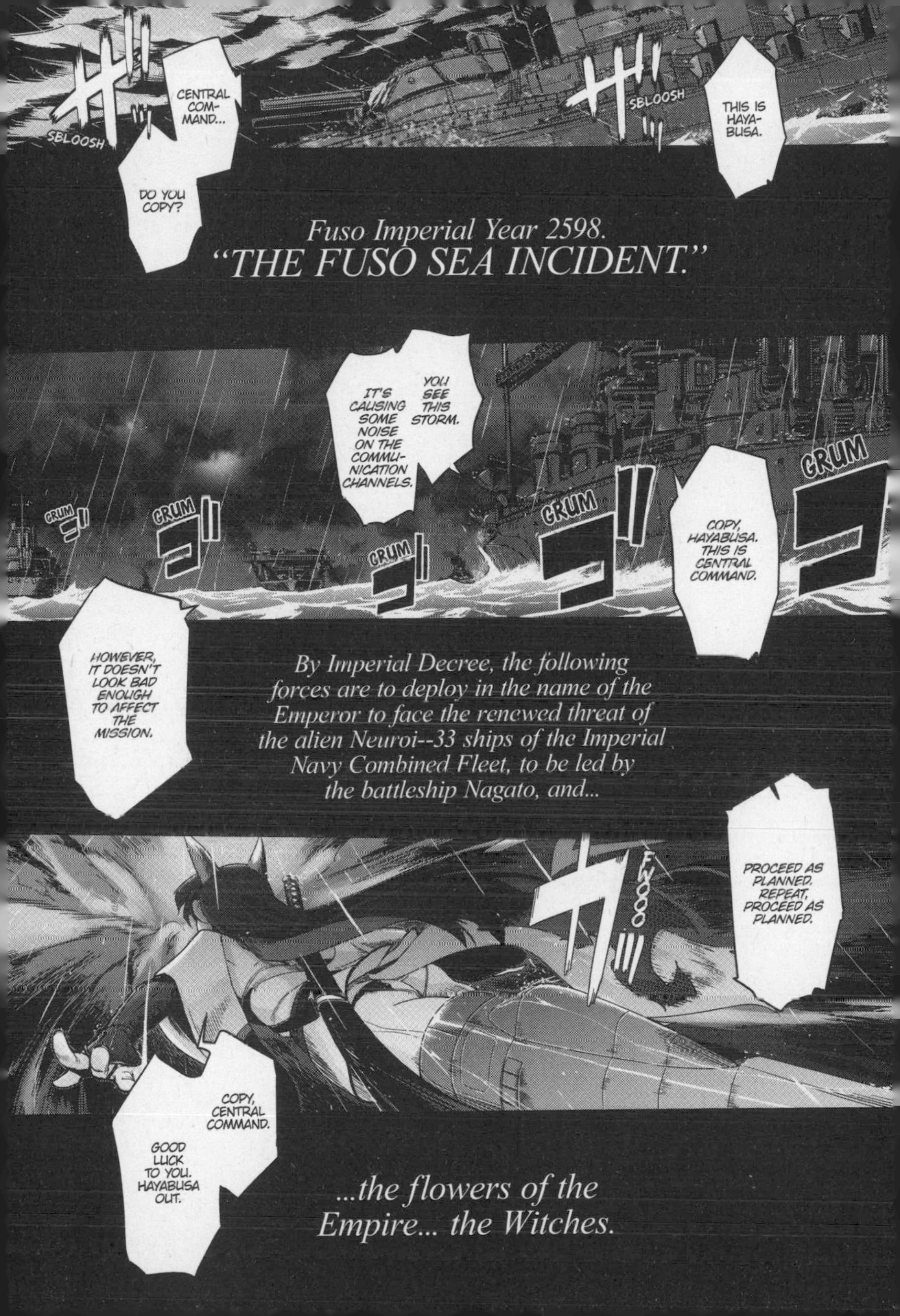
THIS IS HAYABUSA.
SBLOOSH
CENTRAL COMMAND...
SBLOOSH
DO YOU COPY?
Fuso Imperial Year 2598.
"THE FUSO SEA INCIDENT."
COPY, HAYABUSA. THIS IS CENTRAL COMMAND.
GRUM
YOU SEE THIS STORM.
IT'S CAUSING SOME NOISE ON THE COMMUNICATION CHANNELS.
GRUM
GRUM
GRUM
GRUM
HOWEVER, IT DOESN'T LOOK BAD ENOUGH TO AFFECT THE MISSION.
By Imperial Decree, the following forces are to deploy in the name of the Emperor to face the renewed threat of the alien Neuroi--33 ships of the Imperial Navy Combined Fleet, to be led by the battleship Nagato, and...
PROCEED AS PLANNED. REPEAT, PROCEED AS PLANNED.
FWOOO
COPY, CENTRAL COMMAND.
GOOD LUCK TO YOU. HAYABUSA OUT.
...the flowers of the Empire... the Witches.

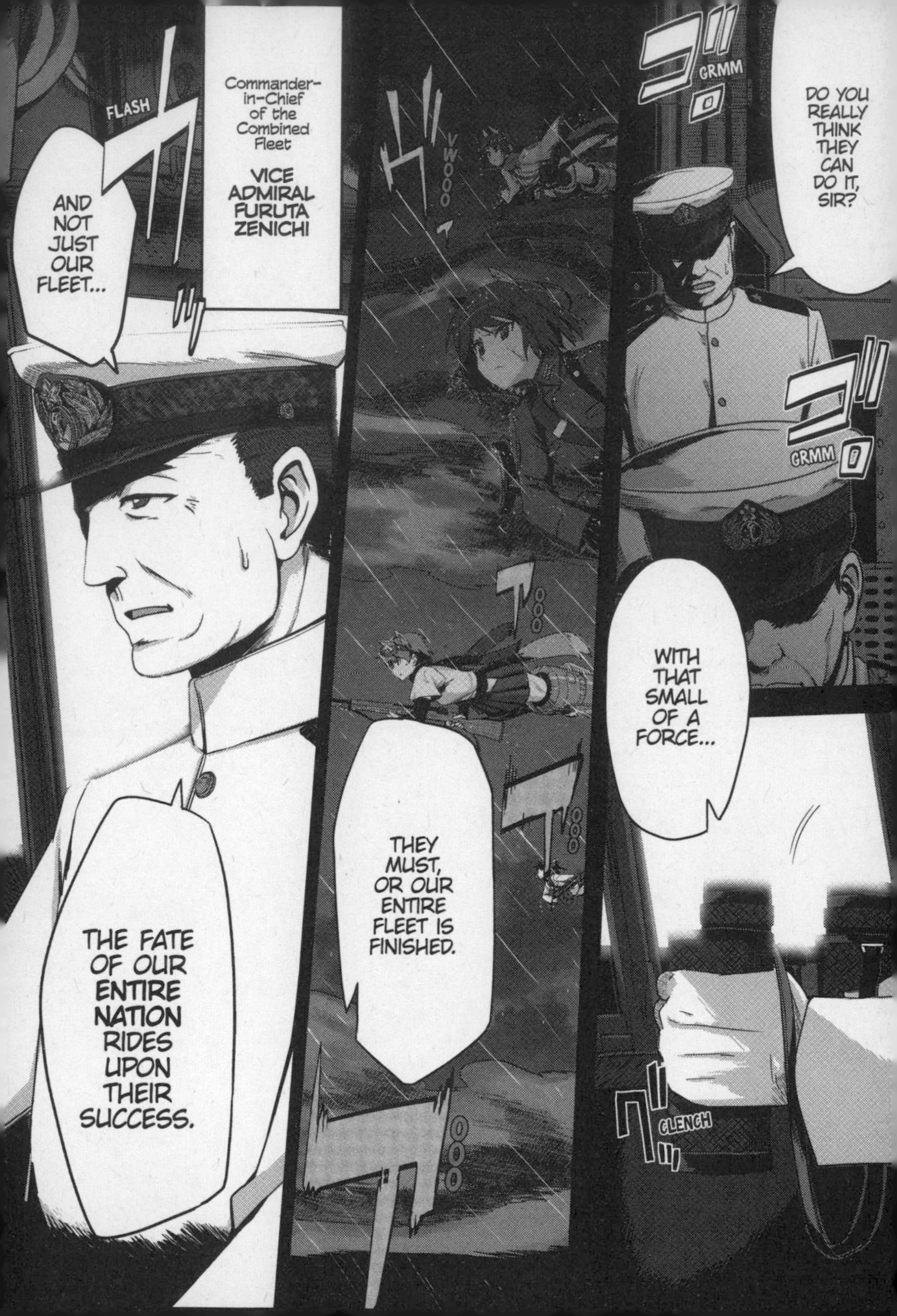
GRMM
DO YOU REALLY THINK THEY CAN DO IT, SIR?
GRMM
WITH THAT SMALL OF A FORCE...
CLENCH
VWOOO
THEY MUST, OR OUR ENTIRE FLEET IS FINISHED.
Commander-in-Chief of the Combined Fleet
VICE ADMIRAL FURUTA ZENICHI
FLASH
AND NOT JUST OUR FLEET...
THE FATE OF OUR ENTIRE NATION RIDES UPON THEIR SUCCESS.

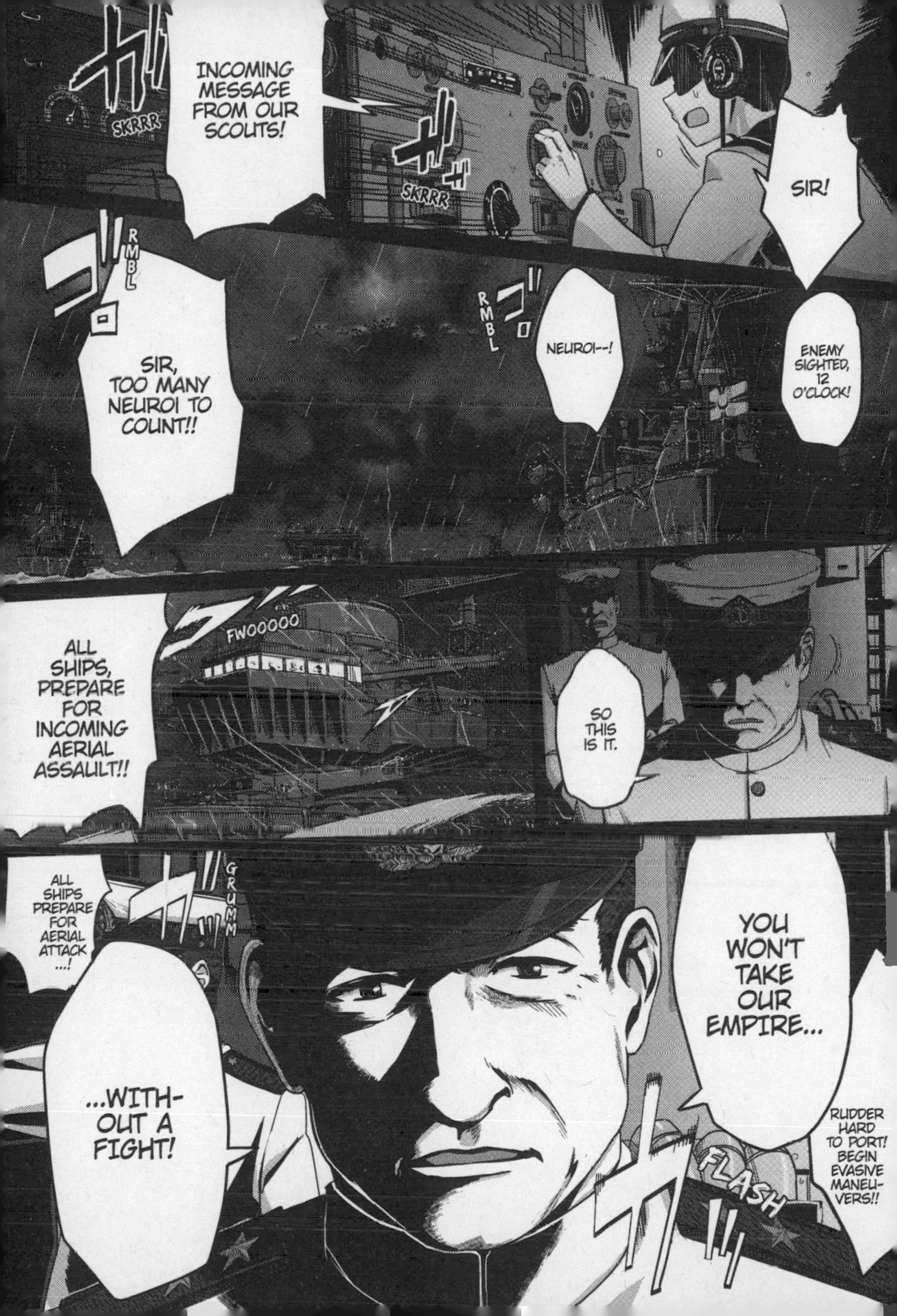
SIR!
INCOMING MESSAGE FROM OUR SCOUTS!
SKRRR
SKRRR
ENEMY SIGHTED, 12 O'CLOCK!
NEUROI--!
RMBL
RMBL
SIR, TOO MANY NEUROI TO COUNT!!
SO THIS IS IT.
FWOOOOO
ALL SHIPS, PREPARE FOR INCOMING AERIAL ASSAULT!!
YOU WON'T TAKE OUR EMPIRE...
RUDDER HARD TO PORT! BEGIN EVASIVE MANEUVERS!!
FLASH
...WITH-OUT A FIGHT!
GRUMM
ALL SHIPS PREPARE FOR AERIAL ATTACK ...!

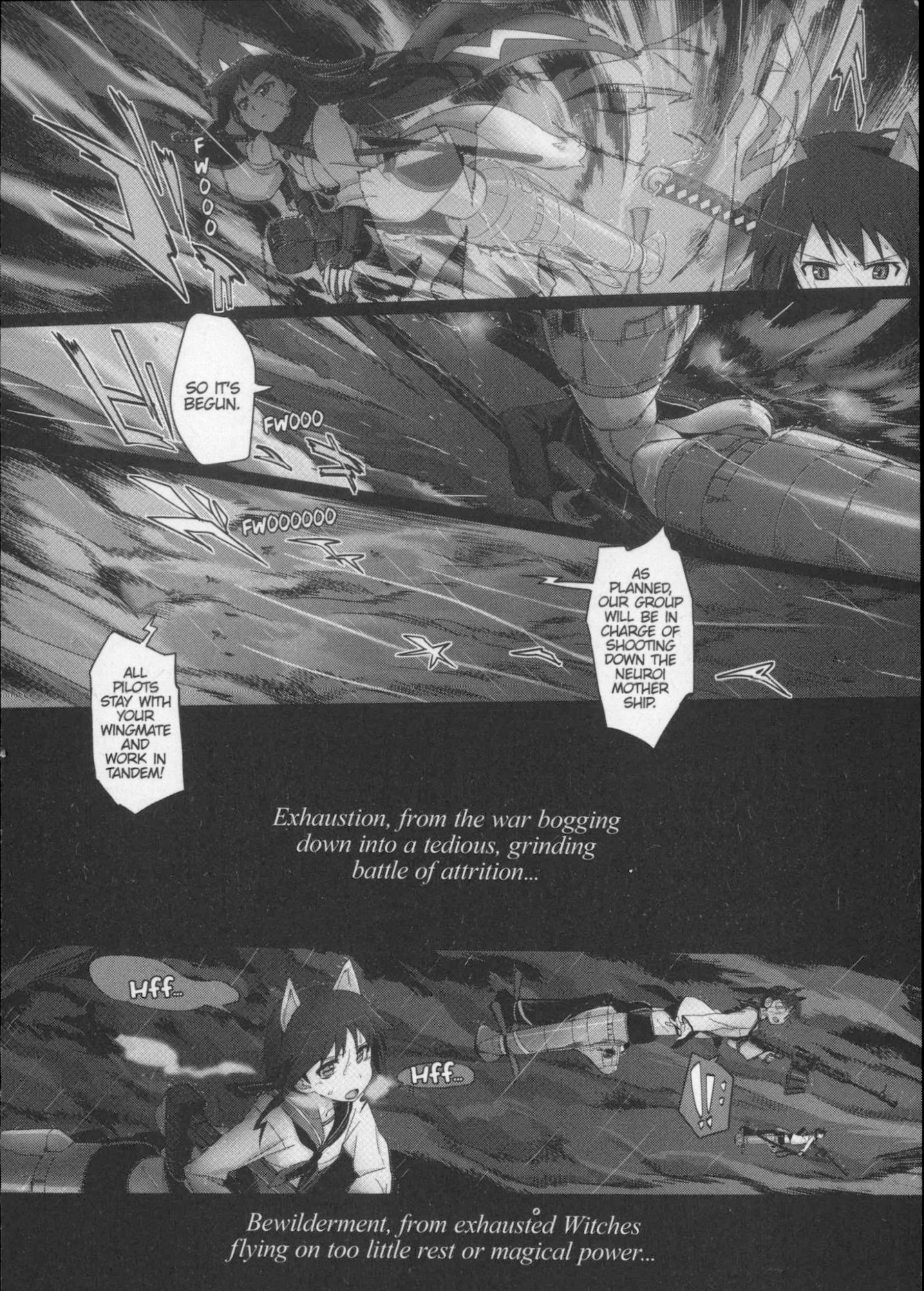
FWOOO
SO IT'S BEGUN.
FWOOO
FWOOOOOO
AS PLANNED, OUR GROUP WILL BE IN CHARGE OF SHOOTING DOWN THE NEUROI MOTHER SHIP.
ALL PILOTS STAY WITH YOUR WINGMATE AND WORK IN TANDEM!
Exhaustion, from the war bogging down into a tedious, grinding battle of attrition...
!
Hff...
Hff...
Bewilderment, from exhausted Witches flying on too little rest or magical power...

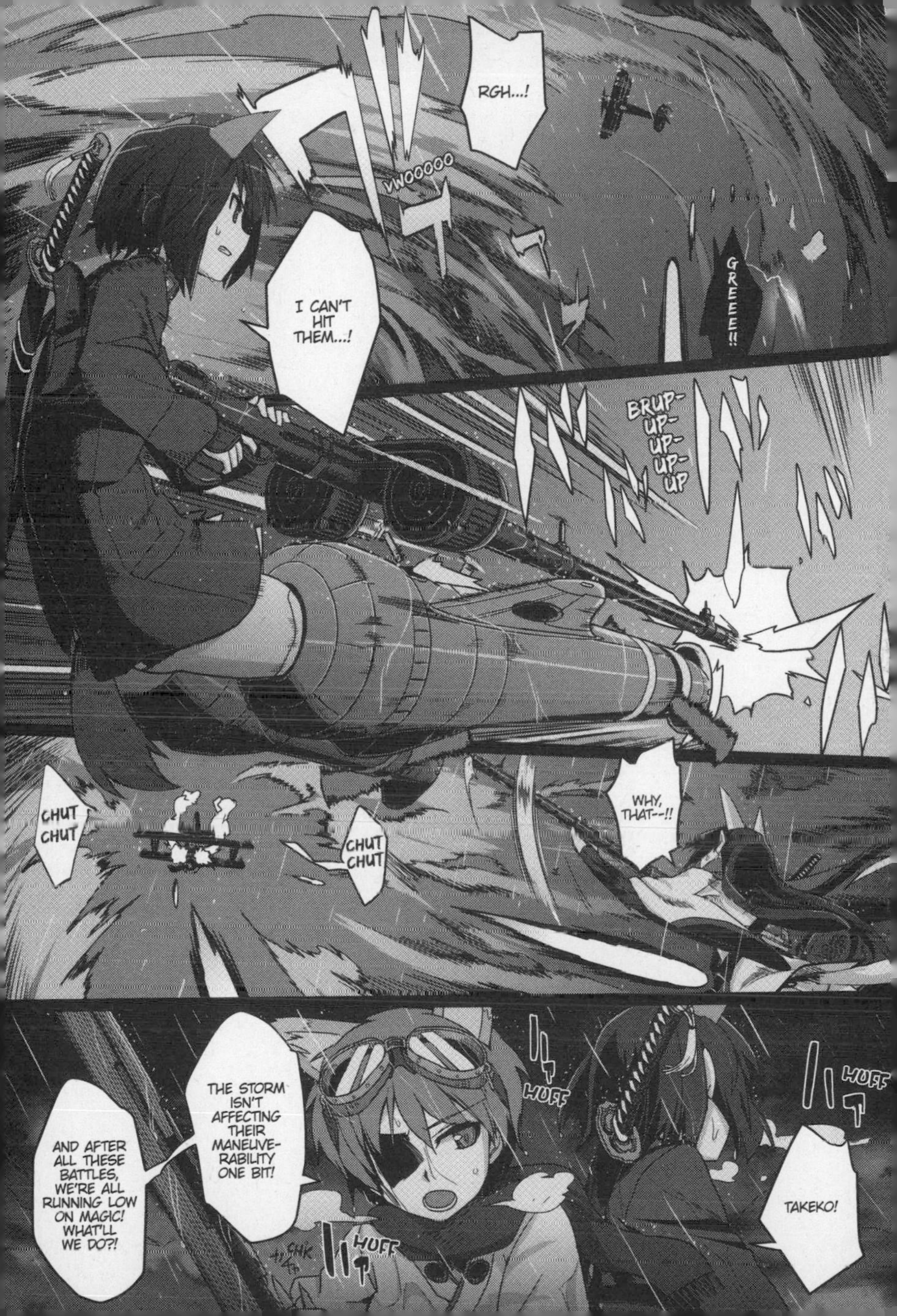
RGH...!
GREEE!!
VWOOOOO
I CAN'T HIT THEM...!
BRUP-UP-UP-UP-UP
WHY, THAT--!!
CHUT CHUT
CHUT CHUT
HUFF
TAKEKO!
HUFF
THE STORM ISN'T AFFECTING THEIR MANEUVE-RABILITY ONE BIT!
AND AFTER ALL THESE BATTLES, WE'RE ALL RUNNING LOW ON MAGIC! WHAT'LL WE DO?!
HUFF
CHK

Sur-rounded by their compan-ions, falling one by one...

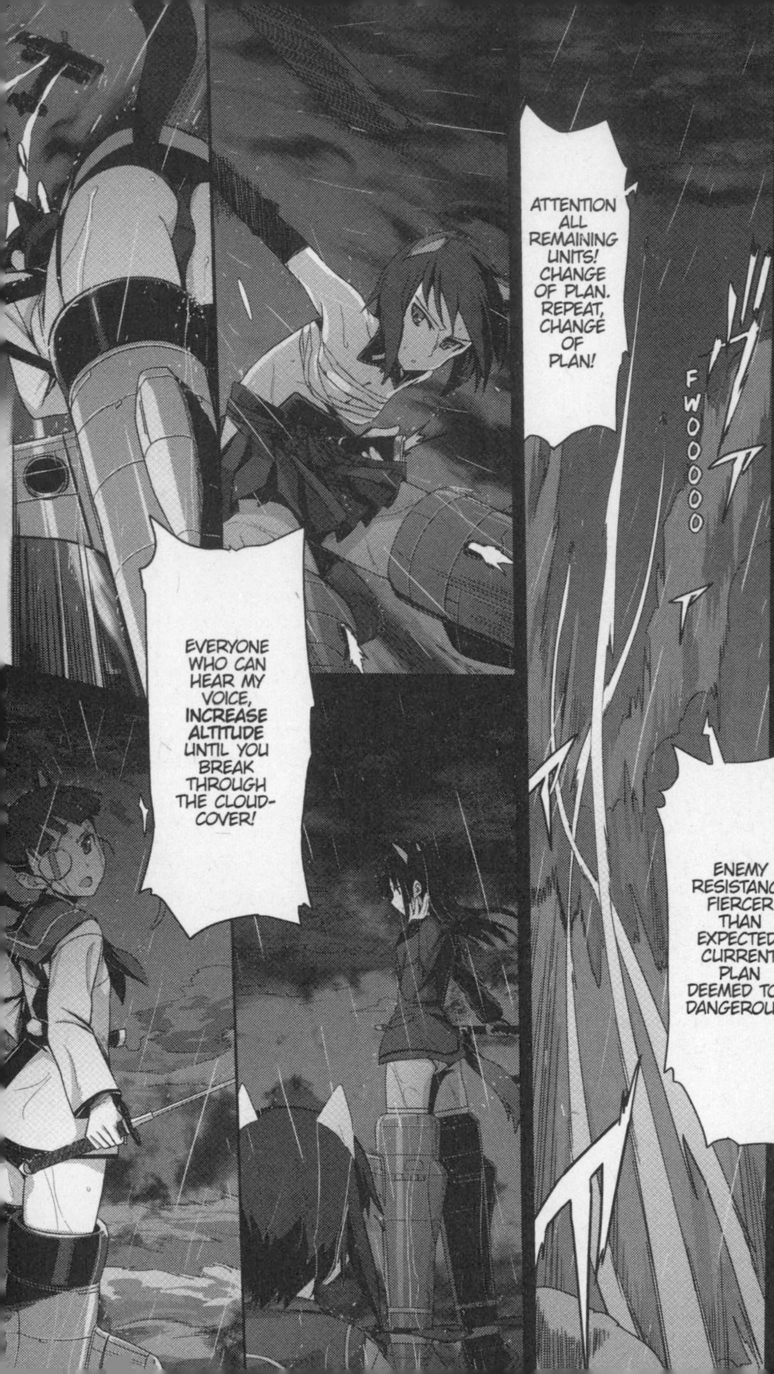
ATTENTION ALL REMAINING UNITS! CHANGE OF PLAN. REPEAT, CHANGE OF PLAN!
FWOOOOOO
ENEMY RESISTANCE FIERCER THAN EXPECTED! CURRENT PLAN DEEMED TOO DANGEROUS!
EVERYONE WHO CAN HEAR MY VOICE, INCREASE ALTITUDE UNTIL YOU BREAK THROUGH THE CLOUD-COVER!

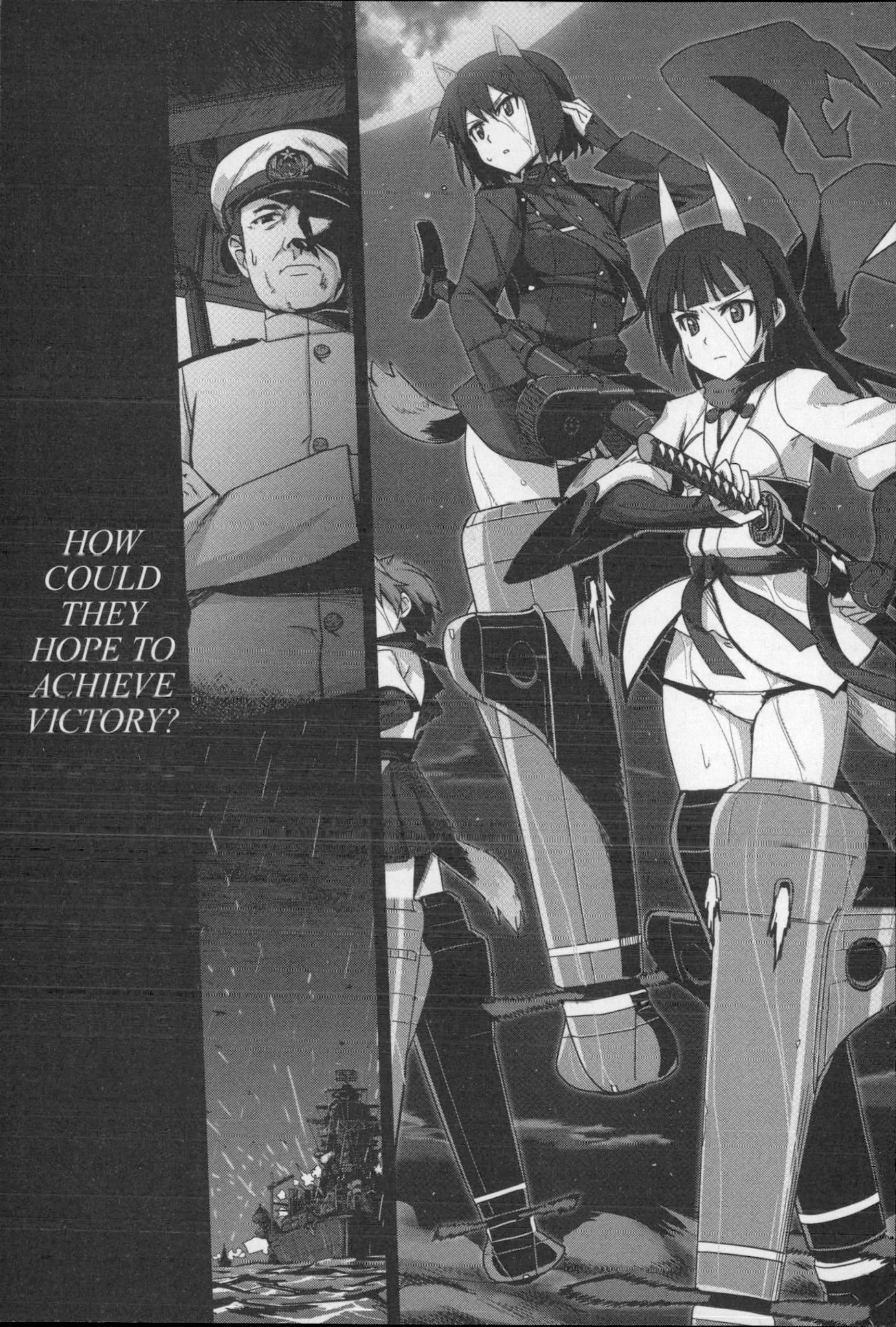
HOW COULD THEY HOPE TO ACHIEVE VICTORY?

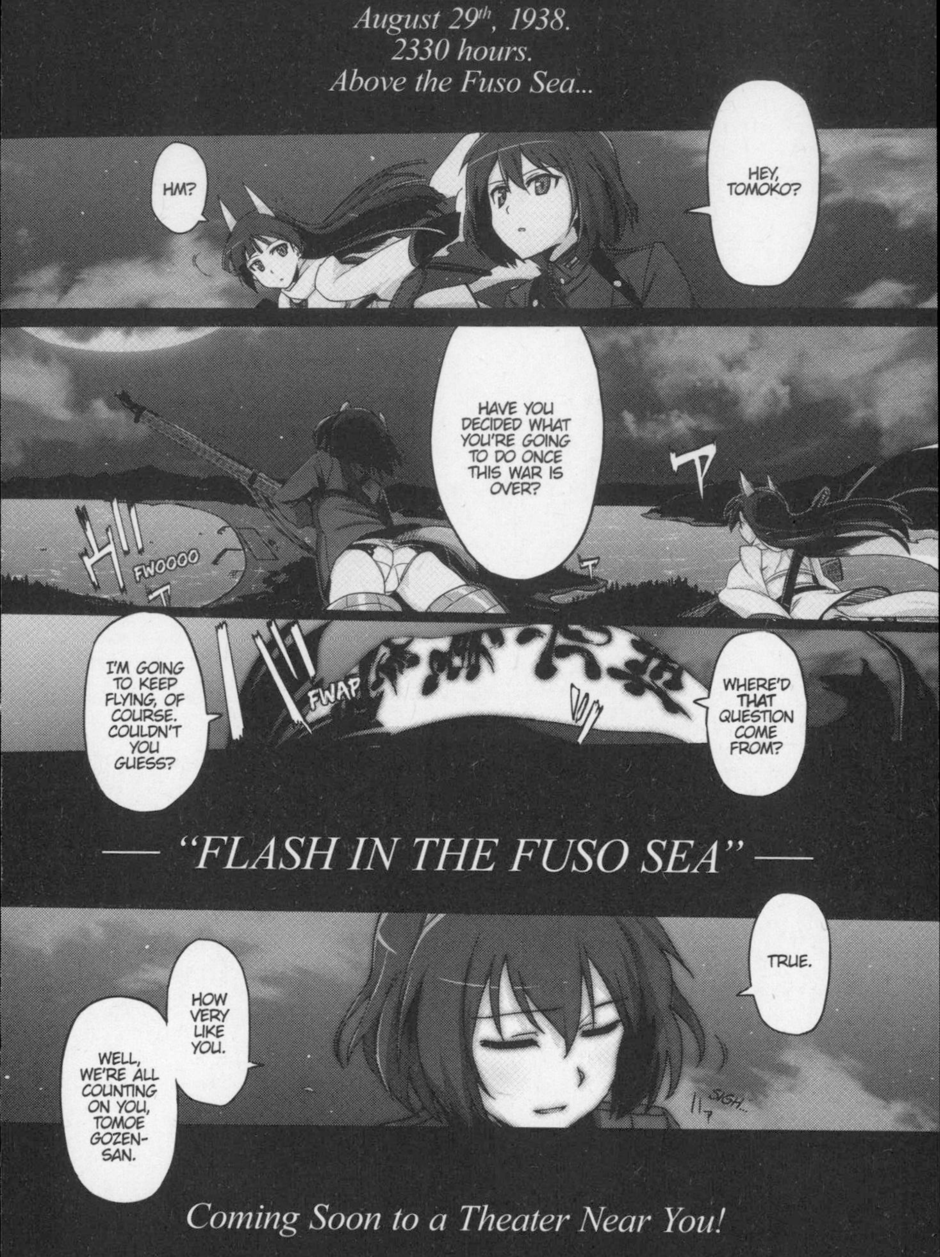
August 29th, 1938.
2330 hours.
Above the Fuso Sea...
HEY, TOMOKO?
HM?
HAVE YOU DECIDED WHAT YOU'RE GOING TO DO ONCE THIS WAR IS OVER?
FWOOOO
WHERE'D THAT QUESTION COME FROM?
FWAP
I'M GOING TO KEEP FLYING, OF COURSE. COULDN'T YOU GUESS?
— "FLASH IN THE FUSO SEA" —
TRUE.
HOW VERY LIKE YOU.
WELL, WE'RE ALL COUNTING ON YOU, TOMOE GOZEN-SAN.
SIGH...
Coming Soon to a Theater Near You!

Chapter 00:
Flash in the Fuso Sea
[Mission Complete]

ABOUT STRIKER UNITS
By: Takaaki Suzuki

 FUSO NAVY

Nagashima A4N Type 95 Carrier-based Striker Unit

The Nagashima A4N, a bi-fin striker unit developed by Nagashima Aircraft Company, was a direct upgrade of the earlier Nagashima A2N. Developed before the widespread acceptance of the Miyafuji Theory, its engine could not be incorporated inside the unit, and was carried in an external backpack. Compared to the large backpack unit of the Nagashima A2N, however, the engine was considerably smaller and still boasted a 30% increase in power. That reduction in size boosted the striker unit's overall maneuverability and combat effectiveness. It was that maneuverability and general stability that made the A4N one of the favorite striker units of the Navy Witches. Both the A2N and the A4N were valuable in developing and solidifying a Witch's battle skill and, once the later Miyahishi A5M was officially adopted, they were maintained as training units for recruits.

Miyahishi A5M Type 96 Carrier-based Striker Unit

The Miyahishi A5M, designed by Miyahishi Heavy Industries, was the first single-fin, all metal striker unit. Professor Miyafuji Ichiro was heavily involved in the design of this unit, and, thanks to what would later become widely known as the "Miyafuji Theory," he was able to incorporate the engine into the striker unit itself. The Professor had first been assigned to striker unit design with the Miyahishi 7-shi Experimental Carrier Striker Unit, in which he employed several new design theories. Unfortunately, it was considered too experimental to see official adoption by the Navy. However, it was the 7-shi's monocoque design, with no interior trusses, that gave the Professor the idea on how to create enough space for an internal engine. At first, he redesigned the 7-shi with the internal engine, but the end result was bulky, inelegant and significantly less powerful. Further adjustments were necessary. Those adjustments resulted in the Miyafuji Theory, and were implemented in the Miyahishi A5M. The highly aerodynamic A5M was 50km/h faster than the earlier A4N model, with greater maneuverability and a much faster equip time for Witches. Though many Navy Witches loved the old A4N, as soon as they tried the newer A5M, they all immediately agreed to its adoption.

12-shi Experimental Carrier-based Striker Unit

After the Fuso Navy encountered the new, tougher flier-type Neuroi during the Fuso Sea Incident, it was apparent that a faster, more powerful striker unit was necessary. Thus Specification 12-shi for a new striker unit design was issued to both Nagashima and Miyahishi. However, the spec requirements were much higher than anything considered possible by current techniques. Deeming them impossible to meet, Nagashima dropped out of the design competition. Given that Professor Miyafuji was away in Europe at the time, Miyahishi also considered withdrawing, but he was able to persuade the Professor to work on the design in Europe. Miyahishi immediately sent technicians to Britannia to assist him. The Professor worked with aeronautics researchers from all over Europe to develop a working theory in which magic power created extra usable space inside the unit. Thanks to this theory, leaving space inside the unit for a Witch's legs was no longer a concern, which made it possible to design larger engines and greater-capacity fuel tanks. The end design had far greater power and a much longer cruising distance, giving the Professor hope that the 12-shi specs were, indeed, within reach.

 FUSO ARMY

Kawataki Ki-10 Type 95 Striker Unit

The Kawataki Ki-10 was a bi-fin striker unit designed by the Kawataki Aerospace Company. The primary striker unit of the Fuso Army at the time of the Fuso Sea Incident, it was considered far more maneuverable and agile than the standard. As it had a larger engine than the Nagashima A4N, the Navy's most common striker unit at the time, it was faster, and had better climbing speed and a longer cruising distance. However, striker unit technology was evolving at a rapid pace. At the same time Fuso was putting out the Ki-10, Karlsland was already running test flights for the Bf-109 and Britannia the Hurricane. These units had maximum speeds of over 500km/h, which easily surpassed the Ki-10's top flight speed of 400km/h. Additionally, Fuso's own navy was testing the Miyahishi A5M single-fin which, despite having a far less powerful engine, still topped out at 451km/h. The army quickly pushed for the design of the Ki-10's successor, but in the early days of the war, it was their top-performing striker unit.

Nagashima Ki-27 Type 97 Striker Unit

The Nagashima Ki-27 was an all-metal, single-fin striker unit designed by the Nagashima Aircraft Company. Having seen the success of the navy's Miyahishi A5M, the army required Miyahishi, Nagashima, and Kawataki to create a new striker design employing the Miyafuji Theory. Miyahishi created the Ki-33, a redesign of the A5M, and Kawataki offered the Ki-28, but the army chose the Nagashima Ki-27. The Ki-27 incorporated a large number of new innovations. In order to give it both exceptional speed and high combat effectiveness, it was designed to be both as aerodynamic as possible and also to be exceptionally light. The resulting unit had greater acceleration and climbing ability than the A5M, despite having the same engine. And even with all the weight-saving measures, the Ki-27 was still a durable unit with an exceedingly reliable engine. It could be flown out on multiple deployments in a single day with no risk of engine trouble. It is said that during the Fuso Sea Incident, Navy Witches stationed at the joint base would often express their jealousy of the army's Ki-27.

The Nagashima Ki-27

Ki-43

The Ki-27 was an excellent striker unit, but against the new, faster, more heavily-armored flier-type Neuroi it had limited impact. At that time, the European forces were perfecting speed-based hit-and-run battle tactics and two-unit echelon formations in the Espania theater. Upon learning this, Fuso issued a two-tiered specification for new striker unit designs. One unit had to be a light, fast, and maneuverable unit for use against smaller targets. The other had to be a heavy-fighter unit that was still fast, but more heavily armored. Nagashima developed the Ki-43 as a response to the former specification. This light fighter unit would eventually be designated the "Army Type 1 Hayabusa." Though similar in structure to the Ki-27 it was based on, the Ki-43 made thorough use of the Miyafuji Theory to load a larger fuel tank, giving it a greatly extended cruising range. It was more aerodynamic, but its top speed was not much greater than the Ki-27's. It was also less combat-effective, making it difficult for the Army to put it into wide use. However, given the continual demands for newer models during the Fuso Sea Incident, it was sent to the front as an experimental replacement model.

Ki-44

Developed by Nagashima alongside the Ki-43, the Ki-44 was a heavily armed striker unit. Unlike previous heavy unit designs, the Ki-44 was developed for fighting large-scale Neuroi. Its design focused on acceleration, climbing ability, better armament, and heavier armor. Unfortunately, while Nagashima had experience developing combat-effective units, this was their first attempt at a heavily-armored one. They also had their hands full developing the Ki-43 concurrently, so work on the Ki-44 lagged further and further behind. However, thanks to techniques learned by the technicians who had been sent to assist Professor Miyafuji, and tips learned from the Bf-109 brought over from Karlsland, a prototype unit was eventually completed. This prototype's engine was insufficient, and most of the armaments intended for it were still in development, making it difficult to call the unit a "heavy fighter." Despite that, it was still capable of sending increased magical power to the shields, boosting its defensive capability. It also had excellent diving ability, making it perfect for the increasingly popular hit-and-run tactics. An advanced model of this unit eventually saw use in the European theater.

Type 97 Medium Land Striker Chi-Ha

International debate had long raged about what kind of equipment to create for land-bound Witches. However, the creed of "mechanical armaments a Witch can wear" espoused by Professor Miyafuji gained enough traction that it was applied not just to airborne Witches, but to land-bound Witches as well. Thus the Land Striker was born. Like many aerial striker units at the time, the earliest land strikers had external, backpack engines. However, the Miyafuji Theory allowed land strikers to incorporate internal engines and armaments. The Fuso Army commissioned Professor Miyafuji to develop the Type 97 unit. Only a prototype was available at the time of the Fuso Sea Incident, but it was immediately adopted by the army and put into mass-production. In battle, the unit performed admirably well. Hard-hitting heavy land strikers with external armor and equipment were also developed.

 KARLSLAND

Messerscharff Bf-109E

Karlsland's main striker unit, developed by the Messerscharff Company. The original V1 prototype, along with the previous, mass-produced A1, had the old backpack-style engines. However, with the announcement of the Miyafuji Theory, they quickly created the improved B1. Not stopping there, the V1, A1 and B1 underwent continual improvements. Porting the B1's engine into the C1's design resulted in the D1. However, all of these designs had already been in production when the Miyafuji Theory became widely known, so all were lacking in aerodynamics. Additionally, the much-anticipated DB-601 engine had just been completed, so the E1, with the new engine and a more aerodynamic design, was developed. The prototype for the E1 design was taken to Fuso by Karlsland observers during the Fuso Sea Incident, and was later used as reference in the development of the Ki-44.

STRIKE WITCHES

1937
FUSO SEA
INCIDENT

ABOUT THE CHARACTERS

ART: Shimada Humikane

KITAGO FUMIKA

Affiliation: Fuso Imperial Navy
12th Flying Corps

Rank: Major

Fumika is a kendo instructor at Fuso's Maizuru Community Center and an aerial Witch with the Fuso Imperial Navy. She was Sakamoto Mio's kendo instructor and, once Mio joined the navy as a Witch, her superior officer and flight instructor. One of the officers Fuso sent as an observer to Europe, she is highly intelligent. Many among the Fuso armed forces call her the "War Goddess."

STRIKE WITCHES ZERO
WITCHES PROFILE

WAKAMOTO TETSUKO

Affiliation: Fuso Imperial Navy
12th Flying Corps

Rank: Flight Petty Officer

Tetsuko has been Mio's classmate since they were both kendo students in the Maizuru Community Center. Since their assignment to the same squadron, they have acted as rivals, constantly trying to outdo each other. Tetsuko is aware that increasing her synchronization with her familiar will boost her magical power, but the side effects--like her hair growing longer--annoy her, so she doesn't do it often.

STRIKE WITCHES ZERO
WITCHES PROFILE

ANABUKI TOMOKO

Affiliation: Fuso Imperial Army
1st Airborne Division

Rank: Pilot Officer

Tomoko, nicknamed "Tomoe Gozen," is a famous Witch known for playing the lead role in the movie *Flash in the Fuso Sea.* The costume she wore in that movie appears in the diagram, in contrast to the maiden's *hakama* she typically wears to battle. Her trademark scarf, embroidered with the phrase, "Anabuki Courage," was also changed for the movie.

NECK-GUARD
SLEEVE CONNECTS WITH COLLAR-LOOP HERE.
CHEST-TIE
BELT
ARM-GUARD STARTS ABOVE THE ELBOW
UNDERARM VISIBLE WHEN SHE RAISES HER ARMS.

STRIKE WITCHES ZERO
WITCHES PROFILE

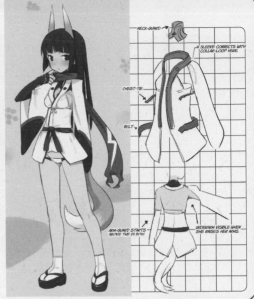

ETO TOSHIKO

Affiliation: Fuso Imperial Army
1st Airborne Division

Rank: Wing Commander

Squad commander for Anabuki, Kato, and the other young aces, Toshiko has exceptional control over her magical powers, especially magical barriers. Her skill is so honed that she can deflect Neuroi attacks with her magical barrier alone. Toshiko and Kitago Fumika have a long history together, hence Fumika's remark, "Eto's scary when she's mad."

STRIKE WITCHES ZERO
WITCHES PROFILE

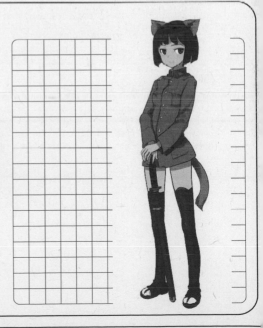

Good Luck, Tomo-chan!! Pt.1

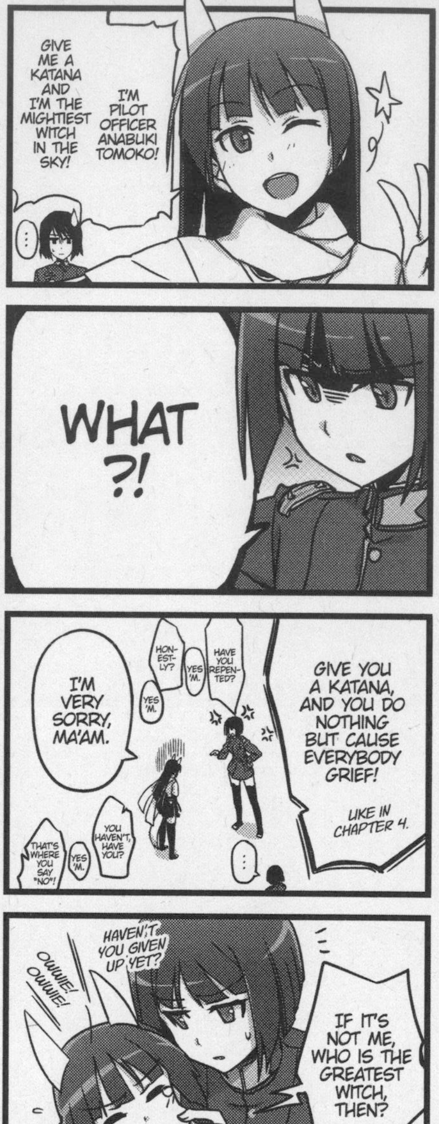
I'M PILOT OFFICER ANABUKI TOMOKO!
GIVE ME A KATANA AND I'M THE MIGHTIEST WITCH IN THE SKY!
...
WHAT ?!
GIVE YOU A KATANA, AND YOU DO NOTHING BUT CAUSE EVERYBODY GRIEF!
LIKE IN CHAPTER 4.
HAVE YOU REPENTED?
YES 'M.
HONESTLY?
YES 'M.
I'M VERY SORRY, MA'AM.
YOU HAVEN'T, HAVE YOU?
YES 'M.
THAT'S WHERE YOU SAY "NO"!
...
IF IT'S NOT ME, WHO IS THE GREATEST WITCH, THEN?
HAVEN'T YOU GIVEN UP YET?
OWWIE! OWWIE!

Good Luck, Tomo-chan!! Pt.2

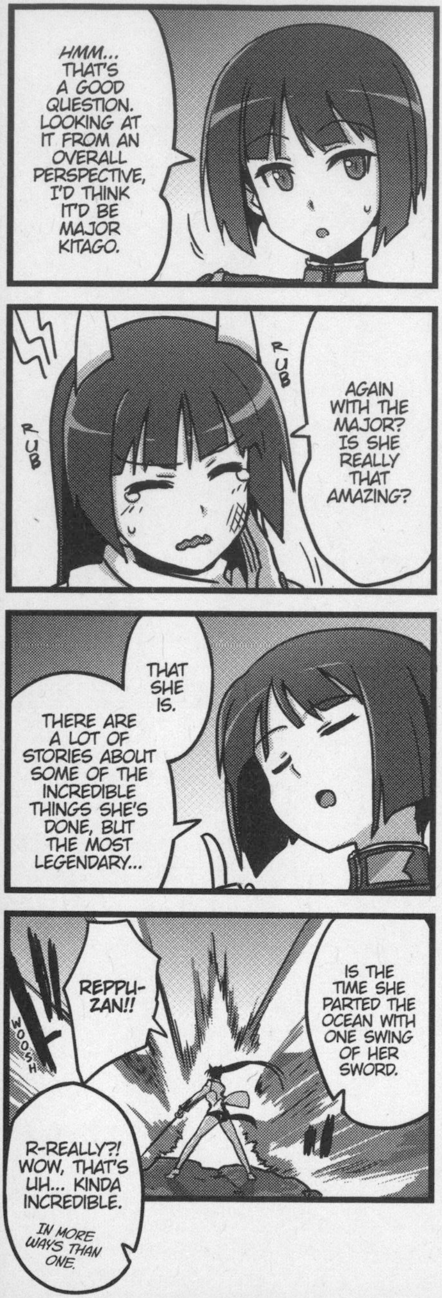
HMM... THAT'S A GOOD QUESTION. LOOKING AT IT FROM AN OVERALL PERSPECTIVE, I'D THINK IT'D BE MAJOR KITAGO.
AGAIN WITH THE MAJOR? IS SHE REALLY THAT AMAZING?
RUB
RUB
THAT SHE IS.
THERE ARE A LOT OF STORIES ABOUT SOME OF THE INCREDIBLE THINGS SHE'S DONE, BUT THE MOST LEGENDARY...
IS THE TIME SHE PARTED THE OCEAN WITH ONE SWING OF HER SWORD.
REPPU-ZAN!!
WOOSH
R-REALLY?! WOW, THAT'S UH... KINDA INCREDIBLE.
IN MORE WAYS THAN ONE.

Good Luck, Tomo-chan!! Pt.3

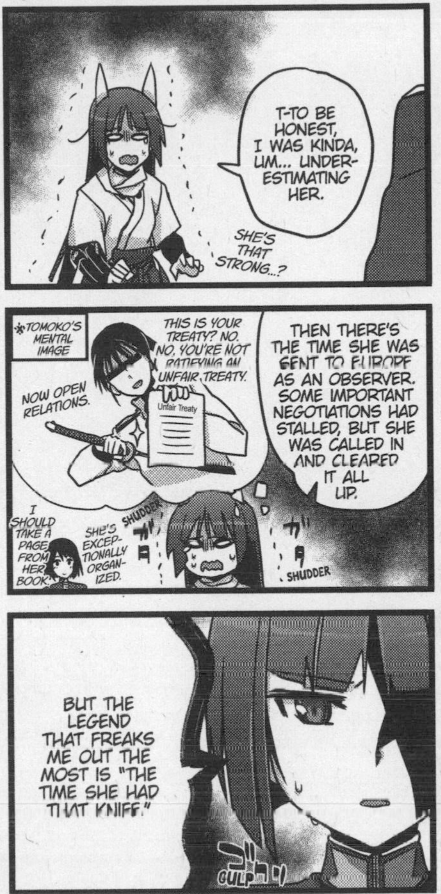
T-TO BE HONEST, I WAS KINDA, UM... UNDER-ESTIMATING HER.
SHE'S THAT STRONG...?
THEN THERE'S THE TIME SHE WAS SENT TO EUROPE AS AN OBSERVER. SOME IMPORTANT NEGOTIATIONS HAD STALLED, BUT SHE WAS CALLED IN AND CLEARED IT ALL UP.
THIS IS YOUR TREATY? NO. NO, YOU'RE NOT RATIFYING AN UNFAIR TREATY.
NOW OPEN RELATIONS.
Unfair Treaty
*TOMOKO'S MENTAL IMAGE
SHUDDER
SHUDDER
SHE'S EXCEPTIONALLY ORGANIZED.
I SHOULD TAKE A PAGE FROM HER BOOK.
BUT THE LEGEND THAT FREAKS ME OUT THE MOST IS "THE TIME SHE HAD THAT KNIFE."
GULP
A MOUNTAIN!!!
COOONG
IF SHE PARTED A SEA WITH HER SWORD, SHE MUST'VE SPLIT A MOUNTAIN WITH THAT KNIFE!!
THAT'S GOTTA BE IT!!

Good Luck, Tomo-chan!! Pt.4

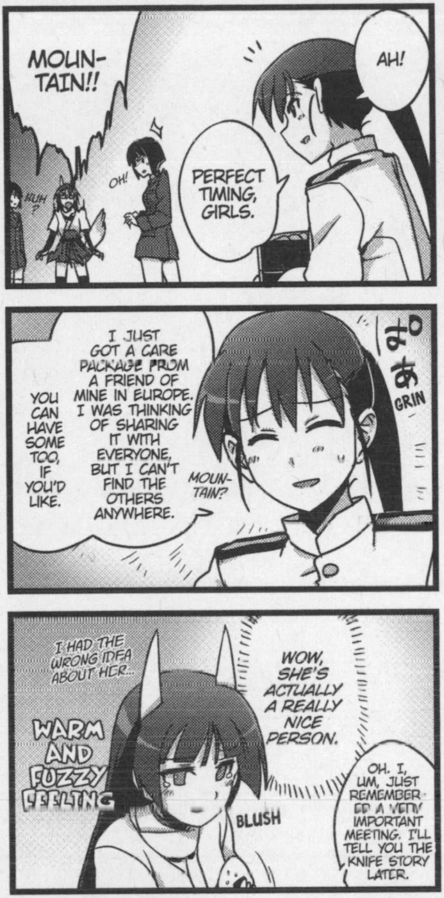
AH!
PERFECT TIMING, GIRLS.
OH!
HUH?
MOUNTAIN!!
ぱあ
GRIN
I JUST GOT A CARE PACKAGE FROM A FRIEND OF MINE IN EUROPE. I WAS THINKING OF SHARING IT WITH EVERYONE, BUT I CAN'T FIND THE OTHERS ANYWHERE.
MOUNTAIN?
YOU CAN HAVE SOME TOO, IF YOU'D LIKE.
WOW, SHE'S ACTUALLY A REALLY NICE PERSON.
OH. I, UM, JUST REMEMBERED A VERY IMPORTANT MEETING. I'LL TELL YOU THE KNIFE STORY LATER.
I HAD THE WRONG IDEA ABOUT HER...
WARM AND FUZZY FEELING
BLUSH
HAVE YOU EVER HEARD OF "SALTY LICORICE"?
THIS IS SUPPOSED TO BE A REALLY POPULAR SNACK IN NORTHERN EUROPE.
SO THAT'S WHAT SHE USED THE KNIFE FOR!!

The End

Afterword

Thank you very much for reading volume 1 of *Strike Witches Zero: 1937 Fuso Sea Incident*. This was full of firsts for me, but with the generous help of a lot of people, I was able to finish this first volume. Humika Shimada-sama and Takaaki Suzuki-sama provided a wonderful world and interesting characters to populate it. The diligent editors at *Musume TYPE* magazine worked hard to help iron out a variety of issues. Takashi Mineda-sama, my assistant, was an invaluable help with every chapter. And the greatest thanks go out to you, the loyal readers, for all of your warm support. I'm going to take my effort up to the next level for volume 2. I hope to see you there!

–Ningen

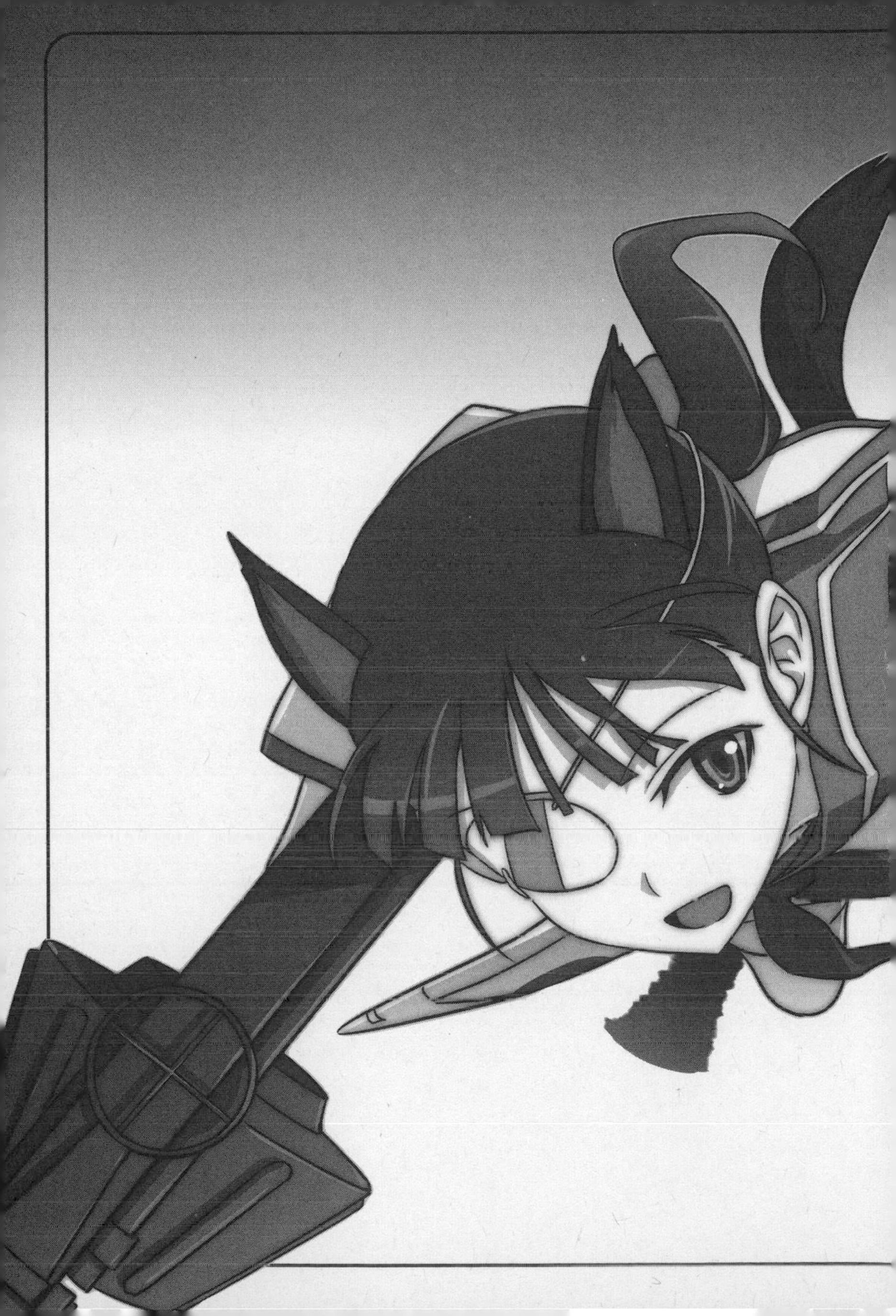

To be continued...

ストライクウィッチーズ零
STRIKE WITCHES ZERO
1937 扶桑海事変

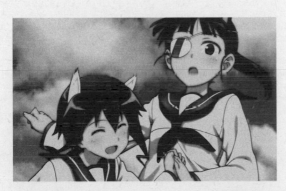

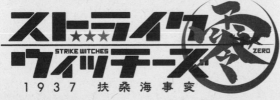

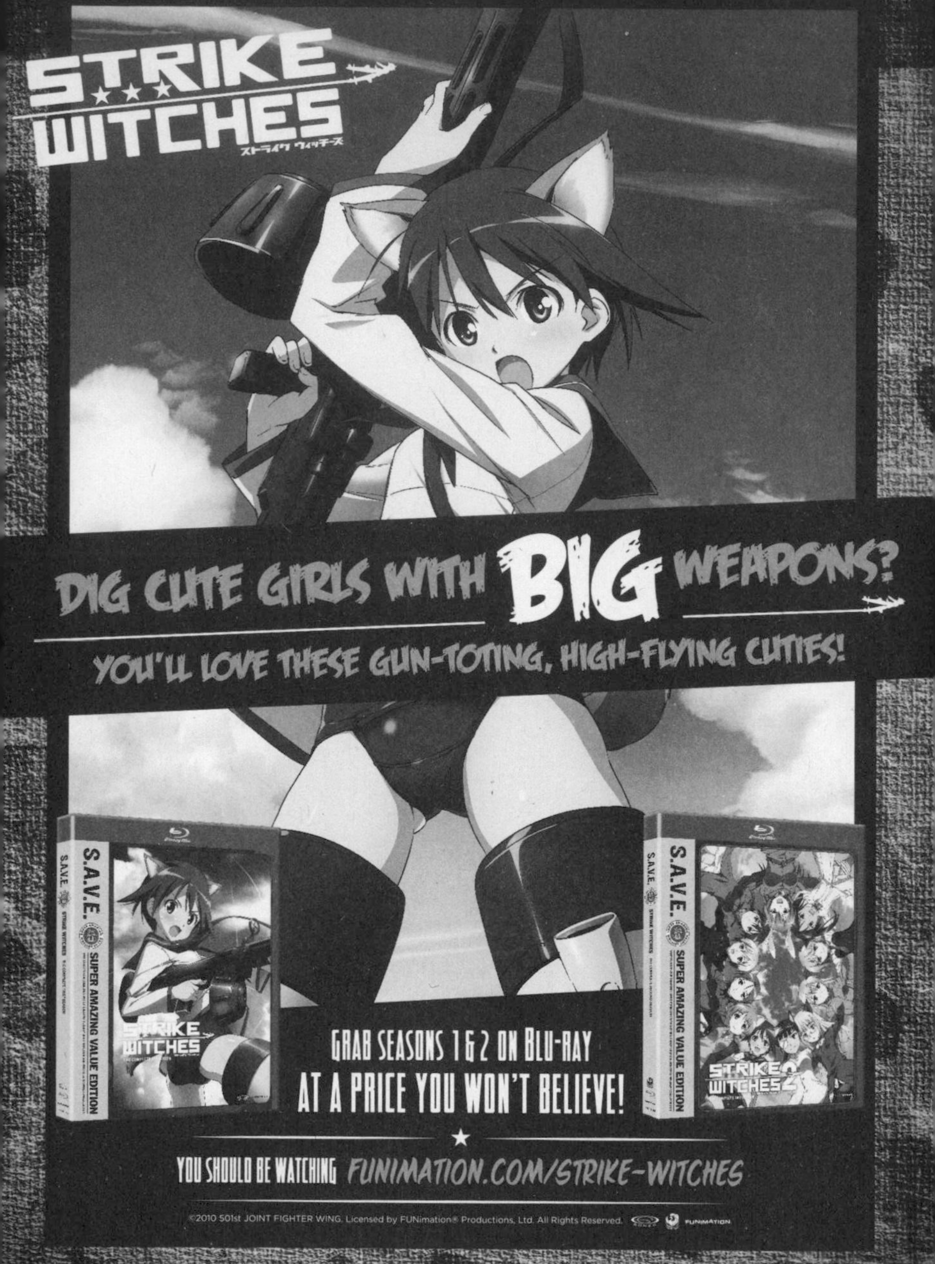
STRIKE WITCHES
ストライクウィッチーズ
DIG CUTE GIRLS WITH BIG WEAPONS?
YOU'LL LOVE THESE GUN-TOTING, HIGH-FLYING CUTIES!
S.A.V.E.
SUPER AMAZING VALUE EDITION
STRIKE WITCHES
GRAB SEASONS 1 & 2 ON BLU-RAY
AT A PRICE YOU WON'T BELIEVE!
S.A.V.E.
SUPER AMAZING VALUE EDITION
STRIKE WITCHES 2
YOU SHOULD BE WATCHING FUNIMATION.COM/STRIKE-WITCHES
©2010 501st JOINT FIGHTER WING. Licensed by FUNimation® Productions, Ltd. All Rights Reserved.
FUNIMATION

SEVEN SEAS ENTERTAINMENT PRESENTS

STRIKE WITCHES
1937 FUSO SEA INCIDENT VOL. 1

art by **Ningen** / story by **Humikane Shimada + Projekt Kagonish**

TRANSLATION
Adrienne Beck

ADAPTATION
Shanti Whitesides

LETTERING AND LAYOUT
Alexandra Gunawan

COVER DESIGN
Nicky Lim

PROOFREADER
Janet Houck
Conner Crooks

MANAGING EDITOR
Adam Arnold

PUBLISHER
Jason DeAngelis

STRIKE WITCHES ZERO: 1937 FUSO KAIJI HEN VOL. 1
© Ningen 2011, © 2010 501st JOINT FIGHTER WING
Edited by KADOKAWA SHOTEN.
First published in Japan in 2011 by KADOKAWA CORPORATION, Tokyo.
English translation rights arranged with KADOKAWA CORPORATION, Tokyo
through TOHAN CORPORATION, Tokyo..

Seven Seas books may be purchased in bulk for educational, business, or
promotional use. For information on bulk purchases, please contact Macmillan
Corporate & Premium Sales Department at 1-800-221-7945 (ext 5442)
or write specialmarkets@macmillan.com.

Seven Seas and the Seven Seas logo are trademarks of
Seven Seas Entertainment, LLC. All rights reserved.

ISBN: 978-1-626920-47-7

Printed in Canada

First Printing: August 2014

10 9 8 7 6 5 4 3 2 1

FOLLOW US ONLINE: *www.gomanga.com*

READING DIRECTIONS

This book reads from *right to left*, Japanese style.
If this is your first time reading manga, you start
reading from the top right panel on each page and
take it from there. If you get lost, just follow the
numbered diagram here. It may seem backwards at
first, but you'll get the hang of it! Have fun!!

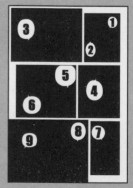